BASIC CRIMINAL PROCEDURES

EDWARD E. PEOPLES, DPA

Instructor Emeritus
Administration of Justice Department
Santa Rosa Junior College

Prentice Hall
Upper Saddle River, NJ 07458

OCT 0 5 2000

Library of Congress Catologing-in-Publication Data

Peoples, Edward E.
    Basic criminal procedures / by Edward E. Peoples. — 1st ed.
        p.   cm.
    Includes bibliographical references and index.
    ISBN 0-13-084774-7
    1. Criminal procedure—United States.   I. Title.
KF9619.P46   1999
345.73'05—dc21   99-13091
                                                                         CIP

Production Supervision: *Kathryn Kasturas*
Managing Editor: *Mary Carnis*
Director of Production and Manufacturing: *Bruce Johnson*
Manufacturing Manager: *Ed O'Dougherty*
Acquisitions Editor: *Neil Marquardt*
Editorial Assistant: *Susan Kegler*
Marketing Manager: *Shannon Simonsen*
Interior Design and Page Layout: *Kathryn Kasturas*
Cover Design: *Marianne Frasco*

Printed in the United States of America

10   9   8   7   6   5   4   3   2   1

ISBN 0-13-084774-7

Prentice-Hall International (UK) Limited, *London*
Prentice-Hall of Australia Pty. Limited, *Sydney*
Prentice-Hall Canada, Inc., *Toronto*
Prentice-Hall Hispanoamericana, S.A., *Mexico*
Prentice-Hall of India Private Limited, *New Delhi*
Prentice-Hall of Japan, Inc., *Tokyo*
Pearson Education Asia Pte. Ltd., *Singapore*
Editora Prentice-Hall do Brasil, Ltda., *Rio de Janeiro*

Dedicated to my wife, Corinne,
for joining with me to share of life
in our process of loving and becoming.

BRIEF TABLE OF CONTENTS

TABLE OF CONTENTS

CHAPTER 4: MIRANDA: ITS MEANING AND APPLICATION   74

CHAPTER 7: THE TRIAL   128

CHAPTER 8: SENTENCING PROCEDURES AND ALTERNATIVES   158

PREFACE

The purpose of this book is to explain and/or describe the basic procedural aspects of the criminal justice system in a way that can be applied within the context of any state's procedural laws. It is designed to be the primary text in college courses entitled Criminal Procedures, Procedures in the Justice System, or a similar title. No prior knowledge of how or why the justice system operates is necessary to use the book. It is written and published with the students' needs in mind. The style is direct and basic, yet the material is well researched and current. However, it is not intended to be the definitive work on the subject. It is an introductory text, and there is ample opportunity for the instructor to include his or her own areas of emphasis.

Although the presentation is directed to the student new to this field, no study of criminal procedures can avoid the vocabulary used by those who work within the sysœtem: law enforcement, judges, lawyers, correctional officers, probation officers, parole agents, and related personnel. To the new student of criminal justice, the vocabulary might initially seem like a foreign language. In fact, it is. It is known as *legalese*, a language created by attorneys, grounded in our English common law heritage, with an overlay of French terms and Latin expressions.

It has been said that to understand criminal procedures, one needs only to know its vocabulary. It is almost that simple; and it is impossible to understand the procedures without learning its vocabulary. Consequently, the real job of the student is to gain a command of the words used to describe and explain the procedures. To help in this learning, a list of key vocabulary terms and concepts is provided at the end of each chapter. Learning these will be useful in understanding the procedures and in preparing for exams. After that, the procedures will become self-evident.

Many of the procedures we follow in criminal justice were not those created to deal with crime and society in the twentieth or twenty-first century. Rather, they were devised to protect us from eighteenth-century England after we declared our independence. If you will excuse the paraphrasing of a recent movie title, our system of justice, with its Bill of Rights, was designed to protect American citizens from the *badness of King George*. Any frustrations that one might feel about the deficiencies of our system come from that fact. Only recently have we had any concern for the victims of crimes or for the impact of violent crime on society.

In Chapter 1 we present an array of basic concepts and historical developments that underpin the procedural aspects of our justice system. These form the basis of much of the content to follow.

Chapter 2 offers a detailed account of the development and current application of one the most significant procedural rules in all of criminal justice: the exclusionary rule. A short chapter is devoted to explaining this rule because of its overriding influence on all police procedures and on the admissibility of evidence in court. The exceptions to the rule are detailed as well.

In Chapter 3 we present a detailed examination of police procedures, from the point of first contact between a citizen and a law enforcement officer, through all the elements of detention and arrest. Chapter 4 is a short chapter devoted exclusively to the *Miranda* decision: its meaning and application in interrogations of suspects by law enforcement officers. Also included is a discussion of when the *Miranda* warning is not needed and how it should be applied in juvenile cases.

Chapter 5 is a short chapter that explains the procedures and requirements necessary in a detention facility where arrested persons are booked and held pending release in some fashion. Depending on the priorities of the instructor, this chapter could be omitted or summarized in a course offering, without affecting the continuity of the book's presentation.

In Chapter 6 we describe the structure of the court system, including the jurisdiction of each court and the procedures that occur. The new consolidation court model, abolishing the lower courts, is presented as well. Following that, the pretrial processes and procedures are described, including the role of the prosecutor, the initial court appearance for all defendants and the preliminary hearing in felony cases, selected pretrial motions by the attorneys, and the primary method of settling most criminal matters, plea bargaining.

In Chapter 7 we examine the trial, from the point of jury selection by both traditional and scientific methods, through the presentation of evidence, to the conclusion of proceedings by the verdict. The role and responsibility of a defense attorney are included. Discussions of a jury of fewer than six persons and the use of a nonunanimous verdict are examined within the context of the trial. The sentencing goals and procedures, along with sentencing alternatives, are presented in Chapter 8. This includes a detailed discussion of two basic sentencing procedures, the indeterminate and determinate sentencing laws, the role of the probation officer in preparing the presentence report, and an examination of probation as the primary alternative to sentencing. The uses and requirements of police searches of probationers are also described.

Chapter 9 offers a variety of postsentencing procedures, including county parole and state parole, the requirements for police in making searches of parolees, the role of the parole board, sex offender registration requirements, the new and controversial sexually violent predator law, and the four most common writs: habeas corpus, certiorari, mandamus and prohibition. An overview of death penalty procedures is presented, followed by a discussion of four acts of executive clemency: pardon, reprieve, commutation, and amnesty. The chapter concludes with a summary of the indemnification procedures by which individuals who are wrongly convicted and imprisoned may receive financial compensation from the state.

A few selected appellate court decisions are summarized in the book because they serve as good examples of the thinking by which the courts create criminal procedures and because they offer additional meaning to the textual material. Many other appellate decisions are cited, merely to document the materials presented and to provide a direction for all who wish to expand their understanding of criminal procedures by individual research.

Throughout the book the word *police* is used when referring to any law enforcement officer. In using this term, there is no intention to slight any local, county, or state peace officer. The word is used simply for convenience and because the generic nature of all law enforcement is to police: to regulate and control human behavior within the confines of the law.

ACKNOWLEDGMENTS

The author gratefully acknowledges the help of the following, who have contributed through their review of the manuscript:

George W. Knox, Chicago State University
Bill Kelly, Auburn University
Wayne L. Wolf, South Suburban College (Illinois)

FUNDAMENTAL CONCEPTS OF LAW

Criminal procedures are founded on a trilogy that includes two legal concepts and a body of law that is as old as our independence and as sacred as our freedom. First, we have an **adversary system** in which two sides (the prosecutor and the defense), having fair and equal access to the same resources and information, compete in open court to arrive at the legal truth. Second, we use the absolute maximum degree of proof that human beings are capable of having to convict a citizen of a crime, **proof beyond a reasonable doubt**. Within this same conceptual framework, we use lesser degrees of proof when less serious intrusions into the citizen's freedom occur, as discussed below. Third, we have a body of law derived from our British legal heritage called **common law**: a body of law that was not written but that has evolved over time in Great Britain through custom, tradition, and court decisions (rather than statutes), to become recognized early in our history as the law of the land. This is not to say that we now have common law or practice the common law. Many states no longer recognize any common laws.

Today, our laws are written down in an array of books called *codes*, and are divided into categories, discussed below. If it is not written in some code, it is not the law. Nevertheless, the basis of the laws we follow today, as well as many appellate case decisions, come from our common law heritage. However, our experiences with British law, both good and bad, strongly influenced the specific laws and legal safeguards that our forefathers enacted. In fact, much of our procedural law, including the Bill of Rights, was created from our bad experiences with English law. It was a defense against the tyranny and legal abuses of the crown's courts and the crown's men.

The Founding Fathers wanted to be certain that similar abuses of the rights of our citizens did not occur under U.S. criminal procedures. One could say that the due process guaranteed in the Bill of Rights, and the procedures that police, courts, and corrections must follow today, were created to protect us from the "Badness of King George," if you will pardon the play on words. Obviously, today's society is far different than colonial America, and the problems of drugs, gangs, and guns and related violence are making it increasingly difficult to maintain order under law.

The parts of this trilogy are bound together by a document that had become the ultimate source of all of our legal rights and wrongs, the **U.S. Constitution**. The reason that the Constitution is the ultimate source of our laws was summed up best in 1803 by Supreme Court Justice John Marshall when he stated that "Any nation created by a document, must hold that document supreme." It is that document that binds us together as a nation under law. Additional terms, concepts, and procedures are also found within this legal framework. We examine a few more of these below: those it is necessary to know before we begin with the actual procedures themselves. Others are integrated within the content of the remaining sections of the book. First, however, we examine certain selected events in our history from which came the major procedures followed today.

A BRIEF HISTORY OF SELECTED PROCEDURES

The purpose here is not to provide an in-depth history lesson. Rather, it is to touch on the origins of selected procedures and processes that are used today and are important to know in appreciating why our current system operates as it does. Only those procedures that grew out of our British common law heritage are discussed, and the focus is on certain aspects of procedural law and the court structure. Consequently, the history of law enforcement and police procedures is not addressed, other than that of the sheriff as that role relates to court responsibilities.

ROLE OF THE SHERIFF

After the fall of the Holy Roman Empire in 395 B.C., various tribes from the continent of Europe began settling the country, primarily the Angles, Saxons, and Jutes. Their system of justice was tribal, had a high degree of citizen involvement, and emphasized restitution given directly to the victim of an offense. Eventually, these tribes merged into one super tribe, the Anglo-Saxons, and by about 870 came to be ruled by Alfred the Great. For the first time, there was a king over the entire land and population, and he began moving the justice system from a tribal and restitutional approach to a state-run system in which the state is the victim.

One of his first acts was to divide England into 52 political subdivisions called *shires*. Then he appointed a knight to be his law enforcement agent in each shire. The term for *agent* was **reeve**. Consequently, by this early date, we have a chief law enforcement officer in each shire, the reeve. Now, if one were to say the two words together, faster and faster, while slurring slightly, it would come out as shire-reeve . . . shire-eeve . . . shireve . . . shirive . . . sheriff. And we have today's **sheriff**, enforcing the king's laws, arresting suspects, holding them for trial, and often acting as judge and executioner as well. Now, of course, other officials hold trial and carry out punishments, but the role has otherwise changed very little in over a thousand years. As an aside, it is interesting to note that in England the sheriff dropped his judicial role in favor of law enforcement, and now the role is just an honorary title. In Scotland today, the sheriff is the local judge but has no police powers.

EARLY METHODS OF TRIAL

Before the coming of the state under Alfred the Great, the Saxons and other tribes had a tribal court, described in our terms as a *hundred court*. As the state evolved, the sheriff came to head this court, and eventually headed the king's court, which he was responsible to form and direct. Early trial methods were swift and rather brutal. One such method, known as **trial by ordeal**, required the accused to stand before the court and either hold his hands in a pot of boiling water or hold a hot iron for a few seconds. Then his hands would be wrapped for two days. Upon the third day, the wraps would be removed and he would show his hands. If burn or scar marks showed, he was found guilty and killed because God had not intervened, as he would with an innocent man, to remove the marks.

A similar method, used if the court was near some water, was to have the accused swim with rocks tied to him, or to tie him up, weight him down with rocks, and throw him into the water. If he managed to swim free, in the first example, or if he managed to undo the rocks and survive, he was guilty because the devil had helped to set him free. One can imagine that the recidivist rate (rate of return to crime) was very low with these methods.

A less severe method, known as **compurgation**, required the accused to purge himself by swearing his innocence, with support of *oath helpers* to support his testimony. Interestingly enough, the number of oath helpers required was 12. Another milder method was called **atonement**, which required the accused to pay compensation, or, as it was termed above, restitution, to the victim. Initially, the amount atoned went to the victim. However, as the state assumed more control over the justice system, the amount was paid directly to the court. This practice was also used extensively in the church courts, which were developing at a parallel with, and in support of, the king's courts. Atonement became a useful way of raising revenue for both. During this period the sheriff presided over the courts and collected the compensation. Also, the hundred court gave way to the practice of the sheriff convening the court, with twelve men sitting to represent the hundred, or the citizens.

THE NORMAN CONQUEST

The next significant development occurred in 1066. From 1042 to 1066, St. Edward the Aetheling (the Confessor) was king of England. As he neared the end of his reign, there were many disputes about who would succeed him. He promised the crown to William, Duke of Normandy (in France). However, just before dying, he changed his mind and appointed Harold of Wessex as king, who was crowned on January 6, 1066. Duke William (a.k.a. William the Conqueror) thought the crown was rightfully his, so he landed his troops at Hastings in southern England, on September 27, defeated Harold, and declared all of England his. William was crowned king of England in Westminster Abbey on Christmas day, 1066.

One of his first efforts to control the citizens was to replace all the Anglo-Saxon reeves (sheriffs) with his own Norman knights. He also redistributed much of the land to his Norman knights. Consequently, his rule in general, and the Norman reeves in particular, were not well received. The people frequently hid men wanted by the sheriff, or helped them to escape after arrest and before trial. In an effort to counter these reactions by the citizens, William initiated a procedure called **recognizance** (a French word), which required the accused, or his family, friends, or townspeople, to post something of value in order to gain the freedom of the accused pending trial. Then, if they helped the accused escape, they would forfeit to the king what they had posted.

Today, we call this procedure **posting bail**, posting an amount of money with the court to gain the freedom of the accused, pending trial. In fact, today we have gone beyond having an accused post money, and in many cases allow him or her to post their word, their promise to return to court when required. We call this procedure releasing the accused on his or her **own recognizance**, or **OR**. If the accused fails to appear, he or she can be charged with a new crime of failing to return, which can be either a felony or a misdemeanor, depending on the level of the original crime charged. Think of it: The word and procedure known as *recognizance* has been a vital part of our justice system for over 930 years.

William also added **trial by battle** as a method of trial and settling disputes between individuals. However, the practice was limited to the knights. Commoners continued to perform ordeals or pay atonement. As the king's power grew, so did that of the church, and the church made increasing use of atonement as the preferred method for one to make up for violating church laws and other sins.

THE STATE BECOMES THE VICTIM

Until the beginning of the twelfth century, victim restitution played an important role in settling disputes. When a party was wronged during the commission of a crime, that injured party was considered the victim, deserving of compensation. That all changed when Henry I took the throne (1116–1132). He announced that from now on "the **King's Peace** shall be maintained throughout the kingdom," and anyone who disturbs that peace by committing a crime is committing a crime against the king. The king (state) became the victim of all crimes, and from that point until only recently, the real victim has been forgotten. The real victim suffered the loss from a crime, but the king reaped the rewards that came from a conviction.

King Henry also created two crime categories: He said that "There will be certain crimes against the king's peace that we will call **felonies**." These were arson, robbery, false coinage, and all crimes of violence. These crimes were punishable by death, and a person wanted for committing any of these crimes was declared an outlaw. Anyone could kill an outlaw and claim any reward that might be offered. In both cases, death or outlawry, the accused was considered to be civilly dead. The person ceased to have any legal life, which meant that he or she could not own property, will or inherit property, or perform anything else that required a legal existence. Once they suffered civil death, the king assumed title of all their property. This practice of declaring a convicted felon civilly dead, stripping them of their civil rights, was practiced in many states as late as the 1970s.

All the lesser crimes were called **misdemeanors** (misbehaviors) and were punishable by atonement or corporal punishment. We no longer use corporal punishment, but we certainly use atonement, or a fine, for most misdemeanors, and the use of a fine is still a way for the state to raise money. Also, consider the fact that the words used to classify two major crime categories we use today are approximately 880 years old and the basic behaviors in each category are about the same.

COURT STRUCTURE AND PROCEDURES EMERGE

Under King Henry II (1154–1189), the king's court was centralized at Westminster, the country was divided into five judicial districts, and knights were appointed as circuit-riding judges to travel about the realm hearing cases. Initially, it was the sheriff's job to present the case in court. However, because the people had so long played a part in their own justice system, going all the way back to tribal times, and because they did not always trust the sheriff, pressure mounted for the people to have a more direct role. Consequently, by about 1176, when a person was accused of a crime, it became the sheriff's job to summon 12 knights from the shire and four from the town or village to hear a preliminary version of the case.

This group came to be known as the **grand jury**. The sheriff was responsible to present enough evidence to this grand jury to convince them that a crime really had occured and that the evidence showed that the accused probably did it. If the grand jury agreed, the accused was held for trial before a circuit-riding judge. Otherwise, the accused was allowed to go free. Consequently, when the judge arrived, he heard only those cases that had been screened by the grand jury in this preliminary type of hearing, which made better use of his time.

Today, every case that is prosecuted in federal court goes through the same process. An assistant attorney general in the district where the crime occurred summons a federal grand jury and presents sufficient evidence to convince them of the same issues: that a crime occurred, that the accused probably did it, and that the case should therefore go to trial. Today, a grand jury often is used also at the state level, particularly in the Eastern states. In other states, the prosecutor has the option of using a grand jury or a similar procedure that is detailed in a later chapter. Suffice it to say here that the way in which federal cases reach trial, and the way that local cases may reach trial, is the same as it was over 800 years ago.

Today, the phrase **probable cause** is used to describe these two aspects that the sheriff, and now the prosecutor, was or is required to prove (1) that a crime occurred, and (2) that the accused probably did it. Today, every felony case requires a probable cause hearing before the accused can be held for trial. The details of this are described in Chapter 4.

There was little, if any, written law controlling crime and punishment in England. Customs and traditions evolved out of the tribal practices and blended with the values of society at the time. Consequently, when judges arrived at a court, heard a case, and rendered a decision, they would follow the customs as much as possible and would write the decisions and their reasons for them in a book. Over time, a body of law developed based on custom and tradition and the application of it to a variety of situations as determined by a judge. We call this *common law* because it was commonly understood as the tradition and practice within the community, and it was what judges commonly followed in deciding cases.

As the decisions of judges grew in number, they provided a basis for deciding future cases that were similar. Judges could look back to see how a similar situation had been judged in the past and could follow the same line of thinking. Today, when a court reviews a case and makes a decision that can be used as an example for deciding future cases that are similar, the decision is called a **precedent**. The use of precedent-setting cases as a reference for deciding future cases is known by the Latin phrase **stare decisis**, or the **Doctrine of Precedent**. Once an appellate court makes a case decision about a police or trial procedure and establishes a procedural rule, it becomes the example against which procedures in future similar cases are decided.

As time passed and the people clamored for an increasing role in their justice system, the practice developed to use one group of citizens as the grand jury and a second group, composed of 12 citizens, as a **petite**, or **trial jury**. Initially, the trial jurors conducted their own investigations, as well as hearing evidence and giving a verdict. This led to abuses in the fairness of trials because the jurors would listen to rumors and hearsay evidence during their investigations. Eventually, they were restricted to hearing the evidence in court, and the evidence was presented by the sheriff. Later, another knight presented the evidence and the sheriff then merely provided law enforcement and court security.

An accused (knight) could have the assistance of a fellow knight in presenting his defense, but only if the crime charged was a misdemeanor. The king had enough authority to prohibit the accused from having assistance in felony cases for many years. Naturally, the king did not want an accused felon having help in his defense because he would have a better chance of not being convicted. Then the king would lose out on obtaining the felon's property. This practice is an early recognition that an accused person stands a better chance at trial with a defense attorney than without one.

THE MAGNA CARTA

Henry II and subsequent kings did not completely support the use of jury trials and, when possible, encouraged the sheriff to act as judge, jury, and executioner. It made it easier for kings to confiscate the properties of convicted felons. One of the worst abusers was King John, who assumed the throne upon the death of his brother, Richard the Lion-Hearted. He moved against commoner and noble alike. The nobles did not seem too concerned when the king abused the rights of a commoner, but when John began abusing the rights of the nobles, they responded quickly to protect their interests. On June 15, 1215, they surrounded King John at a spot just north of Windsor Castle known as the Plains of Runnymead, placed their lances to his body, and offered him a deal he could not refuse. They told John that if he signed the document they laid before him, they would not run him through with their lances. John signed the document, known as the **Magna Carta**, or Great Charter, which listed 37 rights guaranteed to citizens, primarily to nobles and the church. Actually, much of the Magna Carta was copied from an earlier document of Henry I, titled the *Charter of Liberties*, but the Magna Carta is the document remembered and cited as the main source of our Bill of Rights.

One of the principal rights guaranteed in the Magna Carta stated that no free man would be seized or imprisoned, or deprived of his property, without first having the case reviewed and judged by his peers. At the time, that guarantee simply referred to those citizens (peers) to be chosen from the community to form what was termed the grand jury to review the evidence and determine if the case should go to trial. That initial guarantee was interpreted broadly to form the basis of our constitutional due process and was expanded in our Constitution to include the right to both a grand jury and a trial jury of one's peers.

COURT STRUCTURE IS COMPLETED

By the end of the fourteenth century, use of the jury system was fairly well established. By about 1360, the role of coroner was created. A knight was appointed in each shire to view a dead body before burial and investigate suspicious deaths to determine the cause; to list all the property of a deceased; to record the names of those felons convicted or declared outlaws; and to list and confiscate their property for the king. A coroner performs very similar responsibilities today in each county.

During the fourteenth century, society grew more complex, with more population, more crime, and more cases to hear. The workload of the circuit-riding judges exceeded what the judges could hear. Consequently, England was divided into five judicial districts, with a crown court in each district where the judges sat and heard cases. The Peace Knight Act of 1361 authorized the appointments of peace knights in the various cities and towns to hear misdemeanor cases, while the felony cases went to the district crown courts. However, felony cases were first screened by a peace knight and grand jury at the local level, so that only those cases with sufficient evidence to show that a crime occurred, and that the accused probably did it, went on to trial. In felony cases, this amounted to a probable cause hearing before a peace knight in a lower court, after which the lower court judge, the peace knight, would either find that probable cause existed and refer the case to the district crown court for trial, or he would find probable cause lacking and dismiss the case.

We will see in Chapter 3 that the basic model has remained the same and is only now being modified in an increasing number of states to eliminate the two-tier structure. Suffice it to say at this point that the court system and primary roles of the justice system were well established by the end of the fourteenth century. There was by that time a chief law enforcement officer for each county, who also detained prisoners and provided court security; a coroner; a body of law; an adversary system; the use of both prosecution and defense; a two-tier court structure; a jury system; the basic crime categories of felony and misdemeanor, with the state as the victim of crime; the procedure of recognizance, or bail; and the principle of *stare decisis*, or precedent, which provides stability, predictability, and fairness in the application of the law.

The point of this short history lesson is to show that the foundation and structure of our current system of justice was established nearly 600 years ago. What we have done beyond that has increased the complexity of justice, but in many ways might be viewed as being more cosmetic than substantive.

Now we take a quantum leap from the fourteenth century to the present. However, as stated above, today's court system is addressed in later chapters. First we need to bridge that 600-year gap with a look at the one essential link with the past that had the most significant impact on our procedural law, the *Magna Carta*. This document, and its predecessor, the *Charter of Liberties*, hold for us the essence of the rights of all people, and the guarantee of due process and the equal protection that are found in the first ten amendments to the Constitution.

THE BILL OF RIGHTS, 1791

The federal document called the **Bill of Rights** contains the first 10 amendments to the Constitution. By including these in the Constitution, the Founding Fathers intended to guarantee for all the people, certain rights of which they could not be deprived by the government. This was done because the founders thought the English king and his agents had frequently abused their rights when America was a colony. They wanted to be certain that these rights had complete protection under the new form of government they were creating.

Additional amendments have been added to the Constitution over the years, and all of them are equally important. However, for our purposes in studying criminal procedures, only five amendments will be examined. They form the basis of most all criminal procedures that we will study. Note that the Fourteenth Amendment was added 77 years after the original Bill of Rights was written. This addition was necessary to ensure that no one violated the other amendments. It often has been used as the basis for forcing states to comply with the other amendments because most states would not otherwise follow them, nor would they enact their own laws to ensure those same rights.

FOURTH AMENDMENT

The right of the people to be secure in their persons, houses, papers, and effects, against unreasonable searches and seizures, shall not be violated, and no warrants shall issue, but upon probable cause, supported by Oath or affirmation, and particularly describing the place to be searched, and the persons or things to be seized.

FIFTH AMENDMENT

No person shall be held to answer for a capital, or otherwise infamous crime, unless on a presentment or indictment of a Grand Jury, except in cases arising in the land or naval forces, or in the militia, when in actual service in time of war or public danger; nor shall any person be subject for the same offense to be twice put in jeopardy of life or limb; nor shall be compelled in any criminal case to be a witness against himself, nor be deprived of life, liberty, or property, without due process of law;

nor shall private property be taken for public use, without just compensation.

SIXTH AMENDMENT

In all criminal prosecutions, the accused shall enjoy the right to a speedy and public trial, by an impartial jury of the State and district wherein the crime shall have been committed, which district shall have been previously ascertained by law, and to be informed of the nature and cause of the accusation; to be confronted with the witnesses against him; to have compulsory process for obtaining witnesses in his favor, and to have the assistance of counsel for his defense.

EIGHTH AMENDMENT

Excessive bail shall not be required, nor excessive fines imposed, nor cruel and unusual punishments inflicted.

FOURTEENTH AMENDMENT

Section 1. All persons born or naturalized in the United States, and subject to the jurisdiction thereof, are citizens of the United States and of the State wherein they reside. No State shall make or enforce any law which shall abridge the privileges or immunities of citizens of the United States; nor shall any State deprive any person of life, liberty, or property, without due process of law; nor deny to any person within its jurisdiction the equal protection of the laws. (Added July 28, 1868.)

The **U.S. Supreme Court** has used the Fourteenth Amendment often to force the states not to violate the guarantees of the other amendments.The guarantees in the Fourth and Fifth Amendments serve as a springboard for the procedures that have been mandated for law enforcement officers, and they are used in Chapter 3 as the basis for understanding police procedures. The Fourth Amendment, protecting citizens against unreasonable search and seizure, was applied to police procedures through a series of Supreme Court cases that are detailed in Chapter 2.

The application of one guarantee in the Fifth Amendment, the protection against self incrimination, better known as the *Miranda* warning, is the focus of Chapter 4. Included in the *Miranda* warning, of course, is one guarantee from the Sixth Amendment, the right to an attorney. The discussion of that right is divided into two areas: (1) the need for police to inform suspects of that right as a part of *Miranda*, and (2) the history of how the right to an attorney became a reality. Application of the Eighth Amendment is a part of Chapter 7.

The balance of this chapter presents a number of fundamental concepts which, when combined with those described in the introduction and in the history given above, provide the conceptual foundation required to appreciate the criminal procedures presented in subsequent chapters.

BASIC LEGAL CONCEPTS

ELEMENTS OF CRIME

The terms *crime* and *public offense* often are used interchangeably because in the technical sense, today all crimes are offenses against the general public, or public will, just as they were against the King in early England. The public is always the legal victim. **Crime** can be defined as *any act committed or omitted in violation of a law forbidding or commanding it, and for which a penalty is proscribed following a conviction*. This means that some acts become crimes when they are committed, such as burglary or robbery, and some acts become crimes when they are omitted, such as not registering for the draft, not filing an income tax return, or not stopping at the scene of an accident in which one was involved. Obviously, the majority of crimes fall into the category of *prohibited acts that are committed*. Although it is not within the scope of this book to devote much time with the laws of crime and punishment, it is appropriate to define what crime is and how a crime may be divided into its elements.

The **elements of a crime** that form the definition of crime stated above are the act, the law, and the punishment. The criminal act is known by the Latin phrase ***actus resus***. Four additional elements are needed to complete the definition of crime: criminal intent (or negligence), which is the guilty mind, known by the Latin phrase as ***mens rea***; the concurrence of the act and the intent; the social harm; and the fact that the harm was caused by the act. We can list these elements in order as follows:

    1. The act, or *actus resus*

    2. The intent, or *mens rea*

    3. The law prohibiting the act

    4. Concurrence between the act and the intent

5. The social harm (to a victim)

6. The cause of the harm being the act

7. The punishment following conviction

When proving a crime in court, a prosecutor must show that the act occurred and that the act caused the harm. Criminal intent is either implied in the act or must be proven separately, depending on the specific crime charged. For example, burglary is the act of entering a place (house, barn, building, etc.) with the intent to commit theft or any felony. A person can enter a house with the intent to steal, to assault, to kidnap, to murder, or any other felony, and the crime may be charged as a burglary. However, the intent is the key element that must be proven, and that is not always easy. Consequently, the police report submitted to the prosecutor to support the charge(s) must be complete and accurate so that the prosecutor knows what elements are there for prosecution.

DEGREES OF CRIME

There are three levels of crime; that is, three levels or degrees of seriousness of the act: felony, misdemeanor, and infraction. Actually, it is not the act itself that determines the level of crime. It is the seriousness of the punishment received following a conviction of the act that determines its level.

A **felony** is a crime that is punishable by execution or by imprisonment in the state prison. A **misdemeanor** is a crime punishable by a fine or a sentence of up to one year in jail, or both jail and a fine. An **infraction** is a crime *punishable* by a fine; one cannot lose his or her freedom as the result of an infraction conviction. In some states, these categories are further divided into classes, such as a Class A or Class B felony, which indicates the seriousness of the crime and the severity of the punishment to follow conviction. In addition to these three basic degrees of seriousness, there is the category known as a **wobbler**, which is a crime that is punishable at the discretion of the court by a term either in prison or in jail.

No other crime categories are described officially in any penal codes, but there are two additional categories in some states. For lack of more creative titles, call these categories Special Felonies A and Special Felonies B. Under subcategory A are crimes that are ordinarily misdemeanors, but when combined with a charge of having a prior conviction, become felonies punishable by a term in state prison. For example, petty theft with a prior theft , a driving under the influence (DUI) charge with four prior DUI convictions, or carrying a concealable firearm without a license and with a prior felony conviction may be charged as felonies, punishable by prison sentences. As examples, as of June 30, 1996, there were 6957 people in state prison in California for petty theft with a prior, and 2728 people in prison for DUIs with priors.

Under the category of Special Felonies B are those felonies that may come under what is termed the *threee-strikes*, or *habitual offender, law*. If an offender is convicted of a felony and has had prior convictions of certain designated felonies, the sentence may be increased substantially. In some states, the additional penalty is mandatory; in other states, the sentencing judge has the discretion to delete one or more of the priors.

ENHANCEMENTS

One dictionary definition of *to enhance* is "to make better, as in value, desirability or attractiveness." Ironically, several years ago, when various state legislatures were seeking ways to increase the severity of punishment for certain crimes, they adopted the term and created what are called **enhancements**. They are designed to *enhance*, *to make better*, the prison sentences given convicted felons. An enhancement is some specific aspect of a crime, or of the criminal's role in the crime, or of the criminal's background (stated in the penal code) that may be added to a criminal complaint which, if proven, will add time to a felon's prison sentence if the felon is also convicted of the basic crime. At the federal level, these are called **harms**, under the Federal Sentencing Guidelines.

Examples of situations that may result in enhancements or harms include the offender who provides another person with a firearm during a crime for the purpose of helping that person commit the crime, anyone who personally uses a firearm in the commission of a felony, anyone convicted of a felony who has had a prior felony conviction, or anyone who commits a crime as a member of a street gang.

There are many other enhancements that are derived from the nature of the victim, such as a crime against a minor under the age of 14, or a pregnant woman, or that result in great bodily injury or a substantial financial loss to a victim. Enhancements must usually be charged and proved separately from the basic criminal charge that brings the accused before the court. Whether to charge them is a decision made by the prosecuting attorney. Also, the prosecutor may charge an enhancement initially, then dismiss it later if warranted by the circumstances, such as a plea bargain agreement, discussed in a later chapter.

MALA EN SE VERSUS MALA PROHIBITA CRIMES

These are Latin phrases that represent two distinct categories of crime. *Mala en se* crimes are those that are inherently evil. They are, by their very nature, evil, bad, or wrong things to do, such as most crimes against a person or against property. Usually, there is wide agreement among the members of society that these acts are evil and must be prohibited by law, such as the laws prohibiting murder, rape, robbery, theft, arson, and assault.

Mala prohibita crimes are those acts that are not really evil, bad, or wrong but still pose a threat to society and need to be controlled. Most traffic offenses fall into this category.

There is a group of crimes that lie somewhere between the two extremes of a continuum, from totally evil to completely harmless, that control conduct, only because a sufficient majority thinks that legal control is necessary because harm results from those acts. However, others think that these behaviors pose no threat or harm and should not be controlled. These acts, usually called **victimless crimes**, fall within this category: gambling, drug use, prostitution, and related crimes of vice. Are these evil and wrong or just acts that need legal control?

TYPES OF LAWS

Laws can be put into one or more of several categories, depending on the point of view being considered. Several of the more commonly used categories are described below.

Substantive law is the body of law that defines crime and punishment. It governs the behavior of the citizens within society and tells the citizens what they cannot do or what they must do, to obey the law. If one violates the substantive law, it is a crime. Substantive laws are found in the penal code, health and safety code, vehicle code, business and professions code, and fish and game code, to name but a few. Their primary purpose is to protect society and protect law-abiding citizens from the lawbreakers.

Procedural law, on the other hand, has nothing to do with regulating the behavior of citizens. It is the body of law that lays out the step-by-step procedures that must be followed by police officers, court personnel, correctional officers, and other officials in processing an accused person through the system. Procedural laws are the laws that must be obeyed by the officers and agents who work within the justice system to protect the constitutional rights and due process of every citizen at every level of involvement in the system, from the point of initial police contact, through arrest, booking, trial, and punishment.

Substantive law, then, protects society from the citizen who might threaten the social order and safety of others, whereas procedural law protects the citizen from any government effort to deprive him or her of any rights or freedoms, without due process.

Statutory law refers to any law that originates in a legislature. A law (bill) is introduced in a senate or assembly, referred to an appropriate committee for consideration, then voted in as law by the majorities in both houses (the senate and assembly). It thus becomes a law, a statute.

We can mix two categories of law by saying that the vast majority of laws passed by the legislature are laws that regulate some type of behavior by either criminalizing a behavior that threatens society or decriminalizing a behavior that is no longer viewed as a threat. Therefore, most statutory law is also substantive law.

Case law is the body of law that results from a court case and is actually created by judges. In a typical case, a person is arrested, tried, and convicted of a crime. Either during or after this process the person (or his or her attorney) believes that he or she has been denied a constitutional right or protection along the way and appeals the case to a higher court, either within the state or federal system. Judges on the higher court review the records of the case, read and listen to arguments by the attorneys representing the person who appealed and the person representing the state (the prosecutor), then decide who is right. This decision may result in creating a procedure that must be followed by law enforcement officers or the lower courts in all future situations that are like the one appealed.

PROCEDURAL VERSUS SUBSTANTIVE LAW

Again, we can mix two types of law categories, by saying that most procedural law is created by case law decisions, and that rarely do case decisions affect the substantive law. When a person appeals his or her case from a trial court, he or she usually is not challenging the substantive law, only the procedural law. For example, if a man is arrested, accused, tried, convicted, and sent to prison for murder, and then appeals his case, he is not claiming that the substantive law prohibiting murder is wrong and should be changed. He is claiming that some procedures used by the police or the court violated his constitutional rights in some way and therefore that his conviction was the result of an illegal activity by police or the court and should be reversed. If the appellate court agrees, it will throw out his conviction either because existing procedural law had been violated, or because the procedures violated a right protected by the Constitution but not yet controlled by an existing procedural law. In the latter case, the court will create a new procedure to be certain that the constitutional right in question is protected in all future cases.

Many examples of this will be studied in subsequent chapters, and we will see that most current procedures that police, courts, and correctional officers must follow were created by case decisions made within the last 35 years.

THE SOCIAL CONTRACT

The **social contract** refers to a theory that attempts to explain and/or describe the origin and maintenance of organized society and the legal relationship between the citizens and the government. In its simplest terms, the theory holds that the state, with its government and laws, was created and is maintained through the mutual agreement entered into by all the citizens and the ruler (state), as a way of having social order, protection, and freedom. The main principles are the equality of all citizens before the law, the merging of individual interests with those of the state, and the necessity that each person surrender certain rights for the good of society. Citizens recognize that at times there is a conflict between having freedom and maintaining social order and safety, and that they cannot have both complete freedom and safety, because they are sometimes in conflict with each other. Also, they cannot enjoy either one to the fullest, because of the type of society that would result. Imagine what life would be like at either end of the following continuum:

The Social Contract Continuum

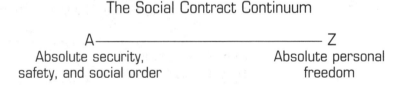

A——————————————————— Z
Absolute security,   Absolute personal
safety, and social order   freedom

Establishing absolute order and security could severely limit which freedoms would be enjoyed by the individual. However, absolute freedom could lead to anarchy and a complete absence of social order and security. Consequently, when entering this social contract, citizens agree to give up some of their freedoms to the state to gain the desired level of safety and security. As an example, citizens could have said to each other: "I won't steal from you and you won't steal from me; then we will all be protected from thieves."

To put it in a contemporary legal framework: "I won't drive over 65 mph and you won't drive over 65 mph; then we will all be protected from speeders." We all agree to give up the freedom to drive as fast as we want in order to be safe from the carnage that would result. In agreeing to give up some of our freedoms, we also give consent to the state to take appropriate action against us if we break our part of the contract. For its part, the state will not invade the privacy of the individual unless it has some overriding interest, as defined by the rules of the contract, the law.

The social contract theory is primarily the work of a French philosopher, Jean-Jacques Rousseau (*Le Contract Social*, 1762), supported by two English philosophers, Thomas Hobbs and John Locke, together with John Stuart Mills' philosophy of *utilitarianism*, which had as its theme "the greatest happiness for the greatest number." For Rousseau, *state* was the term used to mean the general will of the people, the common good. These two theories about the relationships between the individual and the state, the Social Contract and utilitarianism, embody principles underlying our current system of justice.

Like any theory, these are only as good as they can be made useful by applying them to real-life situations. Without elaborating any further on the social contract, we can see how practical this approach is because it portrays exactly what we need and must deal with in today's society. The trick in applying it is knowing how to balance the two needs. How do we balance the needs of the state with that of the individual? How much freedom are you willing to give up to ensure your own safety? It probably would vary somewhat with each person answering this question. Therefore, we use Mills' notion of the greatest good for the greatest number, and build into the contract, laws or procedures for determining that. As a reader, where would you place the balancing point?

The Social Contract Continuum

Recalling the symbol of justice—the statue of the woman standing blindfolded holding the scales of justice in her outstretched hand—it will be obvious that she is trying to balance those same needs. Read the decisions of the U.S. Supreme Court in any search and seizure case, or other right-to-privacy cases, and it will be equally obvious that the justices are trying to balance those needs as well. Chapter 3 deals with police procedures, including the authority to stop, arrest, search, and interrogate. All of these steps in police procedures are controlled by case law that can be examined within the context of this safety–freedom continuum, or social contract teeter-totter. We will see that as the Supreme Court became more involved in creating procedural law over the last 45 years, the balancing point has shifted back and forth, from a primary concern for individual freedom during the 1960s and 1970s, to an increasing concern for public safety and social order in the 1980s and 1990s; from a Court concerned with due process to one more concerned with law enforcement and crime control.

PARTIES TO A CRIME

Individuals can become involved in a crime, can be a party to a crime, in one of two ways: (1) as a principal, or (2) as an accessory.

Principals are all the persons involved in the commission of a crime, whether felony or misdemeanor, and whether they directly commit the crime or help (aid and abet) in its commission. It could also include those who have advised and encouraged the commission of the crime; or those who advised, counseled, or encouraged others who are of a vulnerable age or are in a vulnerable condition, such as younger minors, lunatics, or idiots; or who, by fraud, contrivance, or force, occasion the drunkenness of another for the purpose of causing him or her to commit any crime, or who, by threats, menaces, command, or coercion, compel another to commit any crime. This definition of a principal is worded so as to include anyone who participates in the commission of any crime in any manner, either in planning it, committing it, or encouraging another to commit it.

Accessories are persons who, after a felony has been committed, knowingly and willingly harbor, conceal, or aid a principal in such felony, with the intent of having the principal avoid or escape from arrest, trial, conviction, or punishment. An accessory is not involved in the actual crime at all. Rather, after a crime has been committed, an accessory comes on the scene knowingly to assist the principal (felon), with the *intent* of letting the principal avoid arrest, prosecution, or punishment. An example comes from an early scene in the O. J. Simpson case in California. Simpson was wanted by the police as the principal in two murders. At one point before his arrest, his friend, Al Cowling, drove Simpson up and down the Los Angeles freeways at about 30 miles per hour, with the police swarming all around them, waiting for Simpson's Bronco to stop. Eventually, Simpson was arrested. Authorities considered charging Cowling as an accessory because he certainly did provide some sort of assistance to Simpson by driving him around for so long. However, he was not charged, undoubtedly because it would not have been possible to prove the element of *intent*. If he had intended to help Simpson avoid arrest, he would have led the police in a far different type of chase.

In that case, the crime of being an accessory is a wobbler, punishable by a fine, jail, or up to three years in prison. An accessory can be charged, tried, convicted, and punished regardless of what happens to the principal. If Cowling had led police on a wild chase to help Simpson avoid arrest, he might now be sitting in prison while Simpson wanders about freely after being found not guilty by a jury.

DEGREES OF PROOF

Different **degrees**, or standards, **of proof** are necessary at various steps in criminal procedures, depending on the seriousness of the action taken against a citizen and the impact it has on the citizen's freedom from the point of police contact to conviction in court. The following continuum represents the points where we could place these proofs:

1	2	3	4	5	6
No legal Sufficiency					Complete sufficiency

A police officer might have a hunch, a gut feeling, about some situation or some person, but that does not provide a basis for legal action. It should not be ignored, however, by the officer.

REASONABLE SUSPICION

An officer may be confronted with a situation in which a person arouses in the officer a suspicion that the person might be involved in a criminal activity that just occurred, is occurring, or is about to occur, based on objective facts presented by the situation. This goes beyond a hunch, because there must be some factual basis for the officer's suspicion that the officer can explain in court, if necessary. Factors such as the time of day, location of the event, behavior of the person suspected, officer safety, or the officer's experience might combine to provide the factual basis.

There is no specific rule here that can be applied to every situation. *Reasonableness* is the guiding principle, and each situation must be judged by itself, considering the totality of the circumstances. The question to be answered is: Given any law enforcement situation, is it reasonable to conclude that an officer, any officer, would become suspicious? Here the word *suspicion* provides an officer with the *basis for investigation* to determine if the suspicion is correct. In Chapter 3, **reasonable suspicion** is described in detail as the legal basis required in certain specific police procedures.

PROBABLE CAUSE

Probable cause and *reasonable cause* are interchangeable terms and mean the same thing. Probable cause is a concept that comes into play in a variety of procedures. It is the basis of a valid search and seizure of evidence, of obtaining a valid arrest or search warrant, making an arrest, or of a judge holding someone for trial. It consists of facts and trustworthy information, sufficient in themselves, to warrant a person of reasonable caution to believe that (1) a crime has been committed, and (2) the person under consideration has committed it (in the case of an arrest) or that contraband does exist in the location to be searched (in the case of a search and seizure of evidence or obtaining a warrant). A definition of probable cause used by one state's standards and training commission is: "a set of facts that would cause a person of ordinary care and prudence to honestly believe and strongly suspect that the person being arrested may have committed the crime." The problem with this definition is the fact that a police officer is not a person of "ordinary care and prudence." He or she becomes far more suspicious in any given situation than the ordinary person. In any event, the word *cause* provides an officer with the *basis for action*. This is discussed in greater detail in Chapter 3 as the basis for police to make an arrest or to obtain an arrest warrant.

PREPONDERANCE OF EVIDENCE

Preponderance of the evidence is a degree of proof used in court and means a probability, or sufficiency of belief, of 51 percent or greater, to make a decision. It allows for some doubt or some evidence to the contrary. Consequently, it is used in various proceedings short of an actual criminal trial in which a person's guilt would be established. For example, if a defendant challenges the legality of a confession used as evidence, the state would have to convince the judge by a preponderance of the evidence that the defendant was advised of his or her rights before questioning, and waived them freely and voluntarily.

CLEAR AND CONVINCING EVIDENCE

Clear and convincing evidence lies somewhere between probable cause and reasonable doubt, but closer to the latter. It means that there is enough proof to show a high probability of belief to justify a conclusion. For example, it might be used in juvenile proceedings to determine whether a very young juvenile knew the wrongfulness of an act.

BEYOND A REASONABLE DOUBT

Beyond a reasonable doubt means that there is sufficient evidence to prove the case to the point of conclusive belief, beyond any conclusion reached by any other explanation. This is the degree of proof necessary to prove a defendant guilty of a crime. If two explanations seem reasonable and of similar comparison, a jury is instructed to believe that which favors the defendant. Therefore, a verdict represents a conclusion based on an explanation supported by the evidence that is far more reasonable to accept than any other explanation and conclusion. It is not absolute, but conclusive belief, so as to eliminate other beliefs from consideration.

ADDITONAL LEGAL CONCEPTS

EX POST FACTO AND RETROACTIVE LAWS

The Latin phrase **ex post facto** means *after* the fact. It is a phrase that refers to a law that is passed making some behavior a crime, aggravating or increasing the sentence for a crime, or lowering the degree of proof required for a conviction of a crime, and having that law apply to past cases. This is prohibited by the U.S. Constitution. However, if a law is passed, or a court decision made, that decriminalizes an act, lowers a sentence, or decreases some legal requirement, it may be applied **retroactively**, that is, to past cases. If a law works to the advantage of the accused, it can be applied retroactively. It cannot be retroactive if it disadvantages the accused or adds a greater penalty. It would not be fair to punish a person for a past act. This does not apply when adding an extra penalty for an enhancement because of a prior conviction.

JURISDICTION AND VENUE

Jurisdiction always refers to the *authority* of an agent or agency to act in some capacity. Often, that authority is limited by a political boundary. For example, a city police officer has jurisdiction (authority) to police within the city limits, a sheriff has authority to act within a county, and a state police officer or trooper has authority to act statewide. We will note in the discussions of the courts that each one has certain types of jurisdiction, their authority to act.

Venue always refers to either the county in which the crime occurred or from which the jury is drawn. A change of venue means a change in the location of where the trial will be held and the jury drawn.

CORPUS DELICTI

The *corpus delicti* is the *body of the crime*, any crime. It consists of two elements: (1) there was harm or loss to a victim, and (2) the harm or loss was caused by criminal means. This must be proved in the case of every crime, in addition to proving that the accused did it. This prevents a person from being convicted on his or her own confession alone, without proving that a criminal act occurred.

INDEPENDENT STATE GROUNDS

The phrase **independent state grounds** describes a legal concept by which a state, through its legislature, can enact laws that provide greater procedural protection for people accused of crimes than that required by the Constitution, but not less. In other words, the Constitution, and the U.S. Supreme Court's interpretations of what the rights in that document actually mean, set the minimum procedural standards that must be provided in any criminal proceeding. If a state wants an accused person to have more rights or greater protections, it can enact laws to provide them. We note examples of this in subsequent chapters, where some states provide greater protections in many procedural areas than is required.

SUMMARY

This chapter began with a brief history that traced the development of our court structure and highlighted the concepts and procedures that form the basis of today's criminal procedures. These are listed following this summary, as a way of indicating the concepts and vocabulary that one should know from the reading, and before we examine applications of the procedures themselves. Additional concepts and vocabulary are provided throughout the book as we progress from the point of initial police contact with a suspect in Chapter 3 to the final forms of release from contact to the convicted person in Chapter 7.

The case decisions by appellate courts have created many procedural rules that have had the most profound effect on law enforcement and the efforts of police to solve crimes and provide sufficient evidence to the prosecutor that will lead to a criminal conviction. A majority of these rules have come from U.S. Supreme Court decisions within the past 35 years. Rules decided during the 1960s and 1970s tipped the social contract teeter-totter in favor of individual freedom. That balancing point has been shifting back toward the center, and even a little more toward public safety, in recent years by court justices who have a different orientation. The procedures presented in the chapters to follow will give the reader ample opportunity to discern the priorities of the various courts.

KEY TERMS AND CONCEPTS

Accessory	Felony
Adversary system	Fifth Amendment
Atonement	Fourteenth Amendment
Beyond a reasonable doubt	Fourth Amendment
Bill of Rights	Independent state grounds
Case law	Jurisdiction
Clear and convincing evidence	*Magna Carta*
Common law	*Mala en se*
Corpus delicti	*Mala prohibita*
Crime	Misdemeanor
Degrees of proof	Precedent
Eighth Amendment	Preponderance of the evidence
Elements of a crime	Principal
Enhancement	Probable cause
Ex post facto	Procedural law

Reasonable suspicion
Recognizance
Reeve
Retroactivity
Sheriff
Sixth Amendment

Social Contract
Statutory law
Substantive law
U.S. Constitution
U.S. Supreme Court
Venue

REFERENCES

Friendly, Fred W., and Martha J. H. Elliott. *The Constitution: That Delicate Balance.* New York: Random House, 1984.

Rothwax, Harold J. *Guilty: The Collapse of Criminal Justice.* New York: Random House, 1996.

THE EXCLUSIONARY RULE

The right of the people to be secure in their persons, houses, papers, and effects, against unreasonable searches and seizures, shall not be violated, and no warrants shall issue, but upon probable cause, supported by oath or affirmation, and particularly describing the place to be searched, and the persons or things to be seized.

Fourth Amendment

INTRODUCTION

To study police procedures in their proper legal context, it is necessary at this point to introduce one of the most important rules of law that police must obey, the **Exclusionary Rule**. It is a procedural rule that a law enforcement officer must have on his or her mind in every investigative situation that might involve the collection of evidence. It is also a procedural rule that every defense attorney knows well and will use in an effort to exclude evidence in almost every criminal case. In most instances, when a police officer is subpoenaed to testify in court, it is to testify as to how he or she obtained the evidence, not about the guilt of the accused. How this procedure was created, how it became a binding rule for every police officer to follow, and how exceptions to it have been allowed all make for an interesting story. Therefore, it is presented in detail as a prelude to studying police procedures.

The exclusionary rule is a prime example of a procedural law created by case law; created by a decision of the U.S. Supreme Court. As noted in Chapter 1, the role of the appellate courts, including the Supreme Court, is not to make law but to interpret what existing law means. Specifically, the U.S. Supreme Court has the responsibility of interpreting what the U.S. Constitution means and whether any federal or state laws conflict with the rights therein guaranteed to the people.

Simply stated, the **exclusionary rule** is a rule of law which holds that *evidence seized illegally by the government (police) is inadmissible in a court of law to prove guilt.* The reason that police need to follow this rule is obvious. If they do not follow it, and seize evidence illegally, it cannot be used against a person arrested by the police and accused of the crime. It will result in the **suppression of evidence.** Without the evidence of a crime, the state cannot prove that a crime occurred, and the suspect will go free. One would think, then, that police would never seize evidence illegally because it would ruin their own case, and their efforts would be in vain. The problem with this assumption, however, is the fact that whether police seize evidence illegally often is determined a long time after the fact by an appellate court sitting far away from the scene of the events that produced the evidence. Sometimes police do not realize they are not following the rule. Sometimes they do know, but do not care.

True, there are certain guidelines for police to follow, but there is no absolute rule to govern every situation. Consequently, whether or not evidence is admitted or excluded from a trial depends on how judges interpret the general guidelines as applied to the situation before them. Sometimes, a judge of a higher court will disagree with the trial judge, and a judge at an even higher court might disagree with the other judge, and so on. Sometimes it takes two or three years in this appellate process for the police officer to know if the manner in which the evidence was seized was legal. Even when a case reaches the U.S. Supreme Court, where nine justices sit as the highest legal minds in the country, they might not agree with each other. However, their decision, possibly made by a vote of 5 to 4, will become the law of the land. Three Supreme Court cases are discussed below that demonstrate how and why the exclusionary rule was created and how it affects police procedures. Following that, three more recent cases are presented that explain the exceptions to the rule made by the Court.

CASES LEADING TO THE EXCLUSIONARY RULE

WEEKS v. UNITED STATES, 1914

Weeks was suspected of being involved in illegal lottery gambling. On December 21, 1911, in Kansas City, Missouri, local police went to his residence while Weeks was at work to search for evidence. After being told by a neighbor where the door key was hidden, they entered his home and searched his room and removed various papers and other personal property, which they turned over to a U.S. Marshal. Later that same day, the officers, accompanied by the Marshal, returned to Weeks' residence, where they were admitted by a roomer. They completed a more extensive search and took away many of Weeks' personal effects, including letters and lottery tickets showing his illegal activity.

Weeks was arrested at the express office where he worked at Union Station. He was charged in federal court with the use of the mails for the purpose of transporting illegal lottery tickets, in violation of Section 213 of the *Federal Criminal Code*. He petitioned the court for the return of all his effects, claiming that they had been seized illegally because police did not have a warrant. His petition was denied and he was fined and imprisoned.

Weeks appealed to the U.S. Supreme Court and his case was argued before it on December 2 and 3, 1913, two years after his arrest and conviction. The Court announced its decision on February 24, 1914. Chief Justice Day wrote the opinion for the Court:

> If letters and private documents can thus be seized and held and used in evidence against a citizen accused of an offense, the protection of the Fourth Amendment, declaring his right to be secure against such searches and seizures, is of no value, and, so far as those thus placed are concerned, might as well be stricken from the Constitution...We therefore reach the conclusion that the letters in question were taken from the house of the accused by an official of the United States, acting under color of his office, in direct violation of the constitutional rights of the defendant.

The Supreme Court reversed Weeks' conviction and ruled that the evidence was seized illegally and could not be used in federal court. Consequently, he was not retried. The Court also discussed the seizure of documents by the local police, but declined to address the legality of that because, as Chief Justice Day stated: "...the Fourth Amendment is not directed to individual misconduct by such officials. Its limitations reach the Federal government and its agencies."

Although the Supreme Court did not mention the phrase *exclusionary rule*, its decision created the rule, and the phrase was created later. Notice, however, that in the words of Justice Day, the ruling applied only to federal courts because the court believed that the Constitution applied only to federal procedures. In fact, the prevailing attitude was that all of the amendments to the Constitution applied only to federal procedures. Nevertheless, 20 states adopted the so-called **Weeks doctrine** into their own body of procedural law. Iowa had enacted their own version of an exclusionary rule even before *Weeks*. However, 27 states decided not to follow *Weeks*, and for a majority of local police and sheriffs, it was business as usual, making whatever illegal searches and seizures they wanted for the next 47 years. In fact, federal court allowed the admission of illegally seized evidence if it was seized by local police and not federal officers. Consequently, if federal agents suspected contraband located in a house and wanted to make a search but did not have sufficient probable cause to obtain a search warrant, they would have the local police make the search, then give them the evidence. This practice came to be known as the **silver platter doctrine**, because the federal agents would be handed good evidence on a silver platter.

WOLF v. COLORADO, 1949

In 1944, Dr. Julius A. Wolf, a Denver physician, was charged with conspiring to perform an illegal abortion. He and his co-conspirator pled not guilty. At their trial, the prosecutor introduced into evidence Dr. Wolf's appointment book, which would prove the charge that Mildred Cairo had obtained an illegal abortion from Dr. Wolf. Wolf moved to suppress the appointment book as evidence because it had been seized from his office without a warrant, in violation of Colorado's own version of the exclusionary rule. The trial judge denied his motion. He was convicted and sentenced to a term in prison from 15 months to 5 years. On appeal, his sentence was affirmed by the Iowa State Supreme Court. Finally, in 1948, the U.S. Supreme Court agreed to hear his case.

Justice Felix Frankfurter stated the issue clearly in the introduction to the Court's opinion, which was decided on June 27, 1949:

> The precise question for consideration is this: does a conviction by a State court for a State offense deny the "due process law" required by the Fourteenth Amendment, solely because evidence that was admitted at the trial was obtained under circumstances which would render it inadmissible in a prosecution for violation of a federal law in a court of the United Sates because there deemed to be an infraction of the Fourth Amendment as applied in *Weeks v. United States* 232 U.S. 383?

In a vote of 6 to 3, the Court answered with a resounding "no!" The Court suggested that an exclusionary rule was one remedy to illegal searches and seizure, but it was not the only remedy, and the federal court should not dictate to the states what sort of remedy to use. Justice Frankfurter also noted that if the defendant does not gain satisfaction in his criminal case, "the common law provides for damages against the searching officer…and against persons assisting in the execution of an illegal search."

Consequently, in those states not having their own controls over search and seizure, the police were left to their own devices. For example, in New York, police would stop and search people or places at will without ever obtaining a search warrant. The year following the decision in the case discussed below, they obtained over 800 warrants before searching.

MAPP v. OHIO, 1961

The *Mapp* case stands as a watershed in the history of criminal due process. It established one of the most controversial procedures of our time, the exclusionary rule, as a mandatory procedure in all states. It is revered by defense attorneys and reviled by most law enforcement officers. The last three Republican administrations hoped to reload the U.S. Supreme Court by appointments of individuals who would reverse the vile thing that succeeded in letting the criminals go free. Needless to say, it did not work; that is, not completely. Just how this procedure came to be mandated on the states is a fascinating story.

Ohio was one of those states in which the courts had rejected the Weeks doctrine (*State v. Lindusay*, 1930) as a part of its own criminal procedures in 1936. However, in 1955 the Ohio legislature enacted an exclusionary rule, requiring police to obtain search warrants. And as it is in the case of any warrant, the officer must complete an affidavit stating the probable cause in support of a warrant request and convince a judge to issue the warrant.

At about 2:30 A.M. on the morning of May 20, 1957, a Cleveland police sergeant, Carl Delau, arrived home "a little drunk" from a party and went to bed. Shortly thereafter, he was awakened by a phone call from a man known to him as Don King, a reputed numbers racketeer (Rothwax 1996). King told the sleepy Delau that someone had just bombed his house and wanted to know what to do. DeLau asked how he knew it was actually a bomb, and King replied that his entire front porch and front wall had been blown off of his house. Apparently, Delau indicated that he would report it. Within a few minutes, however, the police dispatcher phoned Delau and told him to get out there to investigate a bombing.

Three days later, Sgt. Delau received a phone tip that the alleged bomber, Virgil Ogiltree, was hiding out at 14705 Milverton Road, Cleveland. That afternoon, Sgt. Delau and two other detectives went to the address, a two-story, two-family flat, identified Ogiltree's car parked near the residence, and staked it out. Finally, the officers got tired of waiting, so they went to the door of the flat occupied by a young black woman, Dollree Mapp, who was known to

Delau from a prior arrest. They knocked on the door, and she called down from the upstairs window to inquire what they wanted. When they told her they wanted to search her house, she said she would call her attorney first, and disappeared from the window. She returned within a few minutes and told Delau that they could not search without a warrant.

Sergeant DeLau and the two other detectives returned to their car and radioed in for a warrant and for some additional officers to help. Three hours later they returned to Miss Mapp's residence, along with six uniformed officers, and again asked Miss Mapp to search, claiming that they had a warrant. When she refused, one officer broke a door window pane, unlatched the door, and they all entered the hallway and moved toward her flat. She rushed down to meet them and demanded to see the warrant. When one officer held up a piece of paper, claiming it was the warrant, she grabbed it out of his hand and shoved it down inside the front of her sweater.

Stories about what occurred next vary. According to Sgt. Delau, the warrant was visible, protruding from her sweater, so he grabbed it back. She then became unruly and had to be restrained with handcuffs. According to Miss Mapp, the officers handcuffed her, held her in a corner, then reached under her sweater after the warrant. Regardless of who is correct, the police obtained the piece of paper they claimed was the warrant, cuffed her, and thoroughly searched her residence, including drawers, closets, and cabinets. Ogiltree, the bombing suspect was not found because he was not there. However, the police did find "pictures of both male and female nude models with all their organs totally undressed," some pencil sketches of nudes, and four books: *London Stage Affair, Affairs of a Troubadour, Memoirs of a Hotel Man,* and *Little Darlings.* Police also searched her basement and found illegal gambling material. She was arrested and charged with both possession of the betting material, a misdemeanor, and possession of obscene materials, a felony. On their way out, police also searched the flat next to Mapp's, where they found Ogiltree hiding and arrested him for the bombing.

Miss Mapp was tried on the misdemeanor in police court and was acquitted. Her felony trial began in September 1958, and she was charged with "unlawfully and knowingly having in her possession certain lewd and lascivious books, pictures, and photographs." Her attorney questioned the legality of the search, and when police indicated that the so-called warrant had disappeared, he moved to suppress the evidence, claiming that the officers actually did not have a warrant. No one seemed to bring up the fact that if the police did have a real warrant, it would not have mentioned any "obscene" material anyway.

The trial judge denied the motion to suppress, and Mapp was convicted and sentenced to seven years in prison for possession of obscene material in her own home. Her attorney appealed to the Ohio State Supreme Court on the basis that the Ohio obscenity statute violated the First Amendment and therefore was unconstitutional. Four of the Ohio justices agreed, but their votes were not enough to reverse her conviction. Upon further appeal, the U.S. Supreme Court agreed to hear the case in 1961.

The basis of the appeal by her attorney, and his written and oral arguments before the Court, centered on the constitutionality of Ohio's broadly worded obscenity statute and Mapp's First Amendment right to free expression and the right to possess any written materials or drawings in the privacy of her own home. Her attorney did not make this a Fourth Amendment search and seizure issue. Many of the questions raised by the justices during the oral argument by the state's attorney were about the fact that mere possession of obscenity in one's own home was a felony. That really concerned the justices.

When Mapp's attorney attempted to explain that the obscene material did not even belong to her but to a former roomer, Justice Felix Frankfurter interrupted to ask exactly what the issue before the court was, and asked if the legality of the search and seizure was before the Court. Her attorney seemed somewhat flustered by the mention of this new issue. Nevertheless, he did start to argue that it was illegal, when Justice Frankfurter interrupted him again to say: "Are you asking us to overrule the *Wolf* case in this Court? I notice it isn't cited in your brief." The attorney was not familiar with the *Wolf* case, and perhaps not even familiar with search and seizure issues, so he indicated no, that he was not asking the Court to reverse *Wolf*, and he let the issue of search and seizure drop.

Upon completion of the oral arguments by both sides, an unusual event occurred. For the first time in the Court's history, it allowed an oral argument to be presented by a representative of the American Civil Liberties Union (ACLU) who had submitted a written brief and requested to be heard as *amicus curiae*, a friend of the court. It was as if the ACLU attorney sensed that Justice Frankfurter wanted to make an issue out of the search and seizure by bringing it up himself, so the ACLU attorney began his address to the court by referring to the *Wolf* case and stated:

The American Civil Liberties Union and its Ohio affiliate... [are] very clear as to the question directed toward the appellant that we are asking this court to reconsider *Wolf v. Colorado* and to find that evidence that is unlawfully and illegally obtained should not be permitted into a state proceeding and its production is a violation of the federal constitution's Fourth Amendment and the Fourteenth Amendment. We have no hesitancy in asking the court to reconsider it because we think that it is a necessary part of due process.

After stating this, however, the attorney indicated that his primary purpose in addressing the Court was to urge them to declare the obscenity statute of Ohio unconstitutional, and he proceeded to address that statute as a First Amendment issue in the *Mapp* case.

Later, in the privacy of their chambers, the justices discussed the legality of Ohio's obscenity statute within the context of the First and Fourteenth Amendments, and they unanimously voted to reverse Mapp's conviction and declare the statute unconstitutional (Rothwax, 1996). Justice Tom Clark was assigned to write the Court's opinion. However, the opinion he wrote focused on the Fourth Amendment and the exclusionary rule and did not address the obscenity issue or the Ohio statute at all.

When his opinion was circulated among the other justices to read and sign, Justice Potter Stewart was "shocked" by the change in the written opinion from that which had been accepted as the basis for reversal of Mapp's conviction. As Rothwax stated, Justice Clark's opinion "was based on arguments that had never even been briefed, argued, or discussed before the Court (Rothwax,1996, p. 45)." Justice Stewart later indicated that he believed the other justices met together to form a "rump caucus" and agreed to make the *Mapp* case a vehicle by which the Fourteenth Amendment could be used to make the Fourth Amendment and the exclusionary rule binding on the states.

Regardless of the objections of Justice Stewart and several other justices, the opinion written by Justice Clark was approved by a 5 to 4 majority (the Warren Court, with its due process orientation) and held that

...the Fourth Amendment's right of privacy has been declared enforceable against the States through the Due Process Clause of the Fourteenth, it is enforceable against them by the same sanction of exclusion as is used against the Federal Government. Were it otherwise, then, just as without the *Weeks* rule the assurance against unreasonable federal searches and seizures would be "a form of words," valueless and undeserving of mention in a perpetual charter of inestimable human liberties, so too, without that rule, the freedom from state invasions of privacy would be so ephemeral and so neatly severed from its conceptual nexus with the freedom from all brutish means of coercing evidence as not to merit this Court's high regard as a freedom implicit in the concept of ordered liberty.

With this decision, the exclusionary rule was imposed on the states and on all state and local law enforcement officers as the primary procedural law that guides their actions. It is against this rule that much of the efforts by police are judged legal or illegal. Any evidence seized illegally, in violation of the Fourth Amendment, cannot be used in court to prove guilt. The sole purpose of the rule is to *police the police*—to deter police from violating the rights of citizens guaranteed in the Fourth Amendment.

The theory holds that if the police know their evidence cannot be used if they seize it illegally, they will follow the law. It is a rule of procedural law that was railroaded through the Supreme Court by a majority of activist justices seeking to impose their version of due process on the rest of the legal community. It is also a rule of law that demonstrates just how delicate the balance is between individual freedom and social protection, and how a simple majority of the Court can decide just where that balancing point will be.

One of the Supreme Court bailiffs in the *Mapp* case had agreed to phone Dollree Mapp when the justices reached their decision. He phoned her every Monday morning for 12 weeks after her case was argued to say that no decision had been made. But finally, on the thirteenth Monday, he called her with the decision and, according to her, "that was the day that the Supreme Court washed my conviction down the drain." Dollree Mapp is all but forgotten by most people, but the rule that the justices created from her case remains on the mind of every law enforcement officer, every attorney, and every judge, every day.

As indicated above at the beginning of the *Mapp* case presentation, how it developed makes for an interesting story. By way of conclusion, Dollree Mapp did not live happily ever after when her conviction was reversed. She was convicted of drug possession in New York in 1973 and was sentenced to a term in state prison of from 20 years to life. After serving 9 years, 4 months, and 17 days in prison, her sentence was commuted to time served and she was paroled. She continued to maintain her innocence of the drug charge and has petitioned the governor for a full pardon. After her release, she went to work in Long Island as a legal aide for prison inmates. As for Don King, who had his front porch and front wall blown away by the bomb, he went on to become one of the country's leading boxing promoters. Sergeant DeLau eventually retired.

EXCEPTIONS TO THE RULE

As the saying goes, for every rule there are many exceptions. This is true for the exclusionary rule, and the Supreme Court has established three exceptions that affect the application of the rule by police in their collection of evidence: (1) the inevitable discovery exception; (2) the public safety exception, and (3) the good faith exception. Each was created from one or more of the case decisions described below.

THE INEVITABLE DISCOVERY EXCEPTION

On Christmas Eve, 1968, a 10-year-old girl named Pamela Powers disappeared from a YMCA building in Des Moines, Iowa, where she had accompanied her parents to watch an athletic event. Shortly after she disappeared, a man later identified as Robert Williams was seen leaving the YMCA carrying a large bundle wrapped in a blanket. A 14-year-old boy who had helped Williams open his car door reported that he had seen "two legs in it and they were skinny and white."

Williams was a local man, known to police, and had recently been released from a mental institution. He became the immediate suspect. His car was found the next day 160 miles east of Des Moines in Davenport, Iowa. Later, several items of clothing belonging to the child, some of Williams' clothing, and an army blanket like the one used to bundle up the girl when Williams carried her out of the YMCA were found at a rest stop near Grinnell, a town between Des Moines and Davenport. A warrant was issued for Williams' arrest.

Police believed that Williams had left the girl or her body somewhere between Des Moines and the rest stop where some of the young girl's clothing had been found. Consequently, on the day after Christmas, officers initiated a large-scale search, accompanied by over 200 volunteers from the local community, who came forward out of concern for the child and her parents. They divided into teams and began the search. They were instructed to check all roads, abandoned farm buildings, ditches, culverts, and any other place in which the body of a small child could be hidden.

Meanwhile, Williams phoned his mother in Des Moines and learned from her that he was wanted by the police. She told him to surrender to the local police in Davenport and that she would obtain an attorney for him. Williams did surrender to local police and was detained on the warrant. The attorney, Henry McKnight, hired by

Williams' parents in Des Moines, arranged for an attorney in Davenport to meet Williams at the Davenport police station. Des Moines police informed the attorney that they would pick Williams up in Davenport and return him to Des Moines. Police were advised by the attorney that his client would not waive his right to remain silent and that officers were not to question him. The officers acknowledged that they understood and agreed not to question Williams on their return trip.

Two Des Moines detectives then drove to Davenport, took Williams into custody, and drove back toward Des Moines. However, before they left the police station in Des Moines, they researched the file on Williams and learned that he was of low intelligence, mentally unstable, and a religious fanatic of fundamentalist beliefs. Like any good detectives, they wanted as much information on their suspect as they could obtain, in order to use it to their advantage in dealing with him.

The Christian Burial Speech

During the return trip, one of the policemen, Detective Leaming, addressed Williams as Reverend Williams and began a conversation saying:

> I want to give you something to think about while we're traveling down the road....They are predicting several inches of snow for tonight, and I feel that you yourself are the only person that knows where this little girl's body is...and if it gets snow on top of it, you yourself may be unable to find it. And since we will be going right past the area [where the body is] on the way into Des Moines, I feel that we could stop and locate the body, that the parents of this little girl should be entitled to a Christian burial for the little girl who was snatched away from them on Christmas Eve and murdered....After a snow storm, we may not be able to find it at all.

Detective Leaming told Williams he knew that the girl was dead but not where the body was, and they needed to find her soon if she was to have a good Christian burial. He concluded the conversation by saying: "I do not want you to answer me....Just think about it...." Leaming's conversation became known as the **Christian Burial speech**.

Later, as the police car approached Grinnell, Williams asked Leaming whether the police had found the young girl's shoes. After Leaming replied that he was unsure, Williams directed the police to a point near a service station where he said he had left the shoes. As they continued the drive to Des Moines, Williams asked whether the blanket had been found, and then directed the officers to a rest area in Grinnell where he said he had disposed of the blanket. After driving a short distance farther, Williams, without any further conversation from Detective Leaming, directed the officers down a gravel road to where he had left the child's body, in a ditch next to a culvert. She had been sexually assaulted and strangled to death.

Williams was indicted for first-degree murder in February 1969. Before trial in the Iowa court, his attorney moved to *suppress evidence* of the body and all related evidence, including the condition of the body as shown by the autopsy. The grounds for the motion was that such evidence was the "fruit" or product of Williams' statements made during the automobile ride from Davenport to Des Moines after Williams' attorney, McKnight, had told police not to interrogate his client without him being present. The motion to suppress was denied.

The jury found Williams guilty of first-degree murder; the judgment of conviction was affirmed by the Iowa Supreme Court (*State v. Williams*, 1970). Williams' attorney then appealed to the U.S. District Court for the Southern District of Iowa. That court concluded that the evidence in question had been wrongly admitted at Williams' trial (*Brewer v. Williams*, 1977). A divided panel of the Court of Appeals for the Eighth Circuit agreed, holding that Detective Leaming had obtained incriminating statements from Williams by what was viewed as interrogation in violation of his right to counsel, and Williams' conviction was reversed.

The court's opinion noted, however, that although Williams' incriminating statements could not be introduced into evidence at a second trial, evidence of the body's location and condition might well be admissible on the theory that the body would have been discovered in any event, even if police had not talked to Williams.

When a convicted person appeals his or her conviction on the basis of a procedural error, wins the appeal, and has the conviction reversed, the person gives up his or her right not to be tried again. A retrial in this case is not considered double jeopardy. Williams' second trial in an Iowa court began in 1977. The prosecution did not introduce Williams' statements into evidence, nor did it seek to show that Williams had directed the police to the child's body. However, evidence of the condition of her body as it was found, articles and photographs of her clothing, and the results of postmortem medical and chemical tests on the body were admitted. The trial court concluded that the state had proved by a preponderance of the evidence that, if the search had not been suspended and Williams had not led the police to the victim, her body would have been discovered "within a short time" in essentially the same condition as it was actually found. The trial court also ruled that if the police had not located the body, the search would clearly have been taken up again where it left off, given the extreme circumstances of this case, and the body would have been found soon because the searchers were only 2 1/2 miles away from the culvert where Williams led them to the body, and they were heading in that direction.

In finding that the body would have been discovered in essentially the same condition as it was actually found, the court noted that freezing temperatures had prevailed and tissue deterioration would have been suspended. The challenged evidence was admitted, and the jury again found Williams guilty of first-degree murder. He was sentenced to life in prison.

Williams appealed his second conviction to the Supreme Court of Iowa, and again, his conviction was upheld. That court held that there was, in fact, a *hypothetical independent source* exception to the exclusionary rule and stated:

> After the defendant has shown unlawful conduct on the part of the police, the State has the burden to show by a preponderance of the evidence that (1) the police did not act in bad faith for the purpose of hastening discovery of the evidence in question, and (2) that the evidence in question would have been discovered by lawful means.

The Iowa court then reviewed the evidence and concluded that the State had shown by a preponderance of the evidence that even if Williams had not guided police to the child's body, it would *inevitably* have been found by lawful activity of the search party before its condition had materially changed. Thus the exception to the exclusionary rule known as **inevitable discovery** was created, but the Williams case was not yet over.

Williams continued with his appeals. The U.S. District Court reviewed the case in 1980, and upheld his conviction. However, the Court of Appeals for the Eighth Circuit reversed the lower court decision, holding that the prosecutor had not shown that "the police did not act in bad faith for the purpose of hastening discovery of the evidence (the first requirement cited above). Consequently, the case is reversed because of that procedural error, and therefore the issue of inevitable discovery is of no importance." That left all the evidence tainted by the original illegal conduct of Detective Leaming, interrogating Williams by way of his *Christian burial speech*.

When an investigating police officer makes one procedural error, any other evidence discovered as a result of the first error becomes tainted and also is inadmissible. This is known as the **fruit of the poison tree** doctrine, which originated from other appellate cases (*Silverthorne Lumber Co. v. United States, 1920; Wong Sun v. United States*,1963). The first procedural error poisons the tree of evidence, causing all the fruit of that tree to become poisoned as well. And without the evidence, there is no basis for prosecution. We will note in a later chapter that questioning the legality of evidence seized is the heart of a defense strategy to have the charges dismissed.

NIX v. WILLIAMS, 1984

Undoubtedly, Williams (or his attorney) thought he had finally won and that the case was over. However, the prosecutor, named Nix, was not to be denied. He appealed the case to the U.S. Supreme Court, and it was heard in January 1984. After much discussion about the Sixth Amendment right to have an attorney present during any police questioning, and about the exclusionary rule and Leaming's interrogation of Williams, the Court focused on the fact that the purpose of the exclusionary rule is to punish police for seizing evidence illegally by not admitting it into court. It is to control police misconduct and to uphold the Fourth Amendment protection against unreasonable search and seizure Granted, the evidence obtained by Detective Leaming's conduct must be excluded. However, "exclusion of physical evidence that would inevitably have been discovered adds nothing to either the integrity or fairness of a criminal trial." The Supreme Court concluded that

> ...it is clear that the search parties were approaching the actual location of the body, and we are satisfied, along with three courts earlier, that the volunteer search teams would have resumed the search had Williams not earlier led the police to the body, and the body inevitably would have been found.

Williams' second conviction was upheld and, after 16 years in the appellate mill, his sentence could be carried out. The inevitable discovery rule became a procedural law of the land, binding on all the states. It is a rule that means, in essence, that if police obtain evidence in violation of the Fourth Amendment but can prove by a preponderance of the evidence that their evidence would have been found in the same condition anyway, by some legal means or independent source, it is admissible in court, and the exclusionary rule does not apply. The complexity of the Williams case is exceeded only by the length of time necessary to complete it. Think how long it took for this case to bring closure for the girl's family.

Chief Justice Rehnquist described the circumstances of the case and delivered the opinion of the Supreme Court in (*New York v. Quarles* (1984). On September 11, 1980, at approximately 12:30 A. M., Officer Frank Kraft and Officer Sal Scarring were on road patrol in Queens, New York, when a young woman approached their car. She told them that she had just been raped by a black male, approximately six feet tall, who was wearing a black jacket with the name "Big Ben" printed in yellow letters on the back. She told the officers that the man had just entered an A&P supermarket located nearby and that the man was carrying a gun.

The officers drove the woman to the supermarket, and Officer Kraft entered the store while Officer Scarring radioed for assistance. Officer Kraft spotted the suspect, who matched the description given by the woman, approaching a checkout counter. He apparently saw the officer and turned and ran toward the rear of the store. Officer Kraft pursued him with a drawn gun but lost sight of him for several seconds. Upon locating the suspect again, the officer ordered him to stop and put his hands over his head.

Three other officers arrived on the scene by that time, but Officer Kraft was the first to reach the suspect. He patted him down for weapons and discovered that he was wearing a shoulder holster, which was then empty. After handcuffing him, Officer Kraft asked him where the gun was, and the suspect nodded in the direction of some empty cartons and responded, "The gun is over there." Officer Kraft retrieved a loaded .38-caliber revolver from one of the cartons, formally placed the suspect under arrest, and read him his *Miranda* rights from a printed card. The suspect, identified as Benjamin Quarles, indicated that he would be willing to answer questions without an attorney present. Officer Kraft then asked Quarles if he owned the gun and where he had purchased it. Quarles answered that it was his gun and that he had purchased it in Miami, Florida.

Quarles was charged with criminal possession of a weapon, but the judge excluded the statement "The gun is over there" and the gun, because the officer had not given Quarles the required *Miranda* warning before asking him where the gun was. The judge excluded the other statements as well because they were tainted by the initial procedural violation by the officer and became fruits of the poison tree of evidence. The Appellate Division of the Supreme Court of New York affirmed the trial judge's decision and rejected an argument by the state that the emergency nature of the situation justified Officer Kraft's failure to read Quarles his *Miranda* rights until after he had located the gun. The appellate court found no indication from Officer

Kraft's testimony that his subjective motivation in asking the question was to protect his own safety or the safety of the public.

We will not go into any detail about the *Miranda* decision or warning at this point; the specifics of that procedure are covered in Chapter 4. Nevertheless, the *Miranda* warning required by police is mentioned because it is a part of the Quarles case and it is assumed that most readers will have a general idea of what it is. The state of New York appealed the lower court's decision to the U.S. Supreme Court, which agreed to hear the case. It was argued in January 1984 and decided in June 1984. In the Court's opinion, Justice Rehnquist stated:

> The Fifth Amendment guarantees that "no person...shall be compelled in any criminal case to be a witness against himself." In Miranda, this Court for the first time extended the Fifth Amendment privilege against compulsory self-incrimination to individuals subjected to custodial interrogation by the police.... The only issue before us is whether Officer Kraft was justified in failing to make available to respondent [Quarles] the procedural safeguards associated with the privilege against compulsory self-incrimination since *Miranda*.

After a detailed review of all the facts and the relevant cases from previous decisions, the Court held

> ...that, on these facts, there is a "public safety" exception to the requirement that *Miranda* warnings be given before a suspect's answers may be admitted into evidence...and that the availability of that exception does not depend upon the motivation of the individual officers involved....Undoubtedly most police officers, if placed in Officer Kraft's position, would act out of a host of different, instinctive, and largely unverifiable motives—their own safety, the safety of others, and perhaps as well the desire to obtain incriminating evidence from the suspect.
>
> Whatever the motivation of individual officers in such a situation, we do not believe that the doctrinal underpinnings of *Miranda* require that it be applied in all its rigor to a situation in which police officers ask questions reasonably prompted by a concern for the public safety....The police in this case, in the very act of apprehending a suspect, were confronted with the immediate necessity of ascertaining the whereabouts of a gun which they had every reason to believe the suspect had just removed from his empty holster and discarded in the supermarket. So long as the gun was concealed somewhere in the supermarket,

with its actual whereabouts unknown, it obviously posed more than one danger to the public safety: an accomplice might make use of it, a customer or employee might later come upon it....In such a situation, if the police are required to recite the familiar *Miranda* warnings before asking the whereabouts of the gun, suspects in Quarles' position might well be deterred from responding. We conclude that the need for answers to questions in a situation posing a threat to the public safety outweighs the need for the...rule protecting the Fifth Amendment's privilege against self-incrimination. We decline to place officers such as Officer Kraft in the untenable position of having to consider, often in a matter of seconds, whether it best serves society for them to ask the necessary questions without the *Miranda* warnings and render whatever probative evidence they uncover inadmissible, or for them to give the warnings in order to preserve the admissibility of evidence they might uncover but possibly damage or destroy their ability to obtain that evidence and neutralize the volatile situation confronting them.

From this abbreviated version of the Court's opinion, it is obvious that the justices were balancing the needs of society for safety with the rights of the individual, Quarles. This **public safety exception** to the *exclusionary rule* shows that in the Court's mind, public safety comes first. In fact, in situations like this, the Court leaves the balancing up to the police officer at the scene, who can best judge when the public safety is in jeopardy. The wording of this opinion also captures a theme that will recur in many subsequent cases decided by the Supreme Court up through 1996: *The subjective motivations of a police officer have absolutely no bearing on the legality of a situation.* The only factors that count are the acts of the officer and the nature of the situation in which he or she is acting. *What an officer thinks or feels is not relevant—only what the officer does.* And public safety does not mean just the general public. It applies equally as well to **officer safety, victim safety**, and **suspect safety** (*United States v. Brady*, 1987; *United States v. DeSantis*, 1989; and *United States v. Carrillo*, 1994), particularly to the admissibility of statements taken without a *Miranda* admonition in an effort to ensure these safeties.

THE GOOD FAITH EXCEPTION

Supreme Court Justice White described the situation and delivered the opinion of the Court in *United States v. Leon*, (1984). In August 1981, a confidential informant of unproven reliability informed an officer of the Burbank Police Department that two persons known to him as Armando and Patsy were selling large quantities of cocaine and methaqualone from their residence on Price Drive in Burbank. The informant also indicated that he had witnessed a sale of methaqualone by Patsy at the residence approximately five months earlier and had observed at that time a shoebox containing a large amount of cash that belonged to Patsy. He further declared that Armando and Patsy generally kept only small quantities of drugs at their residence and stored the remainder at another location in Burbank.

On the basis of this information, the Burbank police initiated an extensive investigation focusing first on the Price Drive residence and later on two other residences as well. Cars parked at the Price Drive residence were determined to belong to Armando Sanchez, who had previously been arrested for possession of marijuana, and Patsy Stewart, who had no criminal record. During the course of the investigation, officers observed an automobile belonging to a Ricardo Del Costello, who had previously been arrested for possession of 50 pounds of marijuana, arrive at the residence. The driver of that car entered the house, exited shortly thereafter carrying a small paper sack, and drove away. A check of Del Costello's probation records led the officers to a suspect, Alberto Leon, whose telephone number Del Costello had listed as his employer.

Leon had been arrested in 1980 on drug charges, and a companion had informed the police at that time that Leon was heavily involved in the importation of drugs into this country. Before the current investigation began, the Burbank officers had learned that an informant had told a Glendale police officer that Leon stored a large quantity of methaqualone at his residence in Glendale. During the course of this investigation, the Burbank officers learned that Leon was living at 716 South Sunset Canyon in Burbank.

Subsequently, the officers observed several persons, at least one of whom had prior drug involvement, arriving at the Price Drive residence and leaving with small packages, observed a variety of other material activity at the two residences as well as at a condominium at 7902 Via Magdalena, and witnessed a variety of relevant activity involving suspects' automobiles. The officers also observed suspects Sanchez and Stewart board separate flights for Miami. The pair later returned to Los Angeles together, consented to a search of their luggage that revealed only a small amount of marijuana, and left the airport. Based on these and other observations summarized in an *affidavit*, Officer Cyril Rombach of the Burbank Police Department, an experienced and well-trained narcotics investigator, prepared an application for a warrant to search 620 Price Drive, 716 South Sunset Canyon, 7902 Via Magdalena, and automobiles registered to each of the suspects for an extensive list of items believed to be related to the suspects' drug-trafficking activities. Officer Rombach's extensive application was reviewed by several deputy district attorneys.

A facially valid search warrant was issued in September 1981 by a state superior court judge. The ensuing searches produced large quantities of drugs at the Via Magdalena and South Sunset Canyon addresses and a small quantity at the Price Drive residence. Other evidence was discovered at each of the residences and in Stewart's and Del Costello's automobiles. The suspects were indicted by a grand jury in the District Court for the Central District of California and charged with conspiracy to possess and distribute cocaine and a variety of substantive counts.

The suspects then filed motions to suppress the evidence seized pursuant to the warrant. The district court held an evidentiary hearing, and while recognizing that the case was a close one, granted the motions to suppress in part. It concluded that the affidavit was insufficient to establish probable cause, but the court made clear that Officer Rombach had acted in good faith. However, it rejected the government's suggestion that the Fourth Amendment exclusionary rule should not apply where evidence is seized in reasonable, good faith reliance on a search warrant.

The district court and a divided panel of the Court of Appeals for the Ninth Circuit agreed and concluded that Officer Rombach's affidavit could not establish probable cause to search the Price Drive residence and the evidence retained suppressed. Upon appeal by the U.S. Attorney General's office, the U.S. Supreme Court agreed to hear the state's case, that the officer should not be punished by having the evidence excluded when he acted in good faith and the error was made by someone else. It was the judge who found that probable cause existed and signed the search warrant. After a very lengthy discussion, the Court held:

This case presents the question whether the Fourth Amendment exclusionary rule should be modified so as not to bar the use in the prosecution's case-in-chief of evidence obtained by officers acting in reasonable reliance on a search warrant issued by a detached and neutral magistrate but ultimately found to be unsupported by probable cause. To resolve this question, we must consider once again the tension between the sometimes competing goals of, on the one hand, deterring official misconduct and removing inducements to unreasonable invasions of privacy and, on the other, establishing procedures under which criminal defendants are "acquitted...or convicted on the basis of all the evidence which exposes the truth."

As yet, we have not recognized any form of good faith exception to the Fourth Amendment exclusionary rule.... But the balancing approach that has evolved during the years of experience with the rule provides strong support for the modification currently urged upon us. As we discuss below, our evaluation of the costs and benefits of suppressing reliable physical evidence seized by officers reasonably relying on a warrant issued by a detached and neutral magistrate leads to the conclusion that *such evidence should be admissible* in the prosecution's case...the officers' reliance on the magistrate's determination of probable cause was objectively reasonable, and application of the extreme sanction of exclusion is inappropriate. Accordingly, the judgment of the Court of Appeals is Reversed (and the evidence is admissible).

Thus the third exception to the exclusionary rule, the **good faith exception**, was created in case law by the Supreme Court, with a majority of justices favoring public safety and law enforcement above the individual freedom of a suspected law violator. Their decision has been reaffirmed in subsequent cases (*Illinois v. Krull*, 1987 and *Arizona v. Evans*, 1995).

SUMMARY

This chapter dealt exclusively with a procedural rule, the *exclusionary rule*, created by the U.S. Supreme Court in an effort to stop law enforcement officers from violating the Fourth Amendment rights of citizens who police might suspect of crimes. To repeat, it is a rule of law which holds that *evidence seized by police illegally cannot be admitted in court to prove guilt.* The *Weeks* case actually created it, but applied it only in federal court cases. In the 1949 *Wolf* case, the Court specifically declined to extend that protection to state courts and make it binding on local law enforcement. Finally, in 1961, the *Mapp* case was used as a vehicle by the Supreme Court to apply the *rule* to all the states, and local law enforcement officers have had to comply with it in the collection of any evidence, whether the evidence is physical or testimonial. The *Mapp* case was decided by a due process-oriented court, headed by Chief Justice Earl Warren, whose concern for fairness and individual rights was paramount.

We have seen in recent years, through the *Williams, Quarles*, and *Leon* cases, that three exceptions to the rule have also been created. This is due primarily to the appointment of an increasing number of Supreme Court justices having a more law-and-order orientation than those before them. This includes Chief Justice Warren Burger, followed by Chief Justice Rehnquist, both of whom hoped to lead the court back to the right and reverse the liberal due process–oriented procedures established under Chief Justice Earl Warren, and thereby, fulfill the plans of Presidents Nixon, Reagan, and Bush, whose appointments to the Court were to facilitate that reversal (Simon, 1995). Burger almost succeeded in convincing a majority of the justices to overturn *Mapp*, but his persuasive powers were not quite enough (Woodward and Armstrong, 1979, pp. 112–121). The full reversal has not occurred, and probably will not. However, a number of decisions like the three just described have chipped away at the foundations of both the Fourth and Fifth Amendments.

KEY TERMS AND CONCEPTS

Christian burial speech	Inevitable discovery
Exclusionary rule	Public safety exception
Fruit of the poison tree	Silver platter doctrine
Good faith exception	Suppression of evidence

REFERENCES

KAMISAR, YALE. "The Exclusionary Rule in Historical Perspective: The Struggle to Make the Fourth Amendment More Than an Empty Blessing," *Judicature*, November 1978.

ROTHWAX, HAROLD J. *Guilty: The Collapse of Criminal Justice.* New York: Random House, 1996.

SIMON, JAMES F. *The Center Holds: The Poser Struggle inside the Rehnquist Court.* New York: Simon & Schuster, 1995.

WOODWARD, BOB, and SCOTT ARMSTRONG. *The Brethren: Inside the Supreme Court.* New York: Simon & Schuster, 1979.

ZALMAN, MARVIN and LARRY SEIGEL. *Key Cases and Comments on Criminal Procedures, 1994 ed.* St. Paul, MN: West Publishing, 1994.

CASES

Arizona v. Evans, 514 U.S. 1 (1995)

Brewer v. Williams, 430 U.S. 387 (1977)

Illinois v. Krull, 480 U.S. 340 (1987)

Mapp v. Ohio, 367 U.S. 643 (1961)

New York v. Quarles, 467 U.S. 649 (1984)

Nix v. Williams, 467 U.S. 431 (1984)

Silverthorne Lumber Co. v. United States, 251 U.S. 385, 392 (1920)

State v. Lindusay, 131 Ohio St. 166, 2 N.E. 2d 490 (1930)

State v. Williams, 182 N.W.2d 396 (1970)

United States v. Brady, 819 F.2d 884 (9th Dist. Ct. App. 1987)

United States v. DeSantis, 870 F.2d 536 (9th Dist. Ct. App. 1989)

United States v. Carrillo, 16 F.3d 1046 (9th Dist. Ct. App. 1994)

United States v. Leon, 468 U.S. 897 (1984)

Weeks v. United States, 232 U.S. 383 (1914)

Wolf v. Colorado, 338 U.S. 25 (1949)

Wong Sun v. United States, 371 U.S. 471 (1963)

3

THE LAWS AND PROCEDURES OF ARREST

The procedures examined in this chapter are those of primary concern to the street officer on patrol in a municipal police agency or county sheriff's department. It begins with the laws of arrest and includes the following: the definition of arrest, the discretion that an officer has in making an arrest, the limits on that discretion, the elements of an arrest, the different requirements in daytime and nighttime arrests, the differences between felony and misdemeanor arrests, the responsibilities of a police officer during and after arrest, exceptions to a peace officer's powers of arrest, and civil and criminal liabilities that might attach to an officer for illegal conduct. A discussion of arrests by private persons, and the responsibilities of police in those situations, is included. We have not included material on search and seizure or search warrants. That content is usually detailed in a separate course.

POLICE–CITIZEN TRANSACTIONS

In the appellate case *Florida v. Royer* (1983), U.S. Supreme Court Justice White addressed the three different categories, or levels, of police–citizen contact: the consensual encounter, the detention, and the arrest transactions. At each level, a peace officer has certain legal authority which is limited by the nature of the particular level. A clear distinction of what is allowed at each level is crucial to effective policing and making a legal arrest. Subsequent cases have continued to uphold these distinctions as the relevant criteria by which to guide police in dealing with citizens.

CONSENSUAL ENCOUNTER

A **consensual encounter** is a voluntary exchange between an officer and a citizen, with no restraint of individual liberty because police do not have any objective justification to stop, detain, or arrest. The citizen is free to leave at any time and free not to cooperate and not to answer questions. According to Justice White, the citizen must have the perception that he or she is free to leave and is not under any legal restraint. If an officer creates an atmosphere of intimidation or one in which a reasonable person would not feel that he or she is free to leave, it might move the encounter from consensual to illegal detention, without legal basis. For example, if the officer blocks the person's exit or asks to see some identification, then retains it during the entire conversation, the person might genuinely not feel free to leave.

CONSENT SEARCH

At the **consent search** level of consensual encounter, any search or seizure of property must be with the consent of the citizen. The consent search is one of the most frequent types of encounters that police have with citizens, either independent of any other contact or immediately following contact for another purpose, such as after a traffic stop. When an officer is talking to a citizen and has a hunch that something illegal might be going on, the officer will say: "Do you mind if I search your trunk?" Or, "Do you mind if I search your car?" The officer who asks for permission knows that he or she does not have the legal authority to demand access. If the citizen refuses to cooperate, that conduct does not give an officer any cause to detain or arrest, and the officer must allow the person to leave. Often, however, the citizen is not aware of this and thinks that he or she must submit to the officer's request. It is amazing how many people agree to let an officer search his or her car, knowing full well that it contains contraband.

If a peace officer elevates a consensual encounter into a detention without legal cause, any evidence seized probably will be excluded from trial under the exclusionary rule. In addition to the evidence being excluded, the officer might face criminal prosecution for false imprisonment or civil liability or criminal prosecution for a violation of civil rights.

DETENTION

Detention is actually seizure of a citizen that is limited in duration, scope and purpose. A **detention** or **stop** occurs when a peace officer compels a person to stop, to stay in one place, or to perform an act.

LEGAL BASIS FOR DETENTION

Any detention of a person by a peace officer must be based on **reasonable** (and articuable) **suspicion** by the officer that the person has committed, is committing, or is about to commit a crime. The person is not free to leave, and has the perception that he or she is not free to leave, but the detention is only for the purpose of settling the issue raised by the suspicion of the officer.

Under ordinary circumstances, the officer does not have the authority to search a citizen during a detention. However, in the *Terry* case, summarized below, the U.S. Supreme Court created certain search procedures that allow a peace officer to **pat search** the outside of a person's clothing if specific conditions described in *Terry* are present.

Terry v. Ohio, 1968

A Cleveland police officer named McFadden was patrolling a downtown business area, on a beat that he had been patrolling for many years, when he observed two strangers, later identified as Terry and Chilton, standing on a street corner. He saw them take turns walking back and forth along the sidewalk, pausing to stare in the same store window for a total of about 24 times. After each one walked back from the store, they talked for a few minutes. Soon they were joined by a third man, identified as Katz, who came and left swiftly. Suspecting the two men of "casing a job, a stick-up," the officer followed them and saw them rejoin the third man two blocks away in front of the store. The officer approached the three, identified himself as a policeman, and asked their names. The men mumbled something, whereupon McFadden turned Terry around, patted down his outside clothing, and found a pistol jammed in his overcoat pocket, which McFadden was unable to remove at the scene.

McFadden ordered the three into the store. He removed Terry's overcoat, took out the revolver, and ordered the three to face the wall with their hands raised. He patted down the outer clothing of Chilton and Katz and felt a hard object in the pocket of Chilton. He reached in the pocket and removed a revolver. He did not find anything in the patsearch of Katz. All three were taken to the police station, and Terry and Chilton were charged with carrying concealed weapons. Katz was released.

At trial, the defense moved to suppress the weapons, claiming that the exclusionary rule prohibited such a search. The prosecution claimed that the guns were seized after a lawful arrest. Although the trial court rejected the prosecution's theory that the guns had been seized during a search incident to a lawful arrest, the court denied the defense motion to suppress and admitted the weapons into evidence on the grounds that the officer had cause to believe that Terry and Chilton were acting suspiciously, that their interrogation was warranted, and that the officer, for his own protection, had the right to pat down their outer clothing, having reasonable cause to believe that they might be armed.

The trial court distinguished between an investigatory "stop" and an arrest, and between a "frisk" of the outer clothing for weapons and a full-blown search for evidence of crime. Terry and Chilton were found guilty, an intermediate appellate court affirmed, and the state supreme court dismissed the appeal on the ground that "no substantial constitutional question" was involved. Eventually, the case was appealed to the U.S. Supreme Court, where the arguments centered around the legality of Officer McFadden's patsearch within the context of the exclusionary rule. The Court's opinion, delivered by Chief Justice Earl Warren, held:

> The exclusionary rule cannot properly be invoked to exclude the products of legitimate and restrained police investigative techniques, and this Court's approval of such techniques should not discourage remedies other than the exclusionary rule to curtail police abuses for which that is not an effective sanction.
>
> The Fourth Amendment applies to "stop and frisk" procedures such as those followed here.
>
> (a) Whenever a police officer accosts an individual and restrains his freedom to walk away, he has "seized" that person within the meaning of the Fourth Amendment.
>
> (b) A careful exploration of the outer surfaces of a person's clothing in an attempt to find weapons is a "search" under that Amendment.
>
> Where a reasonably prudent officer is warranted in the circumstances of a given case in believing that his safety or that

of others is endangered, he may make a reasonable search for weapons of the person believed by him to be armed and dangerous regardless of whether he has probable cause to arrest that individual for crime or the absolute certainty that the individual is armed.

(a) Though the police must, whenever practicable, secure a warrant to make a search and seizure, that procedure cannot be followed where swift action based upon on-the-spot observations of the officer on the beat is required.

(b) The reasonableness of any particular search and seizure must be assessed in light of the particular circumstances against the standard of whether a man of reasonable caution is warranted in believing that the action taken was appropriate.

(c) The officer here was performing a legitimate function of investigating suspicious conduct when he decided to approach petitioner and his companions.

(d) An officer justified in believing that an individual whose suspicious behavior he is investigating at close range is armed may, to neutralize the threat of physical harm, take necessary measures to determine whether that person is carrying a weapon.

(e) A search for weapons in the absence of probable cause to arrest must be strictly circumscribed by the exigencies of the situation.

(f) An officer may make an intrusion short of arrest where he has reasonable apprehension of danger before being possessed of information justifying arrest.

The officer's protective seizure of petitioner and his companions and the limited search which he made were reasonable, both at their inception and as conducted.

(a) The actions of petitioner and his companions were consistent with the officer's hypothesis that they were contemplating a daylight robbery and were armed.

(b) The officer's search was confined to what was minimally necessary to determine whether the men were armed, and the intrusion, which was made for the sole purpose of protecting himself and others nearby, was confined to ascertaining the presence of weapons.

The revolver seized from petitioner was properly admitted into evidence against him, since the search which led to its seizure was reasonable under the Fourth Amendment.

STOP-AND-FRISK

Because of the *Terry* decision, the procedure known as **stop-and-frisk** gives the officer the authority to pat down a person for weapons if the officer has (articulable) reasonable suspicion to believe that the suspect might be armed. This is a patsearch outside the person's clothing for the sole purpose of looking for any weapons that the person might possess.

In a subsequent decision (*Adams v. Williams*, 1972), the Supreme Court extended this stop-and-frisk authority to situations in which the officer's reasonable suspicion is based on information rather than on personal observation. One year later, the Court held that a full body search is permitted after an officer makes an arrest, regardless of the offense and regardless of the apparent danger (*United States v. Robinson*, 1973).

In determining if an officer has **reasonable suspicion to detain**, the circumstances known or apparent to the officer must include specific and articulable facts causing him or her to suspect that some offense has taken place or is occurring or is about to occur and that the person he or she intends to detain is involved in that offense. The circumstances must be such as would cause any reasonable peace officer in a similar position, drawing on his or her training and experience, to suspect the same offense and the same involvement by the person in question.

DETENTION FACTORS

Reasonable suspicion justifies the detention and provides the officer with a **basis for investigation** to determine whether the suspicion is correct. Such suspicion, must, however, be based on objective facts, or factors, that can be stated, not on mere hunches.

A detention is based on two elements:(1) reasonable suspicion by the officer of criminal activity, (2) knowledge by the person stopped that he or she is not free to leave. In addition, there are certain factors about any situation that an officer may consider in forming a legal and articulable basis for reasonable suspicion. It is also important that the officer state all the relevant factors in his or her report to support the legality of the detention and possibly a patsearch, and any evidence that might be seized as a result.

The following are three **detention factor** categories to consider: (1) the appearance of the suspect, (2) the actions of the suspect, and (3) the area in which the suspect is observed. Questions to consider about the **appearance of the suspect** include:

1. Does he or she appear to be under the influence of drugs or alcohol?
2. Does he or she resemble the description of an offender recently given by the victim?
3. Does he or she resemble a wanted person?

4. Does he or she appear to be casing a house, store, building, etc.?
5. Is he or she injured?
6. Is he or she parked in an unusual place, or parked or walking at an odd hour and/or in an odd manner?

Questions about the **actions of the suspect** include:

1. Does he or she appear to be hiding?
2. Does he or she appear to be trying to conceal something?
3. Is he or she running from a crime scene?
4. Did he or she throw something away upon seeing the officer?
5. Did he or she just exchange some object that looked like contraband with another person?
6. Did he or she change his or her driving pattern immediately upon seeing the officer?

Questions to consider about the **area**:

1. Is it a high-crime area ? If so, consider the following:
   (a) What types of crimes are committed in the area?
   (b) What are the frequency and location of the crimes?
2. Is it a residential, industrial, or business area?

These are more than just questions to answer or consider. They represent some of the factors that an officer might have to articulate (to explain) to a judge on the stand under cross examination, to justify making the detention. If a detention cannot be justified by such factors, any evidence obtained might not be admissible in court. Probably, no single factor would be sufficient, and the more factors available, the better. There are no absolute guidelines, and each situation must be considered within the **totality of the circumstances**, a phrase one often finds as the basis for judging the legality of procedures used by police.

If one factor used by an officer to justify a detention is information provided the officer by an outside source, the officer needs to be prepared to describe the source and its reliability to the court, as well. In every situation, an officer should be prepared to explain and/or describe the full array of factors derived from the existing scene that made the officer suspicious. In fact, after a situation has been resolved, the officer would be wise to note those factors present, for later recall in court. Finally, *all of these factors may be considered within the context of the police officer's knowledge, training, and experience.*

A new *stop-and-search* law went into effect in Oregon on February 23, 1998, which allows police to stop and search individuals that police have *reasonable suspicion* to believe have committed a crime or are about to commit a crime. This law goes further than those in most states in allowing searches, and the various interest groups in Oregon are watching police behavior closely to be certain that *reasonable suspicion* is not ethnically driven.

CONSENSUAL ENCOUNTER VERSUS DETENTION

Often, the distinction between a consensual encounter and a legal detention is very slight, and might depend on how a judge interprets the situation. On the other hand, the distinction is obvious in many cases. Selected case summaries are provided below to demonstrate the current interpretations of Supreme Court justices, and they will be useful in learning how appellate courts distinguish between a legal detention based on reasonable suspicion.

A traffic car stop is an example of a legal detention if the officer stops the car with the reasonable belief that the driver might have violated a traffic law.

A recent Ohio case shows how an officer may use a traffic stop to move from a legal detention to a consensual encounter without the motorist being aware of the shift. This new decision, *Ohio v. Robinette* (1996), would probably make Justice White turn over in his grave in view of the fact that he stated in the original *Royer* case that a citizen "must know he is free to leave and free not to respond to questions." That requirement has recently been changed by a case that came from the following set of facts.

An Ohio deputy sheriff stopped Robert D. Robinette for speeding, gave him a verbal warning, and returned his driver's license. Then, without indicating to Robinette that he was free to leave, the deputy asked whether he was carrying illegal contraband, weapons, or drugs in his car. Robinette answered "no" and consented to a search of the car, which revealed a small amount of marijuana and a pill. He was arrested and later charged with knowingly possessing a controlled substance when the pill turned out to be methylenedioxy methamphetamine.

Robinette made a motion to suppress the evidence, claiming that the search was the result of an unlawful detention rather than a consensual encounter, because Robinette did not know he could go or refuse to cooperate. The trial court denied his suppression motion and he was found guilty, but the Ohio Court of Appeals reversed his conviction on the grounds that the search did result from an unlawful detention because Robinette did not know he was free to leave (following the reasoning in *Royer*).

The Ohio State Supreme Court affirmed the decision, establishing a specific rule (*bright-line prerequisite*) for consensual interrogation under these circumstances, stating that after an officer has completed a traffic stop matter, the officer must tell the motorist that he or she is "legally free to go." Then, and only then, said the Ohio Court, can the officer ask for a consent search.

This Ohio decision was in line with the *Royer* requirements, that to truly be a consensual encounter, the citizen must know that he or she is free to go, and then may give consent. However, the prosecutor in Ohio appealed this decision to the U.S. Supreme Court, and it ruled that the Ohio Court erred in its decision because it used an interpretation of the U.S. Constitution as the basis for its decision, rather than using its own State's Constitution. The Supreme Court held that if Ohio wants to have a law requiring its officers to tell citizens they are "free to go" before they ask for consent, it may do so through its own laws (*independent state grounds*). However, that procedure is not required under the Constitution. Robinette's conviction was upheld, and the Court said that an officer does not have to tell a citizen that he or she is free to leave or otherwise indicate that the traffic stop is over.

CONSENT SEARCHES REVISITED

The *Robinette* decision is another example of the Supreme Court's shift toward law and order, and away from due process. It opens up a whole new way for police to gain "consent" to search vehicles. Most citizens believe that they may not leave from a traffic stop until told they may. Therefore, they will not know that they are free to leave and might think that they must submit to search.

Until recently, the laws in some states have allowed the police to go far beyond the *Robinette* type of consent search. In Iowa for example, the code allows a police officer to arrest a motorist if the officer has cause to believe that the motorist has violated any traffic law or motor vehicle equipment law. In that case, (after an arrest) a full search of the person and car would be legal. The Iowa law also provides that the officer may cite the motorist instead of making the arrest, but the decision to cite rather than arrest "does not affect the officer's authority to conduct an otherwise lawful search." Apparently, the police in Iowa would routinely search motorists after issuing a citation. One motorist named Patrick Knowles was cited in Newton, Iowa for driving 43 mph in a 25 mph zone, after which the officer searched his car and found a bag of marijuana and a pot pipe under the driver's seat. The officer admitted that he had no consent and no cause.

In court, Knowles' motion to suppress the evidence as a 4th Amendment violation was denied and he was convicted. His conviction and the search practice of the police were upheld by the Iowa Supreme Court. However, the case was appealed to the U. S. Supreme Court. The tenor of that Court's thinking was suggested during oral arguments on November 3, 1998, when one Justice noted that a person who gets pulled over on a traffic stop and receives a ticket would hardly be prepared for such full-blown scrutiny, and another Justice stated that the police practice sanctioned by Iowa law "does seem an enormous amount of authority to put into the hands of the police."

On December 14, 1998, the Court gave its unanimous decision (*Knowles v. Iowa*, 1998) that there is no justification for an officer to conduct a search of a person or a car during a routine traffic stop and citation. Knowles' conviction was reversed. The Justices noted that if an officer requests the driver or passenger to exit the vehicle, the officer may still make a *Terry* patdown if there is reason to believe that officer safety requires it. This decision stops the routine police search incident to a traffic stop. Consequently, the *Robinette* type of consent search is as far as the police may go.

PRETEXT CARSTOP DETENTIONS

In another recent U. S. Supreme Court decision, *Whren v. United States*, 1996, the Court added to this law enforcement emphasis by sanctioning the use of a **pretext carstop**, as long as it is based on probable cause to believe that the driver has violated some traffic law. The so-called pretext carstop is the use of some very minor traffic violation to stop a car, when the officer's real purpose is to see who is in the car, or to find a way to obtain a consent search of a car if the officer suspects some more serious illegal activity. Examples of a pretext violation include the officer finding a dirty license plate tag, a faulty tail light, or an unlit rear license plate.

WARRANT CHECKS DURING TRAFFIC STOPS

A traffic stop is a legal detention, and a peace officer is allowed to run a warrant check, in addition to a Department of Motor Vehicles (DMV) check, without cause or legal justification. Also, for officer safety, a law enforcement officer may order both the driver and the passengers out of the car during any carstop, pending completion of the detention (*Maryland v. Wilson*, 1997). However, if a warrant check is pending, the officer may not legally delay the motorist to wait for the results of the warrant check beyond the time needed to complete the traffic situation. It might constitute an illegal detention.

If the officer does delay the motorist and a warrant is outstanding, and the officer makes an arrest, any evidence the officer might seize at the scene will be inadmissible under the exclusionary rule. Consequently, if the warrant check is delayed, the officer must either allow the driver to leave or ask for consent to delay. Frequently, an officer will merely engage the motorist in casual conversation, hoping that the warrant check will be completed before the motorist gets impatient and asks to go.

THE ARREST

The third level of police–citizen transactions is the **arrest**, defined as taking a person into custody in a manner authorized by law (and we could add, for the purpose of having the person charged with a crime). An arrest may be made by a peace officer or by a private party, although the laws that affect the arrest in either case vary in certain specific ways that are presented below.

An arrest is made by the actual physical restraint of the person, or by the submission of the person to the custody of an officer. The person arrested may be subjected to whatever restraint is reasonable for his or her arrest and detention.

PEACE OFFICER'S AUTHORITY TO ARREST

State laws are very specific as to when and under what circumstances a law enforcement officer may make an arrest. These can be divided into three categories of **authority to arrest:**

1. When the officer has reasonable cause (a.k.a. probable cause) to believe that the person to be arrested has committed an offense *in the officer's presence*. The officer's authority in these situations usually is the same in both felony and misdemeanor offenses.

2. When the officer has **reasonable (probable) cause** to believe that the person to be arrested has committed a felony, whether or not in the officer's presence. And, whether or not a felony actually was committed. An officer lacks the authority to arrest a person on a misdemeanor offense based

solely on probable cause (*In re Alonzo C.*, 1978). The misdemeanor must have been committed in the officer's presence. Any crime that is punishable by either prison or jail (a wobbler) is treated as a felony for purposes of arrest.

3. On the basis of a warrant. In most states, an arrest for the commission of a felony may be made on any day and at any time of the day or night. An arrest for the commission of a misdemeanor or an infraction often is limited to a certain time frame. For example, in some states, a misdemeanor arrest warrant cannot be served between the hours of 10:00 P.M. of any day and 6:00 A.M. of the succeeding day, unless the warrant is served and the arrest made in a public place, is made when the person is in custody for some other lawful arrest, or the warrant specifically allows for nighttime service.

REASONABLE/PROBABLE CAUSE

When we examine these three circumstances, we find the concept of *probable cause*, that was defined in Chapter 1 as consisting of facts and trustworthy information, sufficient in themselves, to warrant a person of reasonable caution to believe that (1) a crime has been committed, and (2) the person to be arrested probably committed it. (*Probable cause* and *reasonable cause* are used interchangeably in this book.) It is the word *cause* that provides an officer with the **basis for action**, whereas *reasonable suspicion* was a basis for investigation, as stated earlier in the chapter. Probable cause always consists of the two elements noted above.

EXCEPTIONS TO THE REQUIREMENT OF PROBABLE CAUSE IN MISDEMEANOR ARRESTS

There are several exceptions to the requirement that a misdemeanor must be committed in an officer's presence before an arrest can be made. States vary in these exceptions, but the following is a list of the most common exceptions found. The reader must check with his or her own state's law to determine which, if any, apply.

1. When a peace officer is responding to a call alleging a violation of a domestic violence protective order or restraining order (a misdemeanor), and the peace officer has reasonable cause to believe that the person against whom the order is issued has notice of the order and has committed an act in violation of the order.

2. When an officer, responding to a call, has probable cause to believe that the person to be arrested has committed assault or battery upon a spouse or other person with whom he or she is cohabiting, or upon the parent of his or her child.

3. When the officer has reasonable cause to believe that a person has been driving under the influence of alcohol and was involved in an accident.

4. When the officer has reasonable cause to believe that the person has committed assault or battery on school property during school hours.

5. When the officer has reasonable cause to believe that the person is carrying a loaded firearm in a vehicle or in a public place within the city limits.

6. In cases involving juvenile delinquent acts. Legally speaking, juveniles do not commit crimes—they commit delinquent acts. The law in most states gives a peace officer the authority to take a minor into temporary custody (arrest) whenever the officer has reasonable cause to believe that the minor has committed any violation of law. No distinction is made between felony and misdemeanor because they are all delinquent acts and are treated the same for arrest purposes.

PROBABLE CAUSE VERSUS. REASONABLE SUSPICION

The two phrases, or concepts, of probable cause and reasonable suspicion have distinctly different meanings, and provide an officer with two differing bases for dealing with a citizen. Reasonable suspicion occurs either before, during, or after some sort of criminal activity is suspected by an officer and suggests that maybe he or she is up to "something." This suspicion is derived from, and based on, articuable facts. Investigation clears up the suspicion one way or the other. Probable cause, however, always comes into play either during or after a crime has been committed and suggests that he or she "probably did it." It is derived from and based on more conclusive (and articuable) facts. Then the officer has the legal basis for making an arrest.

Even though these two concepts are different, the line dividing them often can be close and sometimes unclear, and their exact distinctions can be elusive. However, this should not be unsettling for an officer when he or she attempts to apply one or both, because the real nature of each arises from the setting in which each occurs. Each situation must be evaluated on its own merits, using the **totality of the circumstances** as a basis for review.

As Chief Justice Rehnquist explained in a recent case (*Ornelas v. United States*, 1996):

> Articulating precisely what "reasonable suspicion" and "probable cause" mean is not possible. They are common sense, non-technical conceptions that deal with "the factual and practical considerations of everyday life on which reasonable and prudent men, not legal technicians, act." As such, the standards are "not readily, or even usefully, reduced to a neat set of legal rules...."
>
> We have cautioned that these two legal principles are not "finely-tuned standards," comparable to the standards of proof beyond a reasonable doubt or of proof by a preponderance of the evidence....They are instead fluid concepts that take their substantive content from the particular contexts in which the standards are being assessed....**The principal components of a determination of reasonable suspicion or probable cause will be the events which occurred leading up to [them], and then the decision whether these historical facts, viewed from the standpoint of an objectively reasonable police officer, amount to reasonable suspicion or to probable cause.**

Once an officer has probable cause to arrest, he or she does not need to effect an arrest at that point—other options are available. However, once probable cause has been established, the officer may immediately search the person for dangerous weapons "whenever he has reasonable cause to believe that the person possesses a dangerous weapon." If a weapon is found on the suspect, the officer shall either return it or arrest the person. If the suspect is in possession of the weapon illegally, he or she may be arrested for that as well as for the original charge that gave rise to the probable cause.

ARRESTS BY WARRANT

An **arrest warrant** is a legal order signed and issued by a magistrate (judge), directed to any peace officer, commanding that the person named in the warrant be arrested and brought before the court, usually to answer to a charge. The warrant is issued at the request of a peace officer or deputy district attorney, who completes a sworn statement, known as an **affidavit**, in which the officer or deputy explains the probable cause in support of the warrant (refer to the wording in the Fourth Amendment). If the magistrate is convinced that probable cause exists, he or she will sign the warrant.

As soon as an arrest warrant is issued, the clock stops running on what is called the **statute of limitations**, the legal time within which a person must be charged with a crime. For a misdemeanor, the time in most states is one year, and for most felonies it varies from three to five years. In many states there is no time limit on prosecuting a person for embezzling public funds or for any crime punishable by execution or life in prison.

To be valid, an arrest warrant must contain the following information:

1. Name of the person to be arrested
2. Legal description of the charge(s)
3. The amount of bail, or no bail
4. The date issued and the judge's signature
5. The court issuing the warrant

Only a peace officer can make an arrest pursuant to a warrant. Obviously, a private person does not have access to warrants. The officer need not have personal possession of the warrant at the time of the arrest. However, before arresting a person on the basis of a warrant, the officer must verify that it is still valid. An officer on patrol will have this verification completed by a dispatcher prior to making the arrest.

As soon as it is practicable, the officer must show a copy of the warrant to the arrested party if that person requests it. In most situations, such as during a routine traffic stop, if a patrol officer makes an arrest on a warrant, the dispatcher will be certain that a copy of the warrant is waiting for the officer at the jail where the subject is booked.

When a person is arrested by a peace officer on the basis of a warrant, the officer must proceed with the person arrested as commanded by the warrant or as provided by law. If the person is arrested on a misdemeanor warrant, however, the person may be issued a citation instead of being physically arrested, in most cases. States often limit an officer's discretion in situations where the offense involves violence or a firearm, the person resists arrest or gives false information or identification, the person is a danger to self or others, the person is under the influence of alcohol or narcotics, or the person refuses to sign the citation. Other limitations might also apply in a particular state.

PRIVATE PERSON ARRESTS

Thus far the discussion of arrest has focused on the authority and procedures of law enforcement officers. However, not all arrests are made by officers, particularly in misdemeanor situations. Any person may make an arrest if the conditions are legal. The phrase *citizen's arrest* is not really the appropriate way to state it because someone might think that it is limited to actual citizens as opposed to noncitizens. The preferred phrase is **arrest by private persons**, which is enough to distinguish it from an arrest by a peace officer.

Situations in which a private person may arrest another person can be divided into two basic categories of authority:

1. For a public offense committed or attempted in his or her presence
2. When a felony has in fact been committed, and the private person has reasonable cause to believe the person arrested committed it

There are two distinctions between the authority of a peace officer and that of a private person in making an arrest: (1) a peace officer is the only one who may serve a warrant, and (2) when a private person makes an arrest for a felony, based upon probable cause, a felony must have been committed, whereas in an arrest by a peace officer, the officer need only believe that one has occurred. A private person faces liability for false arrest or false imprisonment if he or she makes an arrest and no felony actually occurred.

Private person arrests occur frequently in two types of misdemeanor situations:

1. When a security officer of a store detains a shoplifter and calls the police. The security officer must make the arrest (unless the suspect is a juvenile) because it did not occur in the presence of the peace officer.
2. A misdemeanor in which a victim summons a peace officer to the scene of the crime and wants a suspect arrested. Again, the offense did not occur in the officer's presence.

The In-Field Show-up or Drive-by

Situation 2 described above, in which a private person must make an arrest, often includes a common police procedure known as an **in-field show-up**, or **drive-by**. This is a procedure used when an officer arrives at the scene of a misdemeanor crime shortly after it occurs, obtains a description of the suspect, and puts it out over the radio. A second officer, on patrol in the general area where the crime occurred, sees a person who matches the description of the suspect given over the radio. That officer has a reasonable suspicion to stop and detain the person. To clear up the suspicion, the officer at the crime scene has the victim accompany him or her in the police car, and they drive by the location where the suspect is detained. The victim is told that a person is being detained just to see if the victim can identify him or her.

The officer must be careful not to suggest to the victim that the real offender is in custody. If the victim does identify the suspect, the victim will accompany the officer to the police station, and the officer detaining the suspect will take the suspect to the police station. There, the victim will tell the suspect that he or she is under arrest and will sign a private-party arrest form. In some jurisdictions the officer will merely ask the victim if he or she wants the suspect arrested. If so, the victim signs the form and the officer takes custody of the suspect without the victim ever having to face the person.

REQUESTING HELP WHEN ARRESTING

If a peace officer or private person needs assistance to complete an arrest, he or she may exercise an old common law procedure called *posse comitatus*, or power of the county (in effect, to form a posse). Consequently, a peace officer and a private person may request help from anyone (over age 18 and not in military uniform) to help them effect an arrest. In most states it is a misdemeanor offense for a person to refuse to come to the aid of a peace officer who requests help.

When a private person comes to the aid of a peace officer, at the request of the officer, that person has the same authority, rights, and privileges as the officer. As long as that person is acting in good faith, he or she is protected from any civil or criminal liability, even if the officer is acting illegally (*Peterson v. Robinson*, 1954).

ACCEPTANCE BY POLICE OF PRIVATE PERSON ARREST

After a private person makes an arrest, a peace officer is required by law in many states to assume custody of the person. If the officer thinks that the arrest is unlawful, he or she may advise the person making the arrest, but if that person insists, the officer must take custody. If the officer refuses to take custody, the officer may be charged with a crime, usually a felony.

A peace officer assumes no civil liability in accepting custody from an unlawful arrest by a private person. After taking custody, the officer has whatever discretion he or she would have in a regular peace officer arrest. That is, the officer may release the person, give a citation, or book the person in jail.

64

INFORMING THE PERSON ARRESTED

State laws require that anyone making an arrest must provide the arrested person with certain information. The officer (or private person) must inform the person to be arrested of the intention to arrest him or her, of the legal reason for the arrest, and the authority to make it, except when the person making the arrest has reasonable cause to believe that the person to be arrested is then actually engaged in the commission of or an attempt to commit an offense, or the person to be arrested is pursued immediately after its commission or after an escape from some form of custody.

EFFECTING AN ARREST WITH FORCE

When an officer has the legal authority to make an arrest, he or she may use reasonable force to effect the arrest, to prevent escape, or to overcome resistance. A peace officer who makes or attempts to make an arrest need not retreat or stop his or her efforts because of the **resistance** or threatened resistance of the person being arrested. However, the officer may only use reasonable force, which is the amount of force necessary to overcome the resistance posed by the person being arrested. Excessive force by an officer is not legal and can result in serious legal problems for the officer.

ABUSE OF AUTHORITY BY A PEACE OFFICER

The behavior of peace officers is controlled rigorously by law. Not only is his or her authority to act in any situation dictated every step of the way in the state code sections, but abuse of that authority is spelled out in various laws, as well. State laws usually include two areas of behavior by peace officers that are illegal:

1. Acting *under color of authority* (which means using one's peace officer powers to gain a desired result), without actually having legal cause, in two procedural aspects: (a) detaining a person against his or her will without having reasonable suspicion, and (b) arresting a person without having probable cause, or other legal cause
2. Acting under color of authority, but without having legal need, to assault or beat a person

Along with these areas that are controlled by state laws, Title 18 of the *United States Code*, describes circumstances under which a local law enforcement officer may violate federal law:

§241: CONSPIRACY AGAINST RIGHTS

If two or more persons conspire to injure, oppress, threaten, or intimidate any person in any State, Territory, or District in the free exercise or enjoyment of any right or privilege secured to him (or her) by the Constitution or law of the United States, or because of his having so exercised the same; or if two or more persons go in disguise on the highway, or on the premises of another, with intent to prevent or hinder his free exercise or enjoyment of any right or privilege so secured, they shall be fined under this title or imprisoned not more than ten years, or both; and, if death results from the acts committed in violation of this section or if such acts include kidnapping or an attempt to kidnap, aggravated sexual abuse or an attempt to commit aggravated sexual abuse, or an attempt to kill, they shall be fined under this title or imprisoned for any term of years, or for life, or both, or may be sentenced to death.

§242: DEPRIVATION OF RIGHTS UNDER COLOR OF LAW

Whoever, under color of any law, statute, ordinance, regulation, or custom, willfully subjects any person in any State, Territory, or District to the deprivation of any rights, privileges, or immunities secured or protected by the Constitution, or law of the United States, or to different punishments, pains, or penalties, on account of such person being an alien, or by reason of his color, or race, than are prescribed for punishment of citizens, shall be fined under this title or imprisoned not more than one year, or both; and if such acts include the use, attempted use, or threatened use of a dangerous weapon, explosives, or fire, shall be fined under this title or imprisoned not more than ten years, or both; and if death results from the acts committed in violation of this section or if such acts include kidnapping or an attempt to kidnap, aggravated sexual abuse, or an attempt to commit aggravated sexual abuse, or an attempt to kill, shall be fined under this title, or imprisoned for any term of years or for life, or both; or may be sentenced to death.

Fortunately, there are very few incidents in which a peace officer violates the rights of a citizen or abuses a citizen under the color of his or her authority. Unfortunately, it only takes a few situations in which flagrant abuses do occur to taint the reputation of all police. This is particularly true in those situations in which the media get involved and report the facts before they are even known.

ENTRY FOR AN ARREST: KNOCK-AND-NOTICE REQUIREMENTS

Under common law, if a peace officer had the legal authority to arrest a person, the officer also had the authority to break in and/or enter a dwelling to look for that person as long as the officer had reasonable cause to believe that the person was inside. However, that common law procedure is no longer recognized as legal (*Wilson v. Arkansas*, 1995).

Today, the Fourth Amendment guarantees that a person has the reasonable expectation of privacy in his or her own dwelling and other possessions. Unless officers have consent, or some exigent (emergency) circumstances exist, they must have an arrest warrant (*People v. Ramey*, 1976, and *Payton v. New York*, 1980). Police also may not enter the dwelling of a third party to arrest a person, whether or not they have an arrest warrant (*Steagald v. United States*, 1981). In that situation, they would need a search warrant.

When officers do want to arrest a person inside a dwelling with an arrest warrant, they must complete the procedure known as **knock-and-notice**. They must first knock on the door or otherwise announce their presence, identify themselves as peace officers, state their purpose for being there and their authority to carry out that purpose (the warrant), demand entry, then wait a reasonable period of time for the resident to open the door. The phrase *reasonable period of time* means whatever time it normally would take the resident to answer the door. This leaves the officers with a great deal of discretion.

There are three exceptions to the knock-and-notice requirement:

1. If the officers or any occupant would be placed at an increased peril or risk, such as those situations in which the suspect is known to use violence or to possess and/or use firearms
2. If the officers have reasonable cause to believe that some evidence will be destroyed
3. If the wanted person would attempt to flee

Officers need a strong factual basis to justify an entry under any of these situations.

In addition to consent, there are five exceptions to the warrant requirement in which **exigent circumstances** are created:

1. When the situation presents danger and/or serious risk to an officer or to others. Within this context, the gravity of the underlying offense may be considered (*Welsh v. Wisconsin,* 1984; see also *Richards v. Wisconsin*, 1997, which did leave the door open for the possibility of **no-knock** search warrants)
2. When an officer has reasonable cause to believe that evidence is being destroyed, based on reliable information or facts
3. To prevent the imminent escape of the suspect
4. When there is imminent danger of serious damage to property
5. When an officer is in hot pursuit/fresh pursuit

During the 1998 session, the U.S. Supreme Court took up an interesting knock-and-notice case that originated in Oregon, *United States v. Ramirez*, which might have affected police conduct nationwide. At issue, again, was: When must police give the knock-and-notice warning before breaking into a home to serve a warrant, or do certain blanket exceptions exist?

In the Oregon case, in November 1994, state and federal authorities were looking for Alan Shelby, a fugitive who allegedly had assaulted a jail guard and escaped from the Tillamook County (Oregon) Courthouse on November 1. A few days later, an informant told police that he saw Shelby enter the home of a man named Ramirez, so several dozen state and federal law enforcement officers surrounded his house before dawn and prepared to serve a warrant to search for Shelby.

Without knocking, officers broke a window in the garage. Ramirez claimed that he thought burglars were breaking in, so he grabbed a gun and fired several shots. One officer was slightly wounded. The police returned the fire, then broke in. They yelled "police," whereupon Ramirez surrendered. He was charged and convicted in federal court of being an ex-felon in possession of a gun. However, on appeal, U.S. District Judge Ancer L. Haggerty in Portland ruled the search unconstitutional because state and federal officers did not give a knock-and-notice before they entered. Based on precedent, the judge held that there is no blanket exception to the knock-and-notice requirement. He reasoned that if officers had complied by knocking and announcing who they were and their purpose, Ramirez would not have mistaken them for burglars and would not have had a reason for shooting at them. Therefore, the officers would not have been at risk. Also, the officers did not know for certain that Shelby was in the house or that, if he was, he planned an imminent escape, so they did not have sufficient cause to initiate the break-in, thus violating both the Fourth Amendment and Section 3109 of the *U.S. Code*, which requires exigent circumstances to justify the destruction of property in executing a warrant.

The U.S Attorney appealed to the U.S. Supreme Court, and the case was decided on March 4, 1998. The Court ruled that the "Fourth Amendment does not hold officers to a higher standard when a *no-knock* entry results in the destruction of property [and that under *Richards v. Wisconsin*, 1997] a no-knock entry is justified if police have a *reasonable suspicion* that knocking and announcing their presence before entering would 'be dangerous or futile, or...inhibit the effective investigation of the crime.'" Therefore, the Supreme Court held that the actions of the police were justified and reversed the lower federal court's decision to suppress the evidence. Ramirez's conviction in federal court stands, and the *exigent circumstances* justification, based on *reasonable suspicion*, was reaffirmed. Shelby was not found in the house, nor were his whereabouts ever an issue in this case.

Fresh Pursuit

If officers had been chasing Shelby at the time, and actually had seen him enter the home of Ramirez, they could have followed him in without knock-and-notice being an issue because their conduct would have been governed by a procedure known as **fresh pursuit**. This is a situation in which an officer pursues a suspect from the scene of a crime, or from where the arrest is attempted, and the suspect flees to avoid arrest. Once in fresh pursuit, an officer need not stop just because a suspect enters a building to evade arrest, regardless of the nature of the offense. Fresh pursuit is one in which an officer's pursuit efforts are *continuous and uninterrupted*. This pursuit may cross into other jurisdictions without affecting an officer's powers of arrest. In fact, most states participate in what is termed the **Uniform Act of Fresh Pursuit**, allowing officers to cross state boundaries and bring with them their state's authority to arrest. And with the U.S. Supreme Court ruling (*County of Sacramento v. Lewis*) on May 26, 1998, if injury or death results to a suspect being pursued in a vehicle **high-speed chase**, the officer is free from civil liability unless his or her actions "shocks the conscience" or if the motives of the officer are malicious or the harm is intentional.

RESISTING ARREST

If a person being arrested has knowledge, or by the exercise of reasonable judgment, should have knowledge that he or she is being arrested by a peace officer, it is the legal duty of that person to submit to arrest and not resist. However, the person may resist any excessive force used by an officer in effecting the arrest, such as a beating. In this situation, however, the person arrested has the burden of proving that the officer used excessive force.

INTERFERING WITH AN OFFICER

A crime similar to that of resisting arrest is interfering with an officer in the performance of his or her duty. In fact, it is a crime (misdemeanor) in most jurisdictions to interfere with or disobey any public officers in the performance of their duties. This includes police officers, fire officers, ambulance personnel, or any other person authorized to act in public emergency situations. If a person disarms, injures, or kills any officer during any act of resistance and interference, the punishment and/or crime becomes correspondingly more serious. The laws in most states have gone about as far as they can to provide emergency personnel with legal protection in an effort to assist them in carrying out their duties.

EXCEPTIONS TO PEACE OFFICER POWERS OF ARREST

There are two situations in which a peace officer does not have the authority to arrest a person whom the officer believes committed a crime. The first exception to an officer's authority is known as the **stale misdemeanor rule**. An arrest for a misdemeanor committed in an officer's presence must be made right after it occurs, or "within a reasonable time thereafter." This means that the officer must immediately effect the arrest or, if the suspect flees, must pursue the suspect until he or she can make the arrest. If an officer delays an arrest until later for the convenience of the officer, the offense becomes what is termed a *stale misdemeanor*, and the officer loses jurisdiction (*State v. Smith*, 1956). If the officer observes the suspect in a public place at a later time, the officer may detain the person and make an identification but may not make an arrest. He or she must obtain a warrant to make the arrest.

The second exception to an officer's powers of arrest occurs when a person claims, and is eligible to claim, **diplomatic immunity**. By international and federal law, there are certain official representatives of foreign governments who are immune from arrest; that is, who may not be arrested. Since they are here as official representatives of their country's government, they bring their country's soil with them. Wherever they go, they are walking on their soil, and police in this country do not have jurisdiction over any foreign soil. Any peace officer who violates the immunity status may be subject to federal felony arrest and prosecution (§22 *U.S. Code* 252, 253).

There are specific levels of immunity given to foreign representatives, depending on the position and function they serve. Foreign ambassadors and United Nations' representatives are at the highest level and receive the most immunity. Both they and their families are completely immune from arrest and detention.

The next level is that of the consular officers: consul, general, consul and vice-consul. They perform most of the formal functions of their governments and are immune from arrest or detention (and civil liability) only when a criminal act occurs while performing the official duties assigned to them by their government. Their families do not have immunity.

An exception to all of these guidelines includes the consular officers and their families from the Commonwealth of Independent States, China, Poland, Hungary, and the Philippines. They are granted ambassador-level immunity. Also, the employees and staff of Russian and Chinese consulates receive the same level of immunity as that of regular consular officers.

All foreign representatives have official identification cards issued by the U.S. Department of State's (DOS) Office of Foreign Missions (OFM). These cards contain a photograph, identifying information, and a description of the holder's immunity status. Their automobiles are registered with DOS OFM and display distinctive red, white, and blue license plates. These vehicles may not be impounded, stored, or searched, except by consent. An exception to these guidelines occurs whenever the public safety is jeopardized or police action is necessary to prevent a serious crime.

If a patrol officer stops a person who claims diplomatic immunity, the officer should call for a supervisor, document all the information available, initiate an investigation, and allow the subject to leave. Most states have an Office of Emergency Services (OES), which is responsible for the liaison between local police agencies and the U.S. State Department. In a serious crime such as a homicide, the State Department can ask a foreign government to recall its diplomat, and the foreign country may even prosecute its diplomat in its own country if it has a law prohibiting the same crime. Or the foreign country could revoke the diplomatic status of its representative and allow prosecution in this country.

DELIVERY OF A PERSON AFTER ARREST

State laws require that after a person has been arrested, he or she must be taken before a judge or magistrate without unnecessary delay. However, it is a rare occasion when the arresting officer actually delivers an arrested person to a judge after arrest. The arrested person is either cited to appear in court at a later date, or is booked in a county jail, after which the case is referred to the local prosecuting attorney, who determines whether to file charges against the arrested person. If charges are filed, the person will be brought before the judge, magistrate or, in some states, the grand jury, within 48 hours to hear the charges. This satisfies the requirements of the law.

RELEASE PROCEDURES WITHOUT A CHARGE AFTER ARREST

Not all persons arrested are booked in jail; and some are not even charged with a criminal offense. If a crime is not serious and the peace officer believes that the person does not pose a threat to his or her own safety, or to the public safety, and that he or she will appear in court when required, the officer may give the person a **citation**, which is similar to a traffic ticket. It is a **promise to appear**, signed by the person. The use of a citation as opposed to a full arrest is increasingly becoming the more common practice, particularly in states where the jails are overcrowded and in those states where the local sheriffs who run the jails charge other police agencies booking fees that run as high as $200 per subject booked.

If the arresting officer believes that no charges are warranted, such as in cases of public intoxication or disturbing the public peace, he or she may follow the particular procedures provided in his or her state that provide for a direct release of the subject without further action. In these cases, the record of the person is changed from an arrest to a detention and release.

SUMMARY

In this chapter the laws of arrest have been presented from every aspect, starting with the three levels of police–citizen transactions (consensual encounter, detention, and arrest), through all the requirements and limitations of a peace officer and of a private person in the various arrest situations. The knock-and-notice requirement was detailed, as were descriptions of diplomatic immunity and fresh pursuit procedures, and police procedures after arrests for minor infractions.

KEY TERMS AND CONCEPTS

Abuse of authority
Affidavit
Arrest
Arrest by private person
Arrest warrant
Authority to arrest
Consensual encounter
Consent search
Conspiracy against rights
Deprivation of rights
Detention
Detention factors
Diplomatic immunity
Exigent circumstances

Fresh pursuit
Independent state grounds
In-field show-up
Knock-and-notice
Pat search
Posse comitatus
Pretext carstop
Probable cause
Reasonable cause
Reasonable suspicion
Resisting arrest
Stale misdemeanor rule
Statute of limitations
Stop-and-frisk

CASES

Adams v. Williams, 407 U.S. 143 (1972)

County of Sacramento v. Lewis, No. 96-1337 (1998)

Florida v. Royer, 460 U.S. 491 (1983)

In re Alonzo C. , (1978)

Knowles v. Iowa, No. 97-7597 (1998)

Maryland v. Wilson, No. 95-1268, U S. (1997)

Ohio v. Robinette 519 U.S. 417 (1996)

Ornelas v. United States, 517 U.S. 960 (1996)

Payton v. New York, 455 U.S. 573 (1980)

People v. Ramey, 16 C.3d 263 (1976)

Peterson v. Robinson (1954)

Richards v. Wisconsin, No. 96-5955 U.S. (1997)

State v. Smith, 87 So. 2nd 917 (Miss. 1956)

Steagald v. United States, 451 U.S. 204 (1981)

Terry v. Ohio, 392 U.S. 1 (1968)

United States v. Ramirez, 91 F.3d 1297 (1998)

United States v. Robinson, 414 U.S. 218 (1973)

Welsh v. Wisconsin, 466 U.S. 138 (1984)

Whren v. United States, 135 L. Ed.2d 89 (1996)

Wilson v. Arkansas, 131 L. Ed.2d 976 (1995)

Miranda: *Its Meaning and Application*

No person shall be compelled in any criminal case to be a witness against himself…

Fifth Amendment

In all criminal prosecutions, the accused shall enjoy the right to…have the assistance of counsel for his defense.

Sixth Amendment

INTRODUCTION

This chapter deals exclusively with the *Miranda* decision and the effect that it has had on police procedures. The *Miranda* decision ranks alongside the *Mapp* and *Gideon* decisions as one of the three most significant precedent-setting cases in the history of procedural due process. Imagine what it must have been like before 1966, when police could take a suspect into custody, place him or her in an interrogation room at the police station, and question him or her at length without even considering that the suspect had any rights.

Imagine what it must have been like for the suspect. Within that coercive environment, the police could create enormous pressures for a person to confess. Then consider what one of those old-school detectives might think if he were told that he must advise the suspect of the right to remain silent. "How absurd," he might say. "Why should I tell him he has the right to remain silent when I want him to talk freely, to confess? That's the craziest idea I ever heard of."

Most people take it for granted today that police comply with the requirements of *Miranda* and that they have always done so. However, it took many years of effort and several appellate decisions to achieve the full due process required in obtaining a confession. Consequently, before examining *Miranda*, it will be useful to review a summary of the important cases leading up to the 1966 decision. Later in the chapter, the use of the *Beheler* admonition is presented as a current method used by police to avoid having to advise a suspect of any rights.

CASES LEADING TO THE MIRANDA DECISION

THE PROMPT ARRAIGNMENT CASES

Three cases stand out as forerunners to *Miranda*. Two of these are examples of how the U.S. Supreme Court avoided dealing with the issue of confessions obtained by police interrogation, and one case shows the result of making a decision without including any method to enforce it.

The first case is *McNabb v. United States*, (1943), in which two McNabb brothers were convicted of killing a federal revenue agent during a raid on their family's still in the mountains near Chattanooga, Tennessee. They were arrested during the raid, then locked in a strip cell for over 14 hours, then interrogated continuously over the next two days. They finally confessed, were convicted on the basis of their confession, and were sentenced to 45 years in prison. On appeal, the Supreme Court refused to address the legality of their confession, and instead, used the federal arraignment rule, Rule 5a of the Federal Rules of Criminal Procedures, to reverse the McNabbs' convictions. This rule required **prompt arraignment** after arrest. The Court did not want to establish any precedent on custodial interrogation.

In the second case, *Mallory v. United States* (1957), the 19-year-old Mallory, a man of limited intelligence (Robin, (1987 p. 171), was arrested by police in Washington, D.C. on a charge of rape, a capital offense at the time. He was interrogated at the police station by a polygraph operator and a detective for over 10 hours. He finally confessed, was convicted on the basis of his confession, and was sentenced to be executed. On appeal, the Supreme Court again refused to deal with the legality of the confession. The Court again used the federal rule, Rule 5a, to reverse his conviction, holding that Mallory was not arraigned promptly.

The real significance of these two cases, aside from them requiring prompt arraignment, is the fact that no precedent was set in the area of illegal confessions. The Court had the opportunities to address the issue, but declined to do so. There was a strong belief at the time that the Constitution was a federal document and the rights guaranteed therein applied only to federal proceedings.

There was an equally strong belief that the states should be free to determine their own laws and justice system procedures. States rights was a popular, almost sacred theme throughout the nation.

THE ON-THE-SPOT COUNSEL CASE

On the night of January 19, 1960, Danny Escobedo's brother-in-law was fatally shot, and Danny was the prime suspect. He was arrested without a warrant in the early hours of the next morning and was interrogated at police headquarters. He made no statement to the police and was released late that afternoon after his attorney obtained a writ of *habeas corpus*, an order stating that he was being held illegally.

On January 30, Benedict DiGerlando, who was then in police custody on the same charge, and who was later indicted for the murder along with Danny, told the police that Danny had fired the fatal shots, and that he, Danny, and Danny's sister were all in on the crime. Later that evening, Danny and his sister, now the widow of the deceased, were arrested and taken to police headquarters.

Danny was handcuffed in the back of the police car on the way to the police station, when one of the arresting officers told him that DiGerlando had named him as the one who shot the deceased. According to Escobedo's later testimony, the detective also said: "They had us pretty well, up pretty tight, and we might as well admit to this crime," and that Escobedo replied, "I am sorry, but I would like to have advice from my lawyer." A police officer testified that although Escobedo was not formally charged, "he was in custody" and "couldn't walk out the door."

Shortly after Escobedo and the police reached the police station, his lawyer arrived. The lawyer testified about the ensuing events in the following terms:

On that day, I received a phone call from the mother of the defendant and, pursuant to that phone call, I went to the Detective Bureau at 11th and State. The first person I talked to was the Sergeant on duty at the Bureau Desk, Sergeant Pidgeon. I asked Sergeant Pidgeon for permission to speak to my client, Danny Escobedo. . . . Sergeant Pidgeon made a call to the Bureau lockup and informed me that the boy had been taken from the lockup to the Homicide Bureau. This was between 9:30 and 10:00 in the evening. Before I went anywhere, he called the Homicide Bureau and told them there was an attorney waiting to see Escobedo. He told me I could not see him. Then I went upstairs to the Homicide Bureau. There were several Homicide Detectives around, and I talked to them. I identified myself as

Escobedo's attorney and asked permission to see him. They said I could not....The police officer told me to see Chief Flynn, who was on duty. I identified myself to Chief Flynn and asked permission to see my client. He said I could not....I think it was approximately 11:00 o'clock. He said I couldn't see him because they hadn't completed questioning....For a second or two, I spotted him in an office in the Homicide Bureau. The door was open, and I could see through the office....I waved to him and he waved back, and then the door was closed by one of the officers at Homicide...I waited around for another hour or two and went back again and renewed my request to see my client. He again told me I could not....

Danny Escobedo knew that his attorney was at the police station and he asked to speak with him but was told by police that he could see the attorney after the interrogation was over. Eventually, after a lengthy interrogation, Escobedo confessed. Actually, he had been told that if he confessed and named Benedict DiGerlando as the shooter, he would be given immunity from prosecution and could go home. However, after he confessed, he was detained and charged with the murder.

At the trial, Escobedo's attorney made a motion to suppress the confession on the grounds that it had been obtained in violation of Escobedo's Sixth Amendment right to counsel. The trial judge denied the motion and Escobedo was convicted.

The case was appealed to the U.S. Supreme Court, a Court that now had a different composition than the earlier *McNabb* and *Mallory* Courts. This was the Warren Court, and it had a decidedly due process orientation. In its decision (*Escobedo v. Illinois*, 1964), the Court held:

Under the circumstances of this case, where a police investigation is no longer a general inquiry into an unsolved crime but has begun to focus on a particular suspect in police custody who has been refused an opportunity to consult with his counsel and who has not been warned of his constitutional right to keep silent, the accused has been denied the assistance of counsel in violation of the Sixth and Fourteenth Amendments, and no statement extracted by the police during the interrogation may be used against him at a trial.

The Court thought that its decision provided suspects with the constitutional guarantees in the Sixth Amendment. When a person became the focus of an investigation and was a suspect, and requested to speak with an attorney, the questioning had to stop.

However, the decision lacked any provision for determining when the police investigation made the shift from a "...general inquiry into an unsolved crime but has begun to focus on a particular suspect in police custody...." Also, the police were not required to tell the person that he or she was the suspect nor to advise him or her of the right to speak with an attorney. Consequently, the decision requiring **the right to on-the-spot counsel** after police made that "shift" had little, if any, effect on police procedures. It was business as usual in many law enforcement agencies, and police continued to offer confessions into evidence if they were given freely and voluntarily.

THE MIRANDA CASE

The *Miranda warning* was named after the 1966 U.S. Supreme Court decision in which the 1963 conviction of Ernesto Miranda was reversed because the Court believed that he was deprived of his constitutional right to remain silent when questioned by police. The decision was one of the most important cases ever to come out of the Supreme Court. It is one that has often frustrated law enforcement, and one that often has been misunderstood. What follows is an explanation that, hopefully, will clarify exactly what *Miranda* is, and when it is and is not necessary for police to give the admonition to a suspect in a criminal case.

MIRANDA v. ARIZONA, 1966

Ernesto Miranda, a 23-year-old man of Mexican descent, was arrested at his home on March 13, 1963, and taken to the Phoenix Police Station, where he was placed in a lineup. He was immediately identified by a woman as the man who had kidnapped and raped her. He was taken into an interrogation room and questioned for two hours, after which he signed a confession to both crimes. His confession was admitted into evidence at his trial, over objections by his attorney, and he was found guilty of both charges. Miranda was sentenced to two concurrent terms of 20 to 30 years. On appeal, the U.S. Supreme Court held that

...the prosecution may not use statements, whether exculpatory or inculpatory, stemming from custodial interrogation of the defendant unless it demonstrates the use of procedural safeguards effective to secure the privilege against self-incrimination. By *custodial interrogation*, we mean questioning initiated by law enforcement officers after a person has been taken into custody or otherwise deprived of his freedom of action in any significant way. As for the procedural safeguards to be employed, unless other fully effective means are devised to inform accused persons of their right of silence and to assure a continuous opportunity to exercise it, the *following measures are required.*

Prior to any questioning, the person must be warned that he has a right to remain silent, that any statement he does make may be used as evidence against him, and that he has a right to the presence of an attorney, either retained or appointed.

The defendant may waive effectuation of these rights, provided the waiver is made voluntarily, knowingly and intelligently. If, however, he indicates in any manner and at any stage of the process that he wishes to consult with an attorney before speaking, there can be no questioning. Likewise, if the individual is alone and indicates in any manner that he does not wish to be interrogated, the police may not question him. The mere fact that he may have answered some questions or volunteered some statements on his own does not deprive him of the right to refrain from answering any further inquiries until he has consulted with an attorney and thereafter consents to be questioned.

In any case in which a defendant appeals his or her conviction because of a procedural error, and wins the appeal, the person may be retried as long as no evidence is used that was ruled out because of the appeal. That is not double jeopardy. Miranda was retried, without using his confession, and was convicted of the same charges on the testimony of the victim. He was resentenced to two concurrent terms of 20 to 30 years.

That did not mean that he would actually serve 40 to 60 years. It just meant that he would not be paroled right away. Actually, he was paroled in 1972 and returned to his same haunts around Phoenix and Tempe, Arizona. One evening in July 1974, two Tempe police officers observed him driving around town. They stopped him and searched his car and found a loaded handgun and drugs under the front seat. He was arrested and booked into jail, but no charges were filed because the prosecuting attorney found that the stop, search, and seizure were illegal. However, Miranda's parole agent was not held to the same legal standard as the police, and he had Miranda's parole revoked for possession of the gun.

Miranda was paroled again in April 1975, and again returned to his same haunts. One evening in February 1976, while drinking beer in a barrio bar, he got into an argument with a young illegal Mexican who had just entered the country and he stabbed Miranda dead. The bar patrons held the illegal while the bartender called the police. When they arrived, the officers recognized Miranda. They searched his pockets and found several cards with the *Miranda* warning printed on them, cards that he was known to sell near the Maricopa County court buildings. In a touch of irony, one officer stood the suspect against the bar, straddled the dead body of Ernesto Miranda and read the suspect his rights off one of the cards taken from Miranda's pocket.

THE MEANING OF MIRANDA

Our system of justice is called an adversary system because two sides (prosecution and defense) contest against each other in open court, similar to the knights' practice of trial by battle in early England. In theory, the legal truth will emerge from their contest. According to the Supreme Court justices, the privilege against self-incrimination that is guaranteed in the Fifth Amendment shares a similar historical development from England, and is "the essential mainstay of our adversary system, and guarantees to the individual the right to remain silent unless he chooses to speak in the unfettered exercise of his own will" during a period of custodial interrogation, as well as in the courts or during the course of other relevant investigations.

In its reasoning for the *Miranda* decision, the Court explained that when a person is held in custody by law enforcement officers

...the atmosphere and environment of incommunicado interrogation as it exists today is inherently intimidating and works to undermine the privilege against self-incrimination. Unless adequate preventive measures are taken to dispel the compulsion inherent in custodial surroundings, no statement obtained from the defendant can truly be the product of his free choice.

The purpose of the Supreme Court in requiring police to advise an arrested person of his or her rights before questioning was to "police the police." It is similar to the *Mapp* decision in that the Warren Court did not trust the police or what they would do to obtain a confession and conviction. Warren had been a strong law-and-order district attorney in Alameda County, California, where he had firsthand experience with what he could expect of overzealous police officers, and those experiences influenced his thinking and the decisions of the Court.

The *Miranda* warning was suggested by the Court as a guideline to follow in providing the acceptable preventive measures required. Its specific wording is not required, nor is the *Miranda* warning, itself a constitutional right (see *Michigan v. Tucker*, 1974; *Edwards v. Arizona*, 1981, *New York v. Quarles*, 1984; *Moran v. Burbine* 1986; *Duckworth v. Eagan*, 1989; and *Davis v. United States*, 1994).

The only requirement is that police provide sufficient procedural safeguards to satisfy the Court that a citizen's protection against self-incrimination is assured. In the absence of any other procedural safeguards that an agency might have, a law enforcement officer may follow the *Miranda* wording as one way to ensure that a citizen in custody and interrogated by police (hereinafter called **custodial interrogation**) knows of his or her Fifth Amendment protection against self-incrimination, and his or her Sixth Amendment right to an attorney, either hired or appointed, to represent him or her at every stage of a criminal prosecution once prosecution has been initiated. One form of the *Miranda* wording is given below.

THE WARNING

You have a right to remain silent. Do you understand? (Fifth Amendment right)

Anything you say may be used against you in court. Do you understand? (Fifth Amendment right)

You have the right to the presence of an attorney before and during any questioning. Do you understand? (Sixth Amendment right)

If you can not afford an attorney, one will be appointed for you free of charge, before any questioning, if you want. Do you understand? (Sixth Amendment right)

A suspect's statements or confession cannot be admitted as evidence against him or her in trial unless it has been given freely and voluntarily. A confession may not be coerced or given after a threat or a promise of leniency made by police, and not until he or she knows and understands his or her Fifth Amendment protection against self-incrimination *and* Sixth Amendment right to have an attorney appointed and/or present during any questioning. Any evidence obtained in violation of this Sixth Amendment right to an attorney is inadmissible in trial (*Massiah v. United States*, 1964).

Not *Mirandizing* a person in custodial interrogation does not violate his or her constitutional rights. The only time that a person's rights are violated is if a person's statements (confession) made without being advised, or otherwise given involuntarily, are admitted as evidence in what is called the prosecutor's case-in-chief, the prosecution's side of the case during the trial (see *United States v. Verdugo-Urquidez*, 1990).

If an officer obtains information about a person's role in a crime during custodial interrogation without first *Mirandizing* the suspect, the evidence cannot be used against the person at trial during the prosecution's presentation of his or her side of the case. However, it may be used for impeachment purposes at trial if the person testifies in his or her own behalf with information contrary to what was stated to police. Also, evidence derived from the tainted information (confession) obtained by police, such as a gun or other contraband, may be admitted, because it does not fit the *fruit of the poison tree* doctrine (*Oregon v. Elsted*, 1985; *People v. Torres*, 1989; *United States v. Gonzalez*, 1990), although many state trial judges might not agree. In addition, a peace officer knows that under Chapter 42 of the *U.S Code*, §1983, he or she can incur civil liability for depriving a person of rights guaranteed by the constitution under color of authority. However, since *Miranda* is not a constitutional right, no civil liability attaches to an officer for interrogation of a suspect without giving the *Miranda* warning (see *Brock v. Logan County*, 1993).

The requirement to admonish an adult suspect of the *Miranda* warning has been so distorted by its use in cop shows on television and in the movies that it is misunderstood by the general public and by some criminal justice personnel as well. Suspects usually are not *Mirandized* immediately upon arrest.

To reiterate, if a suspect's statements are to be used in trial, *Miranda* must be given only when two specific conditions are present at the same time:

1. When a suspect is taken into custody, or otherwise deprived of freedom in a significant way
2. If and when the person is subject to questioning about a crime as a suspect by a police officer

These two conditions are the elements of *custodial interrogation*. Also, the suspect must know that the person questioning him or her is a law enforcement officer. If the person is not in custody, and knows that he or she is free to leave, *Miranda* need not be given before questioning by police. If the suspect is in custody but police do not question him or her, *Miranda* need not be given.

The phrase above "deprived of freedom in a significant way" means that the person is not free to leave and is restrained in freedom of movement, such as being cuffed and caged in a car, or locked in a room at the station (see, *California v. Beheler*, 1983).

Consider the recent case of *Thompson v. Keohane* (1995) as a clear example of a confession given during noncustodial interrogation.

On September 10, 1986, two moose hunters discovered the body of a dead woman floating in a gravel pit lake on the outskirts of Fairbanks, Alaska. The woman had been stabbed twenty-nine times. Notified by the hunters, the Alaska state troopers issued a press release seeking assistance in identifying the body. Thompson called the troopers on September 11 to inform them that his former wife, Dixie Thompson, fit the description in the press release and that she had been missing for about a month. Through a dental examination, the troopers conclusively established that the corpse was Dixie Thompson. On September 15, a trooper called Thompson and asked him to come to headquarters, purportedly to identify personal items the troopers thought belonged to Dixie Thompson. It is now undisputed, however, that the trooper's primary reason for contacting Thompson was to question him about the murder.

Thompson drove to the troopers' headquarters in his pickup truck, and upon arriving, immediately identified the items as Dixie's. He remained at headquarters, however, for two more hours while two unarmed troopers continuously questioned him in a small interview room and tape-recorded the exchange. The troopers did not inform Thompson of his *Miranda* rights. Although they constantly assured Thompson he was free to leave, they also told him repeatedly that they knew he had killed his former wife. Informing Thompson that execution of a search warrant was underway at his home, and that his truck was about to be searched pursuant to another warrant, the troopers asked questions that invited a confession. Eventually, Thompson told the troopers he killed Dixie.

As promised, the troopers permitted Thompson to leave, but impounded his truck. Left without transportation, Thompson accepted the troopers' offer of a ride to his friend's house. Some two hours later, the troopers arrested Thompson and charged him with first-degree murder. The Alaska trial court, without holding an evidentiary hearing, denied Thompson's motion to suppress his September 15 statements. Deciding the motion on the papers submitted, the trial court ruled that Thompson was not "in custody" for *Miranda* purposes, therefore the troopers had no obligation to inform him of his *Miranda* rights. Applying an objective test to resolve the "in custody" question...the trial court held that, under the *totality of the circumstances*, a reasonable person would have felt free to leave. It also observed that the troopers' subsequent actions—releasing and shortly thereafter arresting Thompson—rendered the question "very close."

After a trial at which the prosecution played the tape-recorded confession, the jury found Thompson guilty of first-degree murder and tampering with evidence. The Court of Appeals of Alaska affirmed Thompson's conviction, concluding, among other things, that the troopers had not placed Thompson "in custody," and therefore had no obligation to give him *Miranda* warnings. The Alaska Supreme Court denied discretionary review.

Thompson filed to the United States District Court for the District of Alaska. The District Court denied his appeal, giving a presumption of correctness under 28 *U.S.C.* §2254(d) to the state court's conclusion that, when Thompson confessed, he was not yet "in custody" for *Miranda* purposes. The U.S. Court of Appeals agreed (1994).

Thompson's appeal eventually reached the U.S. Supreme Court, and his case was argued on October 11, 1995. On November 29, 1995, by a vote of 7 to 2, the Court held that Thompson was not in custody at the Alaska trooper's police station for purposes of *Miranda*. Consequently, *Miranda* did not apply, and his conviction was upheld. Actually, the Alaska troopers and Thompson were engaged in a deliberate consensual encounter (see also *Oregon v. Mathiason*, 1977) in order to question Thompson in the manner they wanted without having to advise him of any rights. This is a common practice in many states under *Beheler*.

THE BEHELER ADMONITION

Many law enforcement agencies have a policy that the arresting officer is not to question the suspect about the crime. The officer merely effects that arrest and transports the person to jail. Consequently, no *Miranda* warning is required. If the person voluntarily offers incriminating information as to his or her role in the crime, it is admissible in court. Any *Mirandizing* will be done by the detectives investigating the case, and they usually will videotape, or at least auditorally tape, the officers giving the warning.

When a suspect has not been arrested, it is a common practice for investigative officers to ask a suspect if he or she would mind coming to police headquarters to discuss a matter. When the suspect arrives, he or she is given what is termed the ***Beheler*** **admonition** or warning (*California v. Beheler*, 1983), which goes something like the following:

Thank you for coming down to the station. We want you to know that you are not under arrest, and that you are free to leave at any time. We just want to talk to you about a matter. Do you mind answering a few questions?

This creates the situation discussed in the *Thompson* case, a consensual encounter. It does not constitute custodial interrogation, because the suspect is not under any restraint and is free to leave. Then, if a confession or incriminating statements are obtained, they are legally admissible. If the suspect does confess, he or she is still free to leave the station at any time. However, after he or she leaves, the officers will obtain an arrest warrant, using the confession as probable cause, and will arrest the suspect.

MORE ON MIRANDA

In the original *Miranda* decision, the Court also stated that if the suspect indicates prior to or during questioning that he or she wishes to remain silent, the interrogation must cease. If he or she requests an attorney, the interrogation must cease and may not resume unless and until the attorney gives permission and is present during any questioning. If questioning does continue, any incriminating statements made by the suspect will not be admitted as evidence to prove guilt at a trial. However, in some states it is admissible to counter a defendant's testimony if he or she does testify at trial. Rarely will this occur, because it is rare for a defendant to take the stand and testify. When an interrogation is conducted without the presence of an attorney and statements are made by the suspect, a "heavy burden rests on the government to demonstrate that the defendant knowingly and intelligently waived his right to counsel."

When a suspect makes statements without waiving his or her rights, the suspect may stop answering questions and invoke his or her privilege against self-incrimination or right to an attorney at any time during the interrogation. However, if the suspect does waive his or her rights, the waiver may be stated *or* implied in the responses to the *Miranda* admonition made by the suspect. That is, the suspect need not actually state that he or she waives his or her rights. He or she may imply a legal waiver merely by responding to a police officer's questions after being advised of the *Miranda* admonition (*North Carolina v. Butler*, 1979).

A person's right to counsel, as guaranteed in the Sixth Amendment, attaches to the person only after he or she has been formally charged in court and becomes the defendant in a criminal action. That is when an attorney will be appointed. Therefore, the police do not provide an attorney if a person requests one after being *Mirandized*. The police must stop any efforts to interrogate the suspect. However, after an attorney has been hired or appointed by the court, after formally charging the defendant, the attorney's representation is case-specific. This means that although police may not question the suspect on the immediate offense without the presence of an attorney, they may question him or her on other, unrelated offenses after *Mirandizing* the person and obtaining a waiver.

WHEN MIRANDA IS NOT REQUIRED

As indicated, during detention situations, the person is not free to leave, and often is asked incriminating questions. However, detention does not constitute an arrest. There are several specific detention situations to take note of:

1. When asking questions of a motorist detained in a routine traffic stop
2. When asking routine questions of a DUI suspect
3. When there is an immediate threat to public safety, officer safety, victim safety, or suspect safety (refer to the discussion of the public safety exception to the exclusionary rule in Chapter 2)
4. When no questions (or the functional equivalent) are asked
5. When asking general on-the-scene questions
6. During lineups, field show-ups, or photo IDs
7. When questioning witnesses
8. When statements are made to a private person, or one believed to be a private person by the suspect
9. When questioning is in an office or place of business, as long as the person is free to leave
10. In simple detention/stop-and-frisk situations
11. Even in an interrogation room of the police station if the suspect knows that he or she is free to leave, is not locked in, and is not under arrest, but instead remains there freely and voluntarily to talk or answer questions

One final word on *Miranda* in adult cases. The private beliefs, thoughts, intentions, or suspicions of a law enforcement officer about a person as a suspect are totally irrelevant to any issue of *Miranda*, just as they are irrelevant in a detention situation. For example, in the *Thompson* case, Alaska troopers suspected him of killing his wife and invited him to come down to the station to pick up her effects because they really wanted to talk to him about his role in her death. However, it does not matter what the officer thinks; it only matters what the officer does.

THE USE OF MIRANDA IN JUVENILE CASES

All the information above on *Miranda* applies only when the suspect is an adult at the time of arrest. Juvenile procedures have more rigorous requirements, in some states, depending on the particular state's law, because of independent state grounds. In California, for example, a minor must be advised of his or her rights regardless of whether he or she will be questioned, and regardless of what the officer might do with the minor after arrest: release, cite and release, refer to some recognized diversion program, or deliver to juvenile hall. In other states, such as Michigan, Nevada, or Washington, police must also advise a parent of those rights and must obtain a waiver from both the minor and parent(s) before questioning, because those states have what is called **interested adult laws** (Cavin, 1992). This extra protection for juveniles is not constitutionally necessary. Actually, the U.S. Supreme Court has held that the *Miranda* requirement is the same for juveniles (*In re Gault*, 1967, and *Fare v. Michael C.*, 1979).

SUMMARY

The purpose of this chapter was to explain what the requirements are for law enforcement officers under *Miranda*. The defining concept is known as *custodial interrogation*, the questioning of a suspect who is in custody or under similar restraints about his or her role in a crime. Several case situations that were forerunners of the *Miranda* decision were also discussed: the *McNabb* and *Mallory* requirement of prompt arraignment, and the Escobedo requirement of on-the-spot counsel. The use of what is known as the Beheler admonition was described as a contemporary approach to questioning suspects without arresting them. The additional situations in which *Miranda* is not required were explained as well, along with the fact that a defendant's waiver of his or her rights after being *Mirandized* may be either stated or implied in the defendant's responses to questions.

The chapter concluded with a summary of how *Miranda* applies in juvenile arrest situations. Federal guidelines for *Miranda* are the same for juveniles as they are for adults, and it is up to each state to offer additional protections if it so desires.

KEY TERMS AND CONCEPTS

Beheler admonition   *Miranda* warning
Custodial interrogation   Prompt arraignment
Interested adult laws   Right to on-the-spot counsel

REFERENCES

Cavin, Jeffery D. "Waiver of a Juvenile's Fifth and Sixth Amendment Rights," *Journal of Juvenile Law*, Vol. 13, 1992.

Robin, Gerald D. *Introduction to the Criminal Justice System*, 3rd ed. New York: Harper & Row, 1987.

Zalman, Marvin, and Larry Siegel. *Key Cases and Comments on Criminal Procedures*, St. Paul, MN: West Publishing, 1995.

CASES

Brock v. Logan County, 3 F.3d 1215, 1217 (1993)

California v. Beheler, 463 U.S. 1121 (1983)

Davis v. United States, 127 L.Ed.2d 563, 114 S.Ct. 1216 (1994)

Duckworth v. Eagan, 492 U.S. 195 (1989)

Edwards v. Arizona, 451 U S. 477 (1981)

Escobedo v. Illinois, 378 U.S. 478 (1964)

Fare v. Michael C., 442 U.S. 707 (1979)

In re Gault, 387 U.S. 1 (1967)

McNabb v. United States, 318 U.S. 332 (1943)

Mallory v. United States, 354 U.S. 449 (1957)

Massiah v. United States, 377 U S. 201 (1964)

Michigan v. Tucker, 417 U.S. 433 (1974)

Miranda v. Arizona, 384 U.S. 444 (1966)

Moran v. Burbine, 475 U.S. 412 (1986)

New York v. Quarles, 467 U.S. 649 (1984)

North Carolina v. Butler, 441 U.S. 369 (1979)

Oregon v. Elsted, 470 U.S. 298 (1985)

Oregon v. Mathiason, 429 U.S. 492 (1977)

People v. Torres, 213 Cal. 3d 1284, 1255 (1989)

Thompson v. Keohane, 516 U.S. 99 (1995)

United States v. Gonzalez, 894 F.2d 1043, 1048 (Calif. 1990)

United States v. Verdugo-Urquidez, 494 U.S. 259 (1990)

BOOKING AND CUSTODY PROCEDURES

The majority of adults arrested are not taken to jail. Most of those charged with infractions and most misdemeanors are cited by police to appear in court. However, each county maintains a jail, usually under the control of the sheriff, which receives adults for one or more of the following purposes:

1. For detention and presentation in court to answer to charges after a lawful arrest by a peace officer.
2. For the detention of persons ordered to jail by a magistrate or judge pending trial.
3. For the confinement of persons sentenced to jail following misdemeanor convictions.
4. For the confinement of persons committed for contempt, or some civil process, or by other authority of law.
5. For the detention of persons committed in order to secure their attendance as witnesses for trial.
6. For the confinement of persons granted probation but ordered to serve some time in jail as a condition of probation.
7. For the detention of persons arrested by county probation officers, county parole officers, or state parole agents and ordered held for probation or parole violation proceedings.

8. For the temporary detention of persons in transit from and/or to other county, state, or federal facilities.

9. The detention of certain juveniles, as specified in the various state codes.

It should be obvious from reading the list of sources of those received in jail that they will be detained for varying lengths of time; some for a few days and some for up to a year or longer. Regardless of the length of time, all those detained or confined must be treated as prisoners under legal custody, subject to all the rights and treatment required by law.

THE JAIL POPULATION

There are over 3300 county jails operating in the United States today, and approximately 20 million persons are booked into jail each year. The states of California and Texas seem to be competing to be the largest in the nation, with California housing approximately 75,000 a day and Texas with nearly 60,000. Overcrowding is a major problem, and many jails are increasing in size and staff at every opportunity. However, jail construction seems to follow the theme expressed in Kevin Costner's movie, *Field of Dreams*: *Build it and they will come.* This could also be expressed as a version of Murphy's law: *The jail inmate population will increase to fill the size of the facilities built to hold it.*

For years, most jail populations were fairly well balanced between felony and misdemeanor offenders. This balance has shifted to the point where 70 percent of the inmates in 1996 were either charged with, or convicted of, felonies. This increase has a decided impact on the type of jail construction needed, with an increased emphasis on security that requires more expensive housing. It also affects jail classification procedures. Ironically, one current philosophy of jail construction and management stresses open, **modular housing**, with its **direct supervision** of inmates, rather than the traditional linear-style cell blocks (Moore, 1997).

In many instances, one correctional officer is placed in charge of 50 inmates in open pods, where the inmates are free to wander about the housing unit, and the correctional officer often wanders among them. This requires a strong and amenable interpersonal style to approaching inmate supervision, as opposed to the authoritarian personality type. It also places a special importance on classification and housing procedures.

CUSTODY

A dictionary defines **custody** as "immediate charge and control exercised by a person or an authority over a ward, suspect or inmate." Another dictionary used the phrase "immediate care or charge." Two aspects of custody are either stated or implied in these definitions: (1) control over a person, and (2) safekeeping of the person. Within the limits necessary to maintain proper control, one does not lose his or her rights and protections just because one is in jail. In fact, it is both the legal and moral responsibility of a person having custody of prisoners to ensure their safety and humane treatment as well as to maintain the control and security of the facility.

BOOKING PROCEDURES

When a person is first brought into a jail after an arrest, he or she is **booked**. This term is derived from the early practice of entering all the relevant information about the person and offense in a large book. Today, computers have replaced the book, but the practice remains relatively the same. Booking is simply a procedure in which the suspect is photographed, fingerprinted, and relieved of all his or her personal property, for which a receipt must be given. The property should be accurately described, but in generic terms so as not to imply worth or value. If the person is to be detained, he or she is provided with jail clothing, and his or her personal clothing is stored for return upon release.

VALIDATING THE LEGALITY OF THE ARREST

The receiving or booking officer should verify that the documents that request or command detention or confinement are legal. These will include an abstract of a warrant; a valid probable cause arrest by a peace officer; a valid adult court commitment document; and valid probation or parole arrest and detainer documents. Valid court commitment documents include an arrest warrant, a sentencing order, or a remanding order. They must contain the court case and docket numbers, the violation, the amount of bail or information as to sentencing time, and the signature of the proper legal authority, the judge or clerk.

For a warrant to be valid, it must either be in the possession of the arresting officer, or its validity must have been confirmed by that officer or a person from his or her agency, and the arresting officer must be in possession of the warrant or abstract at the time of booking. As stated in Chapter 4, by the time an arresting officer reaches the jail, dispatch will have arranged for the abstract or warrant to be there as well. County probation officers will provide their valid arrest and detention orders, as will county parole officers and state parole agents.

When accepting custody from a peace officer after a probable cause arrest, the booking officer will require the arresting officer, or officer doing the transporting after arrest, to provide a copy of the police arrest report or to complete a proper booking sheet containing the arrested person's name, age, and offense. Persons booked and detained while en route to other facilities will be accompanied by a booking or commitment order signed by an authority. The booking officer should note the legality of that order before accepting custody.

Before accepting anyone for booking, the booking officer should be certain that the person to be booked is not in need of immediate medical care or treatment. If immediate treatment is required, the officer should refuse to accept custody and should request that the arresting peace officer take the prisoner to a hospital or medical facility where treatment can be provided before that person is delivered to jail for booking. This procedure should be followed for three reasons:

1. To ensure that treatment is provided to the arrested person as soon as possible
2. To prevent the custodial agency from assuming any liability because of the injury or illness for which the treatment is needed
3. To be sure that the arrested person's insurance company is responsible for the cost of such treatment

Failure of a booking officer to follow this procedure could be very costly to the facility and the county government, and even to the custodial officer if an injury does not receive treatment because of negligence.

MEDICAL PRESCREENING OF ARRESTED PERSONS

Every peace officer is responsible for the care, protection, and safety of each person arrested or otherwise in custody. The initial responsibility lies with the arresting officer to be certain that the person arrested is not suffering from any injury, mental illness, drug overdose or intoxication, or other conditions that might require medication or treatment. If the officer believes that the arrested person is in urgent need of treatment, he or she should immediately take the person to the approved local medical facility, usually the county hospital. The nature of the injury or other condition, and the treatment it is given, should be noted in the officer's report or notebook. When the prisoner has received the required treatment, the officer will obtain a medical release from the medical practitioner in charge and can then transport the person to jail.

The jail intake or custodial person receiving the arrested person should complete a medical questionnaire on each person received. If urgent treatment is required, the person should not be accepted by custody staff. Once custody is accepted, the arresting and/or transporting officer and his or her agency are relieved of any further responsibilities.

PRISONER'S RIGHTS TO PHONE CALLS

Almost immediately after booking, the person is granted the right to communicate with certain people in an effort to gain release from jail and/or assistance of an attorney in answering the charges. Each state's penal code details the procedures that the jail custody staff must follow. It usually includes a time limit within a few hours of custody to allow the person these rights. In addition, these phone calls may not be monitored, eavesdropped upon, or recorded. Any police or corrections officer who deprives an inmate of these rights may be charged with a crime, usually a misdemeanor.

SOLICITING FOR ATTORNEYS OR BAIL BOND PEOPLE

In allowing the phone calls, a peace officer absolutely may not suggest the name of any particular lawyer or bail bond person to call. In addition, the officer may not dial a number for the prisoner. The names of attorneys and bail bond persons usually are posted in the booking area, near the phone from which the prisoner will make his or her other calls. Not only is it an abuse of an officer's position of authority if he or she recommends anyone—friend, relative or business associate—but the act of soliciting for business is prohibited by law as a misdemeanor in most states.

REQUIRED VISITS FOR INMATES

Another legal requirement of custody staff is the obligation to allow jail inmates the rights to have visits on demand with certain types of professionals, including physicians, surgeons, psychiatrists, and psychologists, along with the attorney of record or one requested by the inmate or his or her family.

CITE-AND-RELEASE PROGRAMS

The jails in many jurisdictions are overcrowded and only have room for offenders who present the most serious risk to the community. In addition, it is not necessary to hold some people under lock and key after arrest and during their court proceedings because they do not pose a public threat and/or concern that they might fail to appear in court. Consequently, a procedure known as **cite-and-release** is used to minimize the unnecessary detention of persons brought to jail after a probable cause arrest.

The staff that operates the programs to implement cite-and-release varies from one jurisdiction to another. They might be probation officers, jail custody officers, or nonsworn personnel, usually trained in interviewing techniques. They will interview the prisoner after booking to determine whether the need exists for further detention. They consider the likelihood of the person appearing in court when required. In doing this they look for stability and ties in the area, such as family, property and employment.

They also look at the person's prior record to determine if they ever failed to appear on previous release occasions (any **failure to appear** notices in the record). They also consider the risk to public safety that the person might pose if released. This would include whether they were armed during the commission of the **instant offense** (offense for which they were arrested), the severity of the instant offense, whether they were on probation or parole at the time, and the concerns of any victim, particularly in domestic violence cases.

The cite-and-release staff usually have criteria to use in assessing the worthiness of the person for release, and usually have limits on their release authority. However, in many jurisdictions, a judge is on call to authorize the release if it is beyond the authority of the program staff. If the person qualifies for release, he or she is given a citation to appear in court, similar to what the arresting officer could have given. A court appearance date is provided on the citation. After signing it the person is released without bond or bail.

Those who do not qualify for the cite-and-release program may pursue the traditional options: posting bail with cash, or in some jurisdictions with a credit card, or contracting for the services of a local bail bond person. This person will guarantee the bail for the prisoner. If he or she is released and later fails to appear, the bail bond person probably will contract with a bounty hunter for the person's capture and return.

CLASSIFICATION OF DETAINEES

As people are accepted and booked into jail custody, they may not all be housed together, both for staff and inmate safety and for legal reasons. Each prisoner booked into jail should be evaluated to identify characteristics that can be used in determining where and with whom each may be housed. They should be classified during and/or immediately after booking in order to comply with the law and to ensure everyone's safety and to maintain a secure facility. It is the responsibility of custody staff, not only to protect each other but to protect the prisoners from each other as well. Any classification procedure should be based on consideration of criminal sophistication, seriousness of crime charged, presence or absence of assaultive behavior, age, and other criteria that will provide for the safety of the prisoners and staff.

SEPARATION BY CLASS AND GENDER

People detained in jail pending trial and persons convicted and serving a sentence often may not be mixed together or put in the same room except for the purpose of participating in supervised activities. Persons committed or detained on a civil process, such as a witness or a person being punished for contempt of court, should not be mixed with those detained for criminal matters. Diplomats also might require special consideration. In addition, male and female prisoners, except husband and wife, should not be allowed to sleep, dress or undress, bathe, or perform eliminatory functions in the same room. Male and female prisoners must be separated at all times, unless they are participating in certain recreational or educational activities that are supervised.

SEPARATION BY GANG AFFILIATION

The growth of gangs and gang violence is alarming and it is everywhere. Juvenile and adult gangs often form among those of economically and/or socially disadvantaged families living in the poorer areas of a community. They also seem to cluster along the major transportation corridors throughout a state in order to create favorable drug distribution networks. One of the primary activities of some street gangs is drug sales, and much of the violence is between gangs over the control of drug distribution.

Gangs fight each other over territory as well. There also are gangs formed along racial and even sectional-racial lines, such as the rivalries often found between two Hispanic gangs, those from the north and those from the south, or black gangs against the white Aryan Brotherhood. Many subgroups have developed over the years from these primary gangs, all of which must be identified, classified, and usually separated during detention.

Gangs have expanded their repertoire of crimes, as well, to broaden the threat they pose to the general community. Some gangs, particularly certain Asian gangs, specialize in extortion and home invasion robbery. The victims are often Asians themselves, many of whom do not trust American institutions such as banks and police. Other gangs specialize in carjacking, and still others in party-crashing robbery. The so-called Russian Mafia is becoming an increasing threat as well.

It is beyond the scope of this book to present all the details and complexities of the gang phenomenon. Specific gang recognition characteristics and classification requirements will be provided to detention personnel in their various correctional academies.

SEPARATION FOR INMATE SAFETY

Several categories of prisoners are often separated from the mainline inmates because they might need protection from other prisoners. Besides rival gang members, these would include former peace officers and correctional officers who have been arrested, police informants, homosexuals, youthful and/or vulnerable prisoners, and certain sex offenders, such as child molesters, exploiters, or pornographers. This is particularly true if it is a high-profile case. A good example of this is Richard Allen Davis, who kidnapped, sexually assaulted, and murdered 12-year-old Polly Klass in northern California in October 1993. He required separation and protection in the county jail for nearly three years pending trial, and now requires protection in San Quentin Prison, where he was received on death row in August 1996, because of the nature of his crime and the vulnerability of his victim. In addition to loathing his crime, many inmates blame him for provoking that state's legislature into enacting a three-strikes law because of the publicity and public attention his crime received. Recently he has been attacked by inmates while exercising in the small yard off death row, right under the protection of a gun tower.

Other prisoners might require separation because they pose a threat to their own safety or the safety of others. These would include suicide risks, those with communicable diseases, such as AIDS and hepatitis, along with injured or sick prisoners, those with mental disorders, and alcoholics or addicts who are detoxing. Those who are physically or developmentally disabled also need special classification and treatment.

If an arresting officer has any indication that a person he or she is booking might require special classification, he or she should immediately bring this to the attention of the booking intake staff for their consideration.

DETENTION SEARCHES

PATDOWN AND METAL DETECTOR SEARCHES

Patdown and metal detector searches are the least intrusive searches performed by peace officers and are preferred in cases that present limited risk to officers or to facility safety. Aside from the field patdown by a police officer, pat searches and metal detector searches are performed on misdemeanor and infraction offenders who are booked into jail but who will soon be released. They also are used in screening visitors to prisoners, and in screening private persons who will be touring a jail facility.

STRIP AND BODY CAVITY SEARCHES

Most of the procedures designed to control the behavior of peace officers came into law as the result of isolated cases of serious abuses by a few officers or a pattern of complaints about a particular abuse. However, there were more than a few instances of abuse of prisoners, particularly female prisoners, when it came to requiring strip and/or body cavity searches. Apparently, some females were searched by males while other males watched, and in some cases females would be searched, then released.

In addition, some procedures violated state and federal constitutional rights to privacy and freedom from unreasonable searches and seizures. Just because a person is in jail, he or she does not lose his or her rights. Consequently, many states enacted laws to protect the rights of prisoners by establishing statewide policy placing strict limits on who can be searched and when.

TREATMENT OF PRISONERS BY PEACE OFFICERS

State penal codes provide for criminal penalties for any peace officer who mistreats a prisoner. Mistreatment usually includes the (1) inhumanity to prisoners; (2) assault by public officers; and (3) cruel and unusual punishment. Mistreatment could also include depriving a person of his or her rights under the color of authority.

Examples of mistreatment and the legal consequence can be found in every state and at every level of corrections. For example, in January 1998, a criminal investigation was initiated in Los Angeles, California involving several deputy sheriffs who allegedly *arranged* for certain jail inmates to beat other selected inmates charged with child molestation. Two deputies were suspended and more suspensions are expected, along with criminal prosecution.

On February 26, 1998, eight correctional officers at the Corcoran State Prison in California were indicted by a federal grand jury on nine counts of conspiracy, civil rights violations, and deprivation of rights under color of authority, which could result in life sentences for some of the officers, if convicted. It is alleged that they entertained themselves by arranging for rival prison gang members to be together in the exercise yard. Naturally, this resulted in fights between the rival inmates. Then, as one officer was quoted as saying to another, "It's going to be duck hunting season." The officers shot and killed at least six inmates during these fights.

It was stated in the beginning of this chapter that custody staff have both a moral (or ethical) and a legal responsibility to protect prisoners and to care for them because they are in the charge of the officers. The legal requirements are detailed in the law; the ethical responsibilities are derived from the professionalism of the job.

Hopefully, the personnel selection processes in all the states will strive to ensure employment of persons who have the moral capacity to meet their responsibilities. Those who do not, face state prosecution for violating their state's penal code. In addition, they might well face federal prosecution for a violation of federal civil rights laws. They will also face civil liability for money damages, both for doing what is prohibited and for not doing what is required.

WEAPONS CONTROL IN JAILS

Current law places specific limits on anyone bringing weapons into, or possessing weapons in a custodial institution, including prisons, jails, road camps, or other facilities described in the law. The word *anyone* includes peace officers. Therefore, peace officers need to know the conditions that prohibit and allow them to bring weapons into a jail, and how to secure their weapons when they are not permitted to bring them in. Each state code will have one or more controlling sections.

Each police agency or detention facility will also have its own policy and procedure for securing weapons outside the custodial setting. Usually, a jail will have secure lockers just outside the booking intake area, in which police may lock their weapons. This includes their primary and backup guns, knives, and any other type of weapon. These could be locked in the trunk of the patrol car as well. The baton should be left inside the patrol car. Lockers are also provided in most cases inside the jail lobby area, in which detectives, private detectives, and others entering the jail by the front door may secure their weapons.

SUMMARY

The focus of this chapter has been on the requirements of peace officers, either custodial staff or patrol officers, when dealing with persons in county detention facilities. It began with a look at jail populations and their increasing demands of bed space and institutional security. The booking process was described, including the responsibility of booking staff to validate the legality of the arrest and/or custody, medical prescreening, and the rights of prisoners to phone calls and selected visits. The prohibition against police or detention personnel from soliciting for certain attorneys or bail bond people was discussed as well.

The requirements of classification were described, to include classification by gender and class, by gang affiliation, and for inmate security. The types of detention searches were defined and the law controlling body cavity searches was discussed. The treatment of prisoners was described within the specific laws that prohibit certain types of treatment, rather than any criteria that necessitated certain treatment. This included inhumanity to prisoners, assault by a peace officer, and cruel and unusual punishment. The chapter concluded with an examination of the law controlling the possession of weapons within a detention facility.

In this chapter we stressed the point that when in the custody of police and custody staff, prisoners are in their care. That carries with it the dual responsibility by staff to ensure the safety and protection of prisoners, as well as the security of the facility. Compliance with all the legal requirements will keep them free from criminal prosecution and civil liability, and fulfillment of their ethical responsibilities will help to professionalize an important element of the justice system, the group of peace officers who work within local correctional facilities.

KEY TERMS AND CONCEPTS

Assault by a peace officer
Body cavity searches
Booking
Cite-and-release program
Classification of detainees
Cruel and unusual punishment
Custody
Detention facility
Detention searches
Direct supervision
Failure to appear
Inhumanity to prisoners
Medical prescreening
Metal detector searches

Modular housing
Pat searches
Prisoners' rights to phone calls
Prisoners' rights to visits
Required visits
Separation by gang affiliation
Separation by gender and class
Separation for inmate safety
Soliciting for attorneys
Soliciting for bail bond people
Strip searches
Treatment of prisoners
Validating the legality of arrest
Weapons control in jails

REFERENCES

MOORE, DELANCEY H. "The Complexity of Jail Classification of Gang Members," *American Jails*, March/April 1997, pp. 81–84.

ROWAN, JOSEPH R. "Corrections in the 21st Century," *American Jails*, March/April 1997, pp. 32–34.

THE COURT STRUCTURE AND PRETRIAL PROCEDURES

Within the United States there are two distinct court structures: the federal courts and the state courts. These correspond to the one set of federal laws and federal justice system and to the 50 differing state legal and state justice systems. The chapter begins with a brief description of the federal court structure, then follows with a more detailed presentation of the state courts and proceedings at the state court level. The scope and jurisdiction of each court is detailed first so that the reader will understand which of the procedures described in the balance of the chapter occur in which level of the courts. The remaining portions of the chapter include descriptions of the role and responsibilities of the prosecutor, alternatives to formal prosecution, the formal complaint and grand jury processes, the initial appearance of the accused person before the court, the preliminary screening process in felony cases, and the additional procedures followed in the preparation of a case for trial. The latter portion also includes the role and responsibilities of the defense attorney, defense pretrial motions, and a procedure most often used to settle a case, plea bargaining.

FEDERAL COURTS

U.S. SUPREME COURT

The U.S. Supreme Court is composed of nine members: eight associate justices and one chief justice. Vacancies on the Court are filled by an appointment by the President, with confirmation (approval) by the Senate. Once confirmed, a justice sits for life, or until he or she retires. They are beyond political control and they are not accountable to anyone for their work or their decisions. Their annual term begins on the first Monday of October and runs through sometime in July. Their primary responsibility is to exercise what is called **judicial review** of state and federal court decisions and laws that are questioned by someone's appeal to them. They do not seek out cases to hear, but wait for an appeal from some lower court that the justices believe presents some significant constitutional issue. They are selective and might agree to hear approximately 100 cases of the several thousand that are appealed to them each year.

When someone wants to appeal a conviction, he or she prepares a *writ of certiorari*, a legal document requesting an appellate review of the case. The justices meet behind closed doors and vote on what cases they want to hear. It takes a vote of 4 to hear a case. The one who appealed and the opposing attorney, usually from a state attorney general's office, are notified. Both submit a written argument of their position, which are supported by any prior cases they can find in which precedent was set. Then the case is scheduled for oral arguments before the Court in which each attorney has 30 minutes to present his or her position.

After the oral arguments, the justices meet, again behind closed doors, to discuss and vote for or against the appeal. Many of their decisions are not unanimous. A vote of 5 to 4 is sufficient for a binding decision. After the vote, one justice is assigned to write the majority opinion, which is circulated and signed. When the decision is made public, it becomes law.

U.S. COURTS OF APPEALS

The nation is divided into 12 judicial appellate regions, which includes Guam, the Virgin Islands, the Northern Mariana Islands, and Puerto Rico. Cases from the federal trial courts within those regions are appealed directly to the respective court of appeals. In addition, these courts hear appeals from the various state courts within their regions that pose some constitutional issue.

There are approximately 165 appellate judges, who also are appointed by the President, with confirmation from the Senate, and sit for life. They hear appeals in panels of three judges. Their decisions are binding unless overturned by the U.S. Supreme Court.

FEDERAL TRIAL COURTS

For purposes of federal trials, the nation and its territories are divided into 94 judicial districts. There are 650 judgeship positions within this court structure, but many are unfilled at this time because of political (philosophical) differences between the President who appoints the judges and the controlling party of the Senate, who confirms the appointments. A somewhat similar situation exists in the courts of appeals. Consequently, there is a heavy workload for each court.

The federal trial courts are the felony trial courts for violations of all federal crimes. In addition to the judges, each district court has an assistant U.S. attorney and staff to prosecute the cases, and a U.S. probation officer and staff to assist the court with investigations and the supervision of any offenders who are granted probation after conviction.

There also is a lower trial court, called a U.S. magistrate's court, within each district to serve as the trial court for any federal misdemeanors and to hear the preliminary matters in felony cases, such as arraignment, bail, and supervised release pending trial.

STATE COURTS

In most states, the judicial authority of the courts is distributed among the courts in a four-tier court structure, similar to that of the federal system described above: a state supreme court, a first-level courts of appeal, a felony trial court, and a lower trial court for hearing misdemeanor and/or traffic cases and the preliminary matters in felony cases. This has been the traditional model since the founding of our country, although several states have devised more complex organizations. This traditional structure is examined below, followed by a description of an alternative emerging in several states, the consolidation model.

STATE SUPREME COURT

The authority of a state's supreme court is the highest, and its decisions are binding on all the courts within the state. The court consists of one chief justice and a number of associate justices, ranging from four to eight. In most states, they are appointed by the governor as positions become vacant, and those appointments are confirmed by the state's senate or by a commission established to review and approve judicial appointments. Thereafter, appointees either serve for life or (in some states) their names are placed on the ballot at the next general election and the public votes to either confirm or deny their appointments. If the appointment of a justice is confirmed, his or her name is placed periodically on the ballot for reconfirmation. If the voters deny a confirmation, the governor appoints someone else, and the process begins all over again.

The court is an appellate court, having **appellate jurisdiction**, that exercises judicial review over cases brought to it by appeals from the lower courts. These appeals must raise some issue relative to the state's constitution or laws. In some states, however, death penalty convictions are referred automatically to the court for review. This court does not have the authority to alter, amend, extend, or change any procedure or law established by a U.S. Supreme Court decision (*Fare v. Michael C.*, 1979).

COURTS OF APPEAL

The courts of appeal comprise a network of appellate districts, located to serve a state's population centers and areas from which a substantial number of appeals are raised. The appointment process to the courts of appeal is similar to that of a state's supreme court, and the qualifications are the same as well. These courts primarily have appellate jurisdiction and hear the majority of cases on appeal from the felony trial courts within their districts. Cases are heard by a panel of justices. The panel's decision (the court's opinion) affects the specific case on appeal and can be used as precedent within that district if the decision is published. However, decisions of the panels do not set statewide precedent and are not binding on any court outside the district in which they are made.

FELONY TRIAL COURTS

Each county within a state has a felony trial court, often called a **circuit court** or **superior court**. It is known as the court of **general jurisdiction** because it has the authority to hear any type of case, including criminal, civil, juvenile, probate, or family matters. Each court may have a number of divisions and judges, depending on the case workload. This could vary from a single judge in some rural county to over 200 or 300 judges in the metropolitan areas.

Newly created judgeships and vacancies on any existing bench are filled in one of three ways: (1) by appointment of the governor, or an appointment followed by a nonpartisian election; (2) a partisan election process, in which candidates are associated with a political party ticket and campaign; and (3) what is known as the Missouri plan, in which a commission reviews the qualifications of selected persons and refers the most qualified three to the governor for the final appointment. This last option tends to minimize the political nature of the judicial selection process.

In this book, we are concerned primarily with the courts' jurisdiction in felony cases. However, these represent the least work done by these courts of general jurisdiction. For example, in California during the 1994–1995 fiscal year, over 1.1 million cases were filed in the various superior courts, but only about 150,000 were criminal matters. This example might also serve to indicate the type of law practiced by most attorneys.

LOWER TRIAL COURTS

In many states, each county is divided into districts according to population, and each district is authorized to have some form of lower trial court having limited jurisdiction. These courts are known as **district courts**, or **municipal courts**, or **courts of common pleas**, and hear both designated civil and criminal matters. They are often referred to as the *people's court* because they serve as small claims courts in which a person can bring a civil suit, without the need for an attorney and without having to wade through a lot of legal paperwork. In some jurisdictions, these lower courts are run by a **justice of the peace**, who often sits as a part-time judge in one district while working as an attorney in other districts.

The municipal or district court has original jurisdiction in all misdemeanor and infraction cases, both criminal and traffic. It also has jurisdiction in small civil suits and/or in small claims actions. The judge of the municipal or district court also sits in the capacity of a judicial officer called a *magistrate*, with the authority to preside over preliminary hearings in felony cases (discussed below under pretrial procedures). Also, in noncapital felony cases, when the defendant pleads guilty or no contest, the municipal court judge in some jurisdictions may preside at the sentencing hearing and may sentence the defendant.

As indicated above, the municipal or district court has **limited jurisdiction** in felony cases. Under the traditional two-tier model, the initial appearance and preliminary matters are conducted in the lower court, then the case is forwarded to superior court for trial. The details of this process are presented below in the section on pretrial procedures. However, this two-tier trial model is gradually being replaced by a more efficient structure in which all courts are consolidated into one general court.

COURT CONSOLIDATION MODEL

The primary reason that counties have a two-tier court structure, with the jurisdiction of the lower court limited to hearing misdemeanors and felony prelims, is because that is the way it started. If one will refer back to the history of the court development under Henry I and Henry II, discussed in Chapter 1, it readily will become evident that very little has changed since that structure was developed in that time. In the past five years or so, the courts have been going through a reorganization at the administrative level to improve efficiency. Also, in many counties, superior and municipal court judges are being cross assigned. That is, judges at each level are being assigned to hear cases in the other level: Lower court judges can hear superior court cases, and vice versa.

This cross-assignment approach has helped in reorganizing the work assignments, but it still leaves the two-tier structure in place, which many think is inefficient. Consequently, states are beginning to move toward an alternative model in which the lower court is abolished and all judicial jurisdiction is vested in a single circuit or superior court, with all judges having identical powers. This distributes the workload more evenly and allows each case to be heard and completed in the same court. Oregon is the latest to join this reform effort, as its consolidation model became effective January 15, 1998, On that date, district courts ceased to exist, leaving only the circuit court. District court judges became circuit court judges. Thus Oregon became one of a dozen states to consolidate its court structure. Other states probably will follow soon.

For example, on June 2, 1998, the voters in California approved a senate constitutional amendment that will allow each county to abolish the municipal courts, leaving only the superior courts to hear all the civil and criminal matters, provided that the judges in each county also approve it. Unfortunately, consolidation will proceed on a county-by-county basis, when a majority of judges on the municipal court and superior court benches in each county vote to implement the plan. At this point in time one cannot say if the consolidation will be approved by the judges in each county. It would immediately benefit the municipal court judges because they would become superior court judges, with a new title and a pay increase. It also would greatly improve the efficiency and workload of the court system.

ROLE OF THE PROSECUTOR

PROSECUTING ATTORNEY

Each county has a prosecutor, known as the **district attorney (DA)**, or **county prosecutor**, who usually is elected by the general public every four years. He or she is the only person with the legal authority to charge someone with a crime. His or her role is not just to prosecute criminal cases but *to ensure that justice is done* for the public he or she serves. Therefore, he or she is obligated not to charge a person unless the evidence is sufficient to warrant a trial. The district attorney has a weighty responsibility and a great deal of power—a great deal of power.

The office of the district attorney is staffed by a number of deputy district attorneys (or deputy county attorneys), depending on the size of the office and the prosecution workload. Each attorney is assigned to a specific duty within the department. For example, one might be assigned to a lower court to represent the state during all initial appearances by accused persons. Another attorney might conduct all preliminary examinations. Another might prosecute offenders in misdemeanor trials or handle all traffic matters, while another more experienced deputy might handle only felony trials. Yet another experienced deputy will be assigned to the **complaint desk**.

The deputy assigned to the complaint desk reads the police reports or reviews them with a liaison officer from the police department, then makes several crucial decisions about each person arrested and against whom the police are requesting a complaint. First, he or she decides *whether to charge* the suspect with a crime. The deputy DA looks to see if the reporting officer has described the elements of a crime if there is sufficient evidence to support a charge and if the conduct of the officer was legal.

Next, the DA decides *what to charge*: felony or misdemeanor, or multiple counts. Each separate crime charged is called a **count**. Many crimes are punishable as either a felony or a misdemeanor, at the discretion of the DA. These are called **wobblers** because they wobble on the fence and fall on one side or the other as a result of the punishment given. In some states, a few crimes, such as petty theft, may be charged as either a misdemeanor or an infraction, at the discretion of the DA. Also, the DA needs to review the prior conviction record of the suspect to determine if that person has any priors that can be charged as **strikes**, a prior violent felony conviction, as defined in Chapter 1, or charged under some habitual offender law.

ENHANCEMENTS

In addition to any crime charged, there might be sufficient aspects of the crime, or in the prior record of the accused, to allow the DA to charge one or more **enhancements**, as defined in Chapter 1. In California, for example, if the crime meets the legal definition of a criminal street gang crime, the DA may charge it as a separate offense and, upon conviction of the crime, an extra term of one, two, or three years will be added as the enhancement. If the accused carried a firearm on his or her person or in a vehicle during the commission of a gang crime, an additional enhancement can add one, two, or three more years to the sentence. If a person personally uses a firearm during the commission of any felony, the sentence can be enhanced by three, four, or 10 years.

FACTORS TO CONSIDER IN CHARGING

In deciding whether to charge and what to charge, the DA considers the following factors: the sufficiency of the evidence, the legality of the police officer's behavior, the seriousness of the crime, the wishes of the victim, the risk posed to the public safety, the sentiments in the community regarding the offense, the potential punishment upon conviction and whether punishment is mandatory, the person's role in the crime, the offender's prior record, the willingness of the accused to cooperate with the investigation or prosecution, the motives of the complainant, and the impact of the trial on the victim, particularly if the victim is young. This is not an exhaustive list.

In some instances the DA will charge as many separate counts as he or she can find described in the police report, knowing full well that he or she does not have sufficient evidence to win a conviction, or that if convicted, the defendant could not be sentenced on all the charges. That way, he or she can drop some of the weaker counts as a part of a plea bargain and still end up with convictions on those charges that actually would have held up in court.

In some cases, the DA can find several code violations to describe the same act. For example, if a person is arrested for possession of a loaded and concealed handgun in a town, the DA can charge two crimes: possession of a concealed firearm and possession of a loaded firearm within the city limits. However, since they both arise out of the same act, only one can receive punishment, regardless of whether both receive convictions.

A recent case in April 1997, in Port Washington, Wisconsin, demonstrates how the DA's disregard of community sentiments about a situation and/or his prosecution by the letter of the law rather than the spirit of the law can rile and unify the community in opposition to him. Reportedly, an 18-year-old boy and his 15-year-old girlfriend from the community had a consensual sexual relationship and she became pregnant. They intended to marry and raise their child. The DA prosecuted him for the Wisconsin crime "sexual assault on a child," punishable by up to 40 years in prison. The jury did not want to convict him but were led to believe that they had to if they followed the law, so they did. There was a strong public outcry against the prosecution and a plea for leniency in sentencing. On June 24, 1997, the boyfriend was granted two-years probation and ordered to register as a sex offender. Now the defense will seek a pardon.

A similar situation recently faced the DA in Sonoma County, California. In Petaluma, the town still reeling over the abduction and murder of Polly Klass, a 24-year-old man and his fiancée were in an upstairs room of their house at about 8:00 P.M. on May 7, 1997, when they heard the sound of glass shattering downstairs. The man grabbed a baseball bat and went downstairs, where he found a burglar climbing in the broken kitchen window. He struck the man on the head with the bat, and as the man tried to escape, he chased and struck him at least three more times. In the meantime, the fiancée called the police. When officers arrived, they found the bat-wielding young man standing guard, as it were, over the limp body of the alleged burglar. The burglar was taken to the hospital, where he was treated for a fractured skull and bleeding in his brain. He was unconscious for almost 40 hours. He recovered and was prosecuted on burglary charges, his third strike.

The police arrested the man who hit the burglar on a charge of assault with a deadly weapon because he had become the aggressor when he chased the man trying to escape. The police investigation showed that the burglar had a long criminal record, including burglaries, and he had been paroled from the state prison in Vacaville, California only four hours before his break-in and beating. He also had a blood-alcohol level of 0.21.

The young man claimed that he was defending his home and used force to detain the burglar for police. The people in the community called the man a hero and were outraged at his arrest and possible prosecution. The DA finally decided not to charge the man. He indicated that the arrest by police was based on probable cause, making it the proper action to take, but that he needed proof beyond a reasonable doubt to convict, and that it was lacking in this case.

ALTERNATIVES TO PROSECUTION

The prosecuting attorney has the discretion to file criminal charges or not to file. Depending on the many factors cited above, he or she may simply choose not to file. If the matter is a minor one and actually seems to be more of a civil dispute between two people than a public crime, he or she can call both parties into the office and attempt to resolve the situation without court action. In some cases that are minor but criminal in nature, the DA might reach an agreement with the defense called **filing a case**, in which criminal proceedings are suspended and the case is continued for some period of time, a year for example. If the defendant does not reoffend, charges can be dismissed.

In some cases the DA cannot find a sufficient description of a crime and/or sufficient evidence that will lead to a conviction described in the police report. Consequently, he or she will refer the case back to the originating police agency for further investigation or a more complete report. One can see how crucial the police report is in the charging process. In fact, it is probably the most important document in the arrest–prosecution process. The ability to write comprehensive and literate reports is the most important skill that a peace officer can have in being effective at his or her job. An officer might go an entire career without ever firing his or her weapon, except on the range, but he or she will never go a day without having to write an effective report.

DIVERSION

It is expensive to process a defendant all the way through the system, especially if he or she wants a jury trial. Also, as the result of a criminal conviction, the defendant often ends up with this conviction on his or her record. To avoid spending the time, effort, and money to prosecute a case to its fullest and to avoid a conviction record for certain types of offenders who deserve a second chance, the legislatures in many states have created a variety of diversion laws. **Diversion** is defined as the *temporary suspension of criminal proceedings and the referral of the defendant to some type of education, training, or treatment program.*

The most common diversion program is traffic school, in which a person cited for a minor traffic offense attends several classes to learn about safe and defensive driving. Often, this educational type of program is conducted by either private vendors or local colleges, and the traffic violator pays a fee for the privilege of not going through the formal traffic (criminal) process. After completing the traffic school, the charge is dismissed and the person's record remains clear, providing the additional benefit of not having increased car insurance rates. Other types of programs include diversion for drug possession, misdemeanor theft, prostitution, bad-check charges, contributing to a minor's delinquency by a parent, or programs for the mentally challenged or other special category offenders.

The purpose of these diversion programs is to settle as many cases as possible without having to go to the expense of a trial if they are the types of cases that would result in lenient treatment and/or probation anyway. The state saves time and money and the defendant saves having a criminal conviction. Today's courts are so crowded with cases that almost any creative way to expedite a case out of the system will be considered if justice can still be served.

DEFERRED JUDGMENT

Deferred judgment is a procedure similar to diversion; however, it occurs after conviction and includes cases more serious than a petty offense but ones in which the public is not at risk having an offender remain within the community under certain conditions. In states where this procedure is used, the district attorney has the discretion to enter into an agreement with the defense, in which the defendant admits to all the charges in return for having the judgment (sentence) delayed and, instead, is referred to an approved counseling program.

Upon successful completion, the guilty plea is withdrawn and the charges are dismissed. The defendant would have to demonstrate a strong potential to change his or her behavior to persuade most DAs to consider this option, and long-term counseling usually would be made a condition of deferring judgment. If the crime is intrafamilial, such as child abuse or molestation or domestic battery, both the defendant and victim may receive treatment of some type in an effort to reunify the family.

ACCUSATORY PLEADINGS

COMPLAINT PROCESS

An **accusatory pleading** is the generic name of any legal document used to charge a person with a crime. Three basic types of pleadings are used, depending on the state and where the case is in the court process: the complaint, the information, and the indictment. Some states use the document called a **complaint**, in which a DA names the person being charged, and describes the crime charged along with any enhancements and the date the alleged crime was committed. Both felony and misdemeanor complaints are filed in the lower court within 48 hours after the person is booked into jail. If the defendant is still in jail, he or she is brought into the lower court for the initial court appearance. If the defendant is out on bail, or was cited and released either by law enforcement at the crime scene or by the jail cite-and-release staff, he or she will appear in court on the date stated in the citation.

Some states do not follow the complaint process. Rather, the initial charging document is the **indictment**, which is filed with the grand jury, a body of peers who will determine if sufficient evidence exists to have a trial.

ARRAIGNMENT

The initial appearance of the defendant before the court is called **arraignment**. To *arraign* is a verb that can be conjugated like any other verb. Consequently, one can say that he will be arraigned, or has been arraigned, and the process of actually doing it is called *arraignment*. Typically, one judge hears what is called the **arraignment calendar**, which includes all the cases of defendants who will be arraigned that day. The judge calls each case in turn and arraigns the person called. *To arraign* means to call a defendant before the court and provide him or her with a copy of the complaint, advise him or her of the charges and maximum possible penalty allowed by law, and advise him or her of the right to be represented by an attorney at every stage of the proceedings. The defendant is also advised of his or her right to have an attorney appointed free, or at a nominal cost if the defendant is **indigent** and cannot afford an attorney.

In misdemeanor cases, the defendant need not personally appear but can have an attorney appear instead. However, in that case, the court will require the defendant to sign and file with the court a form titled "Waiver of Defendant's Personal Presence."

TYPES OF DEFENSE REPRESENTATION

The arraignment is the point in the legal process where the Sixth Amendment right to an attorney attaches to the accused. That is, this is the point at which he or she may have an attorney to represent him or her. There are basically four types of **defense attorneys**: private counsel, public defender, conflict attorney, and the contract counsel system.

A **private counsel** is an attorney chosen and paid for by the defendant who can afford one. However, the vast majority of defendants cannot afford an attorney. After arraignment, when the judge asks the defendant if he or she wants an attorney, most defendants say "yes." When the judge asks if he or she can afford one, the answer usually is "no." Therefore, the judge will appoint a public defender to represent the defendant.

A **public defender** is a county-paid attorney who only represents defendants who cannot afford their own attorney. He or she is no better and no worse than a private attorney, although some public defenders have accumulated a negative reputation over the years. Frequently, the public defender can represent the defendant more effectively because he or she works within the system and knows all the players and the processes, both formal and informal.

The main disadvantage of having a public defender is that he or she has very limited time to spend with the client: seemingly, just a few minutes before court. Nevertheless, an experienced public defender has handled almost every type of case and has heard almost every explanation given by a suspect. Also, he or she knows what the **going rate** is for the crime charged and knows best how to work with the judge and opposing DA.

Selecting an attorney is an individual matter. There are excellent and incompetent attorneys in both private and public defense systems, just as there are good and poor levels of competence in any occupation. As a general rule, the public defender system is used in the following states: California, Colorado, Florida, Illinois, Louisiana, Minnesota, Missouri, Nevada, New Jersey, New York, Pennsylvania, Utah, Wisconsin, and Wyoming.

If two or more defendants are being prosecuted for the same crimes, they cannot have the same attorney, or even an attorney from the same office. There will always be a conflict of interest between codefendants. Their roles and motives in the crime are different, and their backgrounds are different. Even husband and wife codefendants have differing interests in the outcome of their case. Consequently, if the codefendants are indigent, the judge will appoint the public defender to represent one and a **conflict attorney** to represent the other. A conflict attorney is an attorney in private practice who is willing to be appointed to represent indigents at the prevailing county pay rate.

In some sections of the country, we find the use of what is called the **contract counsel system**. This is a system used primarily in rural counties in which having a full-time public defender's office might be too expensive. In this system, all appointed defense attorneys are private attorneys who work at the prevailing hourly rate when appointed, and there is no public defender's office. The indigents still receive free attorneys and the counties save money by not having to pay employee benefits, retirement, and vacation time. This system is used primarily in Arizona, Idaho, Kentucky, New Mexico, Oregon, and Washington.

A defense attorney does not defend what his or her client did, or is accused of doing. In fact, the criminal charge against the accused is irrelevant to the responsibility of the defense attorney. *He or she defends the constitutional rights* of an accused person because every person has these rights. That was the purpose of writing the Constitution in the first place, to protect citizens against government actions that might illegally deprive them of their freedom. We all have these rights, and the first thing anyone (even a police officer) will do when charged with a crime is to obtain an attorney to protect those rights. In protecting the accused, it is the responsibility of the defense attorney to be certain that all the actions of the police, the court, and correctional personnel are legal. That is why they challenge the conduct of the police officer in every arrest and search, to test the legality of official conduct. We have had sufficient examples of misconduct to appreciate the need for this system of checks and balances.

SELF-REPRESENTATION

The defendant may waive his or her right to counsel and represent himself or herself, which is called standing in ***propria persona*** (in one's own proper person), which is usually shortened to ***pro per***. Originally, in a 1942 case, *Adams v. United States*, the U. S. Supreme Court held that if a defendant wanted to waive his or her right to counsel, the judge had to be satisfied that the defendant was capable of self-representation before a waiver could be accepted. However, in *Faretta v. California* (1975), the U.S. Supreme Court ruled that when a defendant "knowingly and intelligently" waives his or her right to an attorney, he or she has a constitutional right to **self-representation**. The judge, however, may appoint a standby counsel to assist the defendant, to act as cocounsel, or to take over if self-representation is terminated (*McKaskle v. Wiggins*, 1984). When a person is considering self-representation, he or she should heed the advice of Clarence Darrow, one of this country's great lawyers: "Anyone, even a lawyer, who defends himself has a fool for a client."

DEFENDANT'S RESPONSE TO THE CHARGES

After arraignment, the defendant needs to respond to the charges. The defendant must enter a plea, or refuse to plea and stand mute. In the latter event, the judge will enter a not guilty plea and the matter will proceed.

Defendants may plead **guilty**, acknowledging full responsibility for the acts and outcomes of what occurred, or may plead **not guilty**, denying responsibility for the acts. Another plea, common in misdemeanor cases, is known by the Latin phrase ***nolo contendre***.

This translates into a plea of **no contest**, in which the defendant neither admits nor denies responsibility, but will not contest the charge and is willing to be sentenced as if he or she is guilty. This plea is used in cases in which a possible civil suit for money damages might arise. It separates the criminal from the civil matter, in that the judge may proceed to sentence the defendant, but any civil damages must be proven in a separate court on their own merits.

If a defendant claims insanity, he or she enters what is called a **dual plea**. In effect, the defendant enters a plea of not guilty, *and* not guilty by reason of insanity. When one considers what is meant by these two pleas, it is like saying "I didn't do it, but if I did, I'm not responsible." In this event, there will be two trials, the first to determine if the defendant is guilty or not. If the verdict is not guilty, the charges are dismissed and no one cares about the issue of insanity. If the verdict is guilty, there will be a second trial, usually before the same jury, in which the defendant has the burden of proving that he or she was insane at the moment the act was committed.

Other pleas that are available but rarely used are **once in jeopardy** and **former judgment of conviction or acquittal** of the offense charged. In making the latter plea, the defendant is claiming to have already been tried and acquitted of the same charges or charges arising out of the same act.

If the case is for a misdemeanor, every effort is made to settle it quickly. Even though we operate by the legal principle of *innocent until proven guilty*, one gets the feeling sitting in court that the judge and both attorneys sometimes work on the assumption that the defendant is guilty of something and will plead guilty if an attractive bargain can be found. It is rare to have a misdemeanor go to trial. They are usually continued for some further proceeding, or are diverted or bargained down and settled quickly so that the prosecutor's resources can be devoted to the more serious felony cases. In these misdemeanor cases, the defendant might or might not have an attorney. However, a judge will not accept a plea of guilty unless he or she is satisfied that the defendant knows all his or her rights, voluntarily waives them, and acknowledges that there is a factual basis for the plea.

An attorney usually is appointed or retained in a felony case because the consequences of a conviction might be serious. Typically, an attorney is appointed immediately after arraignment, and he or she assumes command of the case. He or she will stipulate to (agree to) proper arraignment, **waive time** for a speedy trial, and ask that the matter be set for the next stage, the preliminary hearing.

When people are arrested by police and booked into jail, the first thing they want to do is to get out. Some post **bail** and others use the bail bond system. Also, many jurisdictions operate some form of a cite-and-release program on a 24-hour basis, as described in Chapter 5, to reduce the jail population as much as possible. Consequently, many people come to their arraignment from their homes. However, there are a substantial number of defendants who cannot make bail and who do not qualify for cite-and-release. Immediately after arraignment and the appointment of counsel in these cases, the attorney will make a motion to have his or her client released on what is termed **own recognizance** (OR), or at least to have him or her released on a lower bail. Usually, the judge knows nothing about the defendant at this point and wants additional information about him or her in order to rule appropriately on the motion.

The proceedings will be continued for a day or two, and the matter will be referred to the county probation officer, who serves as the investigative arm of the court, for an **OR investigation** and report. A deputy probation officer, working in the investigation unit, will investigate the defendant's background and make a recommendation to the court as to how to rule on the defense's motion, based on the defendant's ties in the area, potential for harm to the victim or others, and the likelihood that he or she will return to court when required. Based on the probation officer's recommendation, the judge may grant the motion for OR release, deny the motion, but lower the bail, raise the bail, or order that the defendant be denied bail. The latter decision is derived from what is termed a **preventive detention law** in many states, by which the judge may deny bail if he or she has a reasonable belief that the defendant poses a threat to the community or will flee the jurisdiction of the court.

In recent years, the county jail populations in most states have increased to the point where there just is not bed space left. Many counties simply cannot afford to build a new jail, given today's high construction costs. The populations inside the jails, which once represented the full range of offenders, from the hard core to the lightweight, are now primarily the serious and violent offenders. Minor offenders are either cited by the police or by the jail's cite-and-release staff. In fact, in many cases some of the less violent serious offenders must be cited out to make room for the more violent. Consequently, there is a category of defendants, whose number is increasing, that cannot be fully trusted in the community but whose behavior is not serious or threatening enough to warrant complete detention.

In response to this, many jurisdictions have established a creative method of releasing these defendants from jail, pending trial, called **supervised OR**. These are offenders who are released without having to post bond, but they must agree to abide by certain conditions and supervision by the enforcement arm of the court, the probation officer, until their case has been settled. Conditions might include anti-narcotic/drug testing, nonassociation with certain other people, a restriction from certain locations, curfew, a requirement to submit to search at any time, and any other condition that the judge or probation officer thinks is appropriate. A violation of any condition could result in the judge revoking the supervised OR status and ordering jail confinement.

This supervised OR will continue until the case is settled by trial or other means, which often will take months or up to a year or more. It is far cheaper to have one probation officer supervise 75 to 100 OR'ed defendants than it is to keep them housed in a jail. Whether the community is as safe is another question. It is a program that usually is money driven. The officer supervising the OR'ed defendant often has a great deal of discretion in overlooking or holding the defendant accountable for violations of the court-imposed conditions. For example, one officer might overlook a dirty test now and again, while another officer might rearrest after the first dirty test. Or one officer might conduct searches of the offender and of his or her residence or automobile on a regular basis, whereas another officer might not have the time or make the effort to search at all. There are no standards for supervision compliance, and officer discretion is the rule.

THE PRELIMINARY HEARING

In those states that use the complaint process rather than the grand jury, the law requires that a felony complaint be set for a **preliminary hearing** within two to 10 days after the initial arraignment. It is often referred to as a **prelim**, or in its abbreviated form, as a **PX**. It is held in municipal court before a judge who serves in the capacity of (or uses the title of) *magistrate* during this proceeding. The use of this term is archaic now, and will probably fade away through disuse. The prelim is a **probable cause** hearing in which the DA must present just enough evidence to the judge to convince him or her that the evidence shows that (1) a crime occurred and (2) that the accused probably did it.

Until recently, the victim of the crime usually had to testify in person in order to establish the elements of probable cause. Now, however, in many states the testimony by a peace officer who has several years of experience and who is directly involved in the investigation of the case may testify in place of the victim and state what the victim said to him or her. This is called **first-person hearsay testimony**, because it is only once removed from the victim's own story. This has provided tremendous relief to young or otherwise vulnerable victims because they do not have to testify in court at this point. However, if the case goes to trial, the victim will have to testify because the Sixth Amendment guarantees that a defendant has the right to face his or her accuser. As we shall see, however, very few cases ever actually go to trial. In addition, if the victim does testify at the prelim and is under the age of 16 years, the judge may close the hearing to the press and public to protect the minor's reputation.

In establishing probable cause, the DA will present whatever physical and/or testimonial evidence is necessary but not all the evidence that is available. The defense attorney may cross-examine any of the state's witnesses and present witnesses on behalf of the defendant. Also, the defendant may waive the right to have a preliminary hearing and have the matter immediately certified to superior court for trial. This is seldom done, however, because the defense gains an opportunity to size up the DA's case and evaluate the witnesses and other evidence at the prelim. The prelim is the heart of any felony case, and this is where the defense will attack the conduct of the police in order to have the evidence suppressed.

The officer will be examined by the defense attorney at length as to the validity of any search warrant, the search and seizure of any evidence, the detention and/or arrest, and any interrogation in which the defendant might have given incriminating statements. As soon as the defense finds a piece of evidence that he or she thinks was obtained illegally, he or she will make a **motion to suppress** the evidence. Sometimes the judge can rule on the motion immediately, but at other times will want the opposing attorneys to write and submit **briefs** (their argued positions on the motion, supported by any precedent-setting cases). If it appears that it will take time to decide on the motion, the judge can schedule the matter for a **suppression hearing**, which is a separate hearing just on the issue of the legality of the evidence. Once the judge rules on the defense's motion to suppress, the prelim is resumed. If the evidence is suppressed, the DA might not be able to establish probable cause, and the case will be dismissed. If the evidence is admitted, the prelim will continue until both attorneys have presented their evidence, and the judge rules as to whether there is probable cause.

If the judge finds that there is not sufficient evidence to establish probable cause, the case is dismissed. This is not the end of the case, necessarily, because if the DA obtains additional evidence, he or she may initiate the process again by filing a new complaint. This is not double jeopardy, because jeopardy attaches (begins) when the trial starts. If the judge does find probable cause, he or she holds the defendant to answer. The phrase **held to answer** means that the defendant's case will be certified to superior court and the person will be **bound over** for trial.

THE INFORMATION

As stated earlier in this chapter, *accusatory pleading* was defined as the generic term for a legal document used to charge a person with a crime or crimes. The most common example of it is the complaint filed in municipal court that initiates the prosecution process. Once a felony case reaches superior court, however, a new charging document is used called the **information**. It looks like a complaint but has a different title, and it lists the crimes that the defendant was held to answer for at the preliminary hearing. These counts might be more or less or different than the original counts in the complaint because the judge at the prelim might dismiss one or more counts or make other changes in the charges.

The information must be filed in superior court within 15 days of the preliminary hearing. When a defendant is held to answer at a prelim, he or she will be advised of the date to appear in superior court. If he or she is still in jail, the detention staff will have a record of the court date and will bring him or her to the court. When the defendant appears in superior court for the first time, he or she is given a copy of the information and is arraigned on the new charging document. This means that the person is advised of the charges again, and of his or her rights at trial. After this arraignment, the defendant may enter a plea or may have the matter continued for further proceedings. At some point, however, he or she will have to enter a plea. Typically, at this point, the defendant is represented by an attorney, who will waive time for a speedy trial, enter a plea of not guilty, and make a motion for (ask for) a **continuance**. That is, the attorney will request that the case be continued until a later date.

The word *continuance* is the most frequently uttered word in the court process. Many cases will be continued and continued for months or a year or two. Usually, it is the defense who requests a continuance. It is to the defendant's advantage. Witnesses might forget what they saw, or move, or die. Any passions that might be aroused within the community over the crime will have had time to cool and the attorney will have sufficient time to investigate the case and prepare a defense. Eventually, the case will be set for trial, but it probably will be settled without a trial.

THE GRAND JURY PROCESS

By law in most states, every county must have a **grand jury**. The number of grand jurors that a county must have also is determined by law, and can vary from nine in very small rural counties to as high as 23 jurors in counties having a large population. Some counties also may have a second grand jury, at the discretion of the presiding superior court judge.

To be eligible to serve on a grand jury, a person usually must be a citizen, over the age of 18 years, a resident of the county for at least one year, possess a command of the English language, and be of sound mind, of ordinary intelligence, and of an honest and fair character.

Grand jurors usually serve for a year. They are not paid any compensation for their time but are reimbursed for any direct expenses related to their work. In most states the grand jury has two functions. First, it is a watchdog over county government and one of its roles is to investigate the actions of government agencies and officials to ensure honesty in local government. In this capacity the grand jury serves in an investigatory and advisory capacity and reports its findings, along with any recommendations, annually to the presiding judge and/or county board of supervisors for review and action, if warranted.

The second function of a grand jury is to serve as a panel to hear evidence in criminal matters at the direction of the district attorney. In some states, notably the eastern states, the law requires the prosecutor to use the grand jury process in every felony criminal matter. In these situations, they would bypass the complaint process and the case would go directly to court for trial. This can be a costly and time-consuming requirement to fulfill.

In those states in which the use of the grand jury is not mandatory, the prosecutor has the discretion to use it. That is, if the DA does not want to prosecute a felony case by the traditional complaint–municipal court arraignment–preliminary hearing route, he or she may convene the grand jury for a secret probable cause hearing. The only persons allowed to be present are the prosecutor, the members of the grand jury, and those witnesses that the DA wants to present. The defendant and his or her attorney are not present, and might not even know that a criminal investigation is under way. If the DA convinces the grand jury that probable cause does exist to show that a crime occurred and that the suspected felon probably did it, the grand jury foreperson signs an accusatory pleading called an **indictment**.

The indictment is filed in superior court by the prosecutor and lists the charges and the name of the accused person. If the person is not yet in custody, a warrant will be issued for his or her arrest.

When arrested, or summoned by the DA to appear in superior court, the defendant is arraigned on the indictment, enters a plea, and the matter is set for trial or other proceedings. There is no prelim and no chance for the defense to view the prosecution's case, except through a motion for discovery.

The grand jury is a secret process, conducted at the direction of the district attorney. Even though the Fifth Amendment to the Constitution guarantees that no person will be tried for an infamous crime without having the case screened first by a grand jury, an accused person has no control over how the prosecution will be initiated: by the traditional procedure or by the grand jury in those states where use of the grand jury is not mandatory.

Actually, no defendant would ever want the grand jury process because it works entirely to the advantage of the prosecution. However, at the federal level, all felony crimes are charged through the indictment process. The defendant has no choice. There are about 1100 federal grand juries, of 23 members. They meet twice a week unless cases require meeting more often, and they meet in secret and are sworn to secrecy about their proceedings. As Nancy Panzke said when she was called to testify regarding her boss, former Rep. Dan Rostenkowski, "You're trapped like a rat. . . . I kept having nightmares about it" (*Chicago Tribune*, February 19, 1998).

PREPLEA REFERRAL

At the request of the defense in some states, in either a felony or misdemeanor case, the judge may refer the matter to the probation department, for what is called a **preplea investigation and report**. It is a tentative and "iffy" procedure. Read the following definition carefully: The *preplea referral* is a temporary suspension of criminal proceedings and the referral to the probation department for an investigation into the background of the defendant to determine *if* he or she *might* make a good candidate for probation *if* convicted.

The probation officer assigned to the investigation reads over the police report, talks to the victim and any witnesses to determine what happened in the offense, then researches the defendant's background, including any prior record, to determine what type of character and potential the defendant has. He or she will interview the defendant in this process, but because it is preplea, and the defendant retains his or her Fifth Amendment protection against self-incrimination, the probation officer may not ask the defendant what or why he or she did what is alleged in the complaint. They may not discuss the offense. Based primarily on this character study, the probation officer recommends to the judge that if the defendant is convicted, the probation department will probably recommend that he or she be granted probation, sentenced to jail, sentenced to prison, fined, or receive any other appropriate sentence. In this manner the defendant has a reasonably good idea what the likely sentence will be. If he or she is willing to accept the recommended sentence, he or she will then enter a plea of guilty. The case will then be re-referred to the probation department to complete the investigation and report, which includes a full discussion of the defendant's role in the crime. Thereafter, the probation officer makes a final recommendation to the judge as to the appropriate sentence.

This procedure works to the definite advantage of the defendant, because he or she can learn what the probable sentence will be before having to plea to the charge. If the final recommendation, or the judge's decision, is different from the initial tentative one, and the defendant does not like it, he or she may withdraw his or her guilty plea and enter the new and different plea of not guilty and ask that the matter proceed to trial. The state does gain a little time and money by this procedure if the defendant likes and accepts the final sentence without having a trial. Otherwise, the defendant is the benefactor. And it consumes a great deal of probation resources.

PLEA BARGAINING

The vast majority of criminal cases, from 90 to 96 percent, are settled without ever going to trial, by the process known as **plea bargaining**. It is a negotiation process between the prosecution and defense (and sometimes, but not always, the judge) to settle the case without a trial, and to the best advantage of both sides, by a plea to some charge in return for some consideration. The types of possible bargains include, but are not limited to, the following:

1. A plea to one count or more of a multiple-count complaint, with the other counts dismissed
2. A plea to a lesser but included offense (e.g., from grand theft to petty theft, from murder first to murder second or manslaughter, from driving under the influence of alcohol to a wet or dry reckless driving charge, from burglary first to burglary second, etc.)
3. A plea to a charge, with the enhancement(s) dismissed
4. A plea to a misdemeanor, reduced from a felony charge
5. A plea to some charge in return for a guaranteed sentence (sentence bargaining), or immunity from prosecution in certain charges in return for testifying against someone else

In whatever form the bargaining takes, the state (the DA) obtains a conviction to something and the defendant usually receives less of a penalty than he or she otherwise would if convicted of all the original counts. The defendant must give up most of his or her Fifth and Sixth Amendment rights in the plea bargaining process, because in pleading guilty or no contest, he or she agrees to waive the right to a trial and all its attending requirements and to the protection against self-incrimination. In fact, before the guilty plea is accepted in court, the parties will go through a litany in which the judge or DA advises the defendant of each and every right the he or she is giving up and the defendant acknowledges that he or she understands these rights and freely and voluntarily waives them. Thereafter, the matter is set for a sentencing hearing.

PRETRIAL MOTIONS

There are a number of **motions** (legal requests) that are made before the trial actually begins or before the case reaches a settlement. The most common ones have already been discussed: the motion for a continuance and to suppress the evidence. Another important motion is the **motion for discovery**. This is a request by one attorney to have copies or access to all the evidence in the possession of the opposing attorney.

Some states limit the use of discovery to the defense and do not allow it for the prosecutor. The reasoning is that it is a necessary element of preparing a defense, because one cannot possibly prepare a defense unless one knows what to defend against. In those states where victim advocate groups have had influence over legislation, the prosecution now has the right to discover what evidence the defense might use as long as it does not include any evidence that might tend to incriminate the defendant.

A **motion to determine the present sanity** of the defendant is made when the defense believes that his or her client is insane now and does not know what is happening to him or her and cannot participate in his or her own defense. It would not be fair to try a defendant in this condition. Psychiatric testimony is used to determine the present sanity, and it has no bearing on the mental state of the defendant at the time of the actual crime. If the defendant is found to be sane, the legal process continues. If found insane, the defendant is sent to a hospital until he or she is sane enough to return for trial.

If a defendant has several legal matters pending in different courts, the defense can make a **motion to consolidate** them all into one court proceeding. This saves time and money for everyone. If the defendant is charged with multiple counts but wants a separate trial for each count, the defense can make a **motion to sever the** counts. This might be granted if the counts are unrelated as to type or as to the time in which they occurred. Similarly, if two or more defendants are to be tried for the same crime, their defense attorneys may make a **motion to sever the defendants**. Each will have a separate trial. That way only a limited amount of evidence, that is relevant to each specific defendant, will be presented at trial.

If the defense wants to challenge the scientific basis for identifying the evidence, he or she can make what is called a **Kelly–Frye motion**. This is done when the defense claims that the scientific foundation of identifying some piece of physical evidence is faulty. None of the foregoing motions are granted automatically.

In cases that involve a charge of assault or battery against a peace officer, or resisting arrest, the defense may make what is termed a **Pitchess motion**, which is a request to have access to the personnel file of the arresting officer. This is done when the defense wants to show that the officer's conduct was overly aggressive and/or brutal and wants to substantiate this by showing that the officer has had a series of complaints of brutality against him or her. The judge will review the personnel file and determine the merits of any information it contains, then will allow the defense to have access only to the information relevant to the motion.

An important motion for the defense in cases that receive extensive pretrial publicity or incur the wrath of the community is a **motion for a change of venue**. This is a motion to change the location of the trial to some other venue (county). If the judge agrees that the defendant cannot receive a fair trial in the original venue, he or she will grant the motion, will choose the new venue, and the entire trial proceedings will be relocated to the new venue.

Another defense motion that is derived from the evidence code in some states is called a **motion to quash inflammatory evidence**. This is a request to disallow the admission of certain inflammatory evidence, such as vivid photographs, that the defense thinks might unreasonably stir the emotions of a jury and result in an unfair trial. The judge will exclude these only if he or she is convinced that the jury would be biased against the defendant by viewing the questioned evidence. After all, regardless of how inflammatory they are, the photographs are a picture of what happened, not out-of-context creations of the DA.

There are a number of other legal motions that a defense attorney may make, but it is beyond the scope of this introductory text to include them all. However, the prosecution does have the opportunity to make one important motion called a **motion to compel exemplars**. This is a request to require the defendant to provide any and all nontestimonial samples of himself or herself, such as samples of voice, hair, semen, prints, blood, or photographs. Obviously, if these exemplars match something found at the scene of a crime and incriminate the defendant, it will make conviction much easier. As long as it does not include statements made by the defendant, the taking of exemplars does not violate the defendant's Fifth Amendment protection against self-incrimination.

TRADITIONAL VERSUS VERTICAL PROSECUTION

Traditional prosecution, as the term is used here, means the assignment of prosecutors throughout the courts based on a function to fulfill. That is, one deputy DA is assigned to a complaint desk, another DA is assigned to handle the arraignment calendar, another DA handles the prelims, and so on. This is the common method that the DA has of allocating resources, and these assignments might be for one to three years. This is the practice followed in most counties. The justification for this is, in part, the need to develop the expertise of a new attorney by having him or her begin with the least complex of cases and procedures and move to the more complex as one gains competence at each level.

Vertical prosecution is a relatively new method in which one deputy DA handles all the cases of a certain type from the point of filing the complaints or grand jury indictments all the way through to trial and sentencing. Jurisdictions are beginning to use this method in sensitive cases such as child molestation or sexual assault. This also allows the victim to deal with only one prosecutor, with whom he or she can develop a rapport, and allows the prosecutor to develop an expertise in certain cases. County prosecutors are using this approach in other types of cases, such as career criminal prosecution, repeat sexual offender prosecution, street gang prosecution, and auto theft.

SUMMARY

The chapter began with a brief description of the federal court structure, followed by an overview of how most states structure their courts along the four-tier model. In many counties the two-tier structure is the traditional method of processing cases, but it is all but disappearing because the courts are being reorganized along more efficient lines by consolidating the jurisdictions of the courts into one court of general jurisdiction.

The responsibilities of the prosecuting attorney in each county were detailed. He or she is the one with the authority, power, and responsibility to represent the people of the community against any accused person and to see that justice is served within the community. The prosecution of a defendant using the traditional complaint–arraignment–prelim process was presented in detail and was contrasted with that of using the grand jury.

Alternatives to formal prosecution that were presented included various diversion programs and the deferred judgment law, as was the manner of settling most criminal matters without a trial by plea bargaining. Along with presenting the role of the prosecutor, the responsibilities of the defense and the types of defense representations were detailed, as was self-representation. This also included a discussion of the various defense motions, and a few by the prosecution, the procedures to reduce bail or have the defendant released on OR or supervised OR, and the pleas that a defendant may enter. We are now ready for trial.

KEY TERMS AND CONCEPTS

Accusatory pleading
Appellate jurisdiction
Arraignment
Arraignment calendar
Bail
Change of venue
Circuit court
Complaint
Complaint desk
Conflict attorney
Contract counsel system
Count
County prosecutor
Court consolidation model
Courts of appeal
Defense attorney
Deferred judgment
Discovery
District attorney
District court
Diversion
Dual plea
Enhancement
Filing a case
First-person hearsay testimony
General jurisdiction
Going rate
Grand jury
Held to answer

Indictment
Indigent
Information
Justice of the Peace
Kelly-Frye Motion
Limited jurisdiction
Lower trial courts
Motion to suppress
Municipal court
Nolo contendre
Own recognizance
Pitchess Motion
Plea bargaining
Preliminary hearing
Preplea investigation and report
Pretrial motions
Preventive detention law
Private counsel
Probable cause
Propria persona
Public defender
Self-representation
State supreme court
Superior court
Supervised OR
Suppression hearing
Vertical prosecution
Wobbler

REFERENCES

DEL CARMEN, ROLANDO V. *Criminal Procedures: Law and Practice*, 3rd ed. Belmont, CA: Wadsworth, 1995.

HOLTEN, N. GARY, and LAWSON L. LAMAR. *The Criminal Courts: Structures, Personnel, and Processes.* New York: McGraw-Hill, 1991.

SCHEB, JOHN M., and JOHN M. SCHEB II. *Criminal Law and Procedures*, 2nd ed. St. Paul, MN: West Publishing, 1994.

CASES

Adams v. United States, 317 U.S. 269 (1942)

Fare v. Michael C., 442 U.S. 707 (1979)

Faretta v. California, 422 U.S. 806 (1975)

McKaskle v. Wiggins, 79 L.Ed. 2d 122 (1984)

THE TRIAL

In all criminal prosecutions, the accused shall enjoy the right to a speedy and public trial, by an impartial jury of the State and district wherein the crime shall have been committed, which district shall have been previously ascertained by law; and . . . to be confronted with the witnesses against him; to have compulsory process for obtaining witnesses in his favor, and to have the assistance of counsel for his defense. . . .

Sixth Amendment

INTRODUCTION

A public myth has been created over the years by the media and entertainment industry about the nature of criminal proceedings and the extent to which cases are resolved by trial. As indicated in Chapter 6, relatively few cases ever go to trial. They are settled by a plea bargain. Nevertheless, many of the serious cases do go to trial: cases in which the defense has too much to lose from a conviction and the prosecution has too much to lose by bargaining. The adversary system is still alive and well, particularly in serious cases. It is here that the two sides clash in battle, each using all the legal skills they possess, and from their contest the legal truth shall emerge.

In this chapter we present the trial procedures, most of which are derived from the portion of the Sixth Amendment quoted above. We begin with a discussion of what constitutes a *speedy and public trial*, then examine the state's burden of proof in a criminal case, followed by a comparison of the relative advantages of a court trial and a jury trial. Next, the selection of jurors, by both the traditional method and a scientific selection process, is presented, as are the selection and preparation of witnesses. We also examine the issues surrounding the number of jurors used in a trial. People who have lived all their lives in a state where a jury is composed of 12 members tend to think that the same requirement applies elsewhere. It does not.

Once the jury is sworn and seated, jeopardy attaches to the defendant, and the actual trial begins. The presentation by the DA is first, followed by the defense and the various strategies used to counter the degree of guilt created in the minds of the jury by the DA. We conclude the chapter in the same manner in which a trial ends, by a discussion of the verdict, including the issues of a unanimous versus a nonunanimous verdict.

A SPEEDY AND PUBLIC TRIAL

A defendant who has entered a plea of not guilty to a misdemeanor charge has the right to have a trial within 30 days if he or she is confined in jail pending trial and 45 days if not confined. In a felony case, the defendant has the right to a trial within 5 to 60 days after after having been arraigned in superior court on the information or indictment. However, in most cases, the defense attorney will **waive time**, meaning that he or she gives up that right for the defendant and will ask that the trial date be continued until a future time. It usually works to the advantage of the defense to delay the trial in a serious case until the emotions of the community have quieted, witnesses' memories have faded, and there has been ample opportunity to investigate the case and prepare an adequate defense. When the attorney waives time, the judge usually will explain to the defendant what that means and ask if the defendant joins in that waiver.

It is unfortunate that in many cases a long delay in bringing a case to trial works a hardship on the victim and on witnesses. This is particularly true in a homicide case. The family of the victim needs closure on the tragedy, which includes having the suspected killer of their loved one tried and, if convicted, punished. Delays work against this and keep the emotional wounds of the victim's family open for months or even years. Of course, the justice system was not established, nor is it maintained, to provide solace and satisfaction to the victim.

A public trial means just that—a trial where the state must prove its case against the accused in an open public forum, free of any government coercion, tricks, and schemes. In addition, members of the public are free to attend to be certain that justice is done in their community. A judge can order any pretrial proceeding closed to the public, and even to the press, if all parties to the case agree, to ensure a fair trial for the accused (*Gannett v. DePasquale*, 1979). However, the judge may not close an actual trial to either the press or the public. The U.S. Supreme Court ruled by a decision of 7 to 1 (*Richmond Newspapers v. Virginia*, 1980) that both the public and the press have an absolute constitutional (First Amendment) right to have access to a trial, and the openness of a trial is an indispensable part of American justice. Space may limit access by all the public who might want to attend, but a representative public will attend in any event. And of course, the press will always be there.

THE ASSISTANCE OF COUNSEL FOR THE DEFENSE

The phrase, the *assistance of counsel for his defense*, is extracted from the **Sixth Amendment**, cited at the beginning of the chapter. It is common today for people to take for granted that an accused person has always had the assistance of counsel for the defense. After all, the police advise everyone they arrest and interrogate of that very right. That is true, in a way. Every person accused of a crime has had the right to an attorney if he or she could afford one. But it is only recently that those who could not afford an attorney actually received the **assistance of counsel**. It took over 30 years, beginning in 1932, and three appellate cases to the Supreme Court, before **indigent** people, those who could not afford an attorney, could have one appointed. It took three U.S. Supreme Court decisions to make the Sixth Amendment binding on the states.

THE SCOTTSBORO BOYS

On March 25, 1931, nine young black men, seven young white men, and two young white women were riding in the same freight car traveling across Alabama, when a fight broke out. The white men were thrown off the train. They immediately notified the sheriff, and in addition to their assaults, claimed that the two white girls were raped. The train was stopped by a sheriff's posse in the small town of Paint Rock, Alabama, and the young black men were arrested. When mob violence seemed imminent, they were moved to Scottsboro, Alabama. There the nine uneducated, illiterate, poor men were tried for the capital offense of rape, without the assistance of counsel. On the first day of the trial, the judge did appoint a local lawyer to assist in their defense, but he was of little use. The nine were tried in groups of three, and it took three days to try and convict all nine, even though medical testimony contradicted the girls' claim of rape. All nine, known as the **Scottsboro Boys**, were sentenced to death.

On appeal, their convictions were reversed (*Powell v. Alabama*, 1932), and the Supreme Court ruled that an indigent is entitled to the appointment of free counsel in capital cases. Later, in a retrial with the assistance of counsel, all nine were convicted again and sentenced to life in prison. Years later, one of the girls recanted her story and admitted that it was a lie. The second girl went to her grave without changing her story. The Scottsboro Boys eventually were pardoned by the governor of Alabama, although not all nine were living at the time.

THE BETTS CASE

In 1941, an out-of-work farmhand on county relief, named Betts, was indicted for robbery in the circuit court of Carroll County, Maryland. He was unable to afford an attorney, so he requested that counsel be appointed for him at arraignment. The judge denied his request and said that it was not the practice in Carroll County to appoint counsel for indigent defendants, except in prosecutions for murder and rape.

Without waiving his asserted right to counsel, Betts pleaded not guilty and asked to be tried without a jury. At his request, witnesses were summoned on his behalf. Betts cross-examined the state's witnesses and presented his own. The latter gave testimony tending to establish an alibi. Although afforded the opportunity, Betts did not take the witness stand. The judge found him guilty and imposed a sentence of eight years.

He appealed, alleging that he had been deprived of the right to assistance of counsel guaranteed by the Sixth Amendment by virtue of the Fourteenth Amendment. His appeal was denied all the way through the state's appellate system and up to the U.S. Supreme Court. Justice Roberts issued the Supreme Court's opinion on June 1, 1942 (*Betts v. Brady*, 1942). The court held that

[t]he Sixth Amendment of the national Constitution applies only to trials in federal courts. The due process clause of the Fourteenth Amendment does not incorporate, as such, the specific guarantees found in the Sixth Amendment....

Thus Betts's conviction was upheld and he remained in prison to serve his sentence. Precedent was set by this case. Indigents accused of felonies in state courts did not have a constitutional right to appointed counsel, unless special circumstances about the case, such as illiteracy or mental incompetence, would make self-representation unfair. For the next 20 years, thousands of indigent defendants were convicted without the assistance of counsel and were sent to prison. Every time a conviction was appealed, the Supreme Court referred to *Betts* as precedent and had to look for special circumstances if a conviction was to be reversed.

THE GIDEON CASE

In 1963 the U.S. Supreme Court did an unusual thing. It reversed itself completely on the Betts precedent in the case of *Gideon v. Wainwright*. In 1960, Clarence Earl Gideon, a 48-year-old itinerant laborer from Hannibal, Missouri, was arrested and charged with breaking into the Bay Harbor Pool Room in Panama City, Florida, and stealing about $65 out of the coin-operated machines, as well as some beer, wine, and Coca-Cola. The charge was felony burglary. He requested an attorney, but the trial judge, Robert L. McCrary, Jr., refused, based on existing practice and precedent. Gideon attempted to defend himself against the skills of the prosecutor, Bill Harris, but he was convicted and sentenced to a term of five years at the Union Correctional Institution in Raiford. Gideon appealed to the U.S. Supreme Court, in his own handwritten petition, with the help of Joe Peel, a former lawyer and city judge who was in Raiford serving time on a murder conviction.

The Supreme Court announced its unanimous opinion on March 18, 1963. Justice Black wrote the opinion, stating that

[t]he right of one charged with crime to counsel may not be deemed fundamental and essential to fair trials in some countries, but it is in ours. From the very beginning, our state and national constitutions and laws have laid great emphasis on procedural and substantive safeguards designed to assure fair trials before impartial tribunals in which every defendant stands equal before the law. This noble ideal cannot be realized if the poor man charged with crime has to face his accusers without a lawyer to assist him.

The *Gideon* decision made it mandatory that judges in state courts appoint free counsel to indigents accused of felonies. The Supreme Court stated that it "was a fundamental right, essential to a fair trial." Gideon's case was set for retrial before the original court in Panama City. The prosecutor, Bill Harris, offered a plea bargain whereby Gideon would plead guilty to the charge in return for a sentence of time served. His defense attorney, a local lawyer named W. Fred Turner, suggested that he take the deal. Gideon refused and demanded a jury trial. With the assistance of Mr. Turner, he was found not guilty and the charges were dismissed. In fact, the testimony at the second trial showed that Gideon might have been framed by the man who testified at the first trial, Henry Cook, who claimed to have seen Gideon in the poolroom when it was burglarized (Los Angeles *Daily Journal*, March 18, 1988, p. 22; Lewis, 1964).

The *Gideon* decision was made *retroactive*, which meant that the officials in every state had to review their prison records to determine who had been convicted without the help of an attorney. Anyone so convicted, and there were thousands, had to be either retried or released.

Gideon had one more brush with the law. He was arrested for vagrancy in Kentucky in 1965, claiming that he had lost all his money on the Kentucky Derby. He spent one night in jail. He died in poverty, and as a family outcast, on January 18, 1972. He was buried in a pauper's grave, with a wooden marker, in Hannibal, Missouri, and not even the remaining members of his family who lived there attended his funeral. Ten years later, however, members of the American Civil Liberties Union (ACLU) felt that Gideon had made such a contribution to the livelihood of so many lawyers that on the tenth anniversary of his death, they collected funds from attorneys nationwide, erected a marble headstone at his grave site and held a belated funeral service commemorating his contribution.

Many thought that the *Gideon* decision meant that anyone charged with a crime could have free counsel, but it actually included only accused felons. It took one more decision to fulfill the Sixth Amendment right.

THE ARGERSINGER CASE

In 1969, another indigent in Florida, named Argersinger, was arrested and charged with possession of a concealable firearm, a misdemeanor punishable by a jail term of up to six months or a $1000 fine. He was not informed of a right to an attorney at arraignment, and he pled guilty. He was given a 90-day jail sentence. He appealed his conviction, even though he was released long before the appeal was ever argued. Justice Douglas wrote the Supreme Court's opinion (*Argersinger v. Hamlin*, 1972), which was released on June 12, 1972, and stated that

[t]he right of an indigent defendant in a criminal trial to the assistance of counsel, which is guaranteed by the Sixth Amendment as made applicable to the States by the Fourteenth, is not governed by the classification of the offense or by whether or not a jury trial is required. No accused may be deprived of his liberty as the result of any criminal prosecution, whether felony or misdemeanor, in which he was denied the assistance of counsel.

The assistance of counsel, a right that people today take for granted, has only been in practice for felons in all the states since 1963, by *Gideon*, and finally in 1972, for all defendants who stand to lose their freedom, by *Argersinger*. That is not very long ago.

Those decisions not only gave indigents a new constitutional protection and released many convicted inmates from prisons and jails, it also created an immediate need for states to establish public defender systems and other appointed counsel methods.

CHALLENGING THE JUDGE

If a judge has personal knowledge about a case that might bias him or her, or has a personal, financial, or other interest in a case, he or she should disqualify himself or herself. Either attorney also may move to disqualify a judge for cause if they can convince the judge, or an appellate court, that the judge is biased. In addition, each attorney can exercise what is called a **peremptory challenge** of the judge's qualifications. This disqualifies a judge without having to provide a reason, and each attorney may exercise one peremptory challenge in each trial. This is a rare occurrence because most judges are fairminded and have the respect of the attorneys within their community.

THE SELECTION OF JURORS

Trial by a jury of *one's peers* is an integral part of our adversary system. However, the term *peers* can mean different things to each person. Does it mean a group of one's own age, or gender, or race, or status? Legally, a **jury of one's peers** is a randomly selected group of qualified individuals from within the venue where the trial will be held. If one's own age or ethnic group or gender is not represented on the jury, but the jury was selected randomly, it is a legal jury. However, it is not legal to exclude any one particular group deliberately.

THE VENIRE LIST

A **venire list** is a list of people within a county who are eligible to be considered as potential jurors. In each county a court administrator or jury commissioner mails out questionnaires to county residents whose names are taken from the list of registered voters and Department of Motor Vehicle records. The people contacted complete the questionnaire, giving a few facts about themselves, including their age, county of legal residence, any felony convictions, and claiming any hardships that they might incur by serving on a jury.

When a jury is needed, the jury commissioner or administrator randomly selects the number that might be needed to arrive at a panel of qualified people, plus several alternates, in the event that problems arise with one of the regular jurors during the trial. These potential jurors are sent a **summons**, commanding them to appear at the jury waiting room at a given date and time. Often, a phone number is listed on the summons that may be called the night before the juror is to appear just to confirm that his or her appearance the next day is necessary. If not, it saves the juror from having to take a day off work or other activities when his or her presence is not needed. Perhaps they will be asked to appear in another day or two.

The number actually summoned depends on the number a state requires on a jury, the nature of the case to be tried, and the length of time it will take. The pool of people summoned might range from 30 people for a simple burglary case to 500 or more for a serious homicide. Those summoned will arrive at the jury waiting room of the courthouse, all primed and ready to serve, or else anxious to be excused for any reason. They soon will come to understand why it is called a *waiting* room.

JURY SIZE

In many states, 12 jurors are required on a felony jury and any number from six to 12 on a misdemeanor jury, if all parties can agree to a number (*Patton v. United States*, 1930). However, it is rare that a defendant would agree to less than 12. Also, the U.S. Supreme Court has ruled (*Duncan v. Louisiana*, 1968) that the Sixth Amendment right to a trial by jury applies only to crimes in which the possible penalty is more than six months' incarceration. This is an example where a defendant receives greater protection under the law in many states than is required by the Constitution, because of independent state grounds.

States such as California require 12 on a felony jury, but that number is not constitutionally required. They use 12 just because that is the way juries started in King Henry's time. The states of Florida, New York, Virginia, and Georgia have long used juries composed of less than 12. The first case to test the constitutionality of this was *Williams v. Florida* (1970) when a bank robber named Williams was convicted by a jury of six and was sentenced to prison. The U.S. Supreme Court found through research that the practice of using 12 on a jury was the result of a historical accident. Consequently, the Court held that 12 were not needed.

Although the Supreme Court ruled that 12 were not needed, it did not say how many were required. By the mid-1970s, over 30 states had reduced the size of their juries, many to as low as six. Georgia even went lower. Finally, the Supreme Court realized that a minimum limit was necessary, and in 1978 it ruled that six is the minimum that a jury must have (*Ballew v. Georgia*, 1978). Today, the following states use a six-person jury in felony trials: Florida, Louisiana, Oregon, and Rhode Island. Utah and Arizona use eight,, and the other states use 12. In misdemeanor trials the number varies from six, seven, or eight to 12.

A strong argument can be made for the use of six on a jury. According to management theory, six is an ideal number for consensus decision making. Twelve can hardly agree where to go for lunch. Those states that have reduced the size of their juries have found that the conviction rates have increased, there are fewer hung juries, it saves time and money, and there is less likelihood that the jury will have a dissenter or holdout. On the other hand, with smaller juries there is less likelihood of minority representation, fewer opinions to consider, and a smaller representation of the community at large, whereas the collective opinion of 12 is better informed and more thorough in its thinking and deliberation. Those who favor twelve on a jury seem to have a defense orientation, whereas those who favor a six-person jury seem to have a prosecution orientation.

QUALIFYING THE JURORS: THE VOIR DIRE PROCESS

Once the prospective jurors are called into a courtroom to be considered for the jury panel, the judge begins a process of qualifying who can serve as a fair and unbiased juror. First, the judge might explain to the potential jurors what the case is about, the names of all the parties involved in the presentation of the case, and approximately how long the trial will last. If anyone knows any of the parties or will suffer hardship by sitting on a jury for the time mentioned, he or she will be dismissed.

After this initial screening is completed, the court clerk will randomly draw numbers, perhaps out of a box, that match the numbers on the jurors' summons stubs. When the number called matches, the person walks up from the audience to sit in the jury box. Anywhere from six to 12 will be called to fill the jury box, and several alternates will be called as standby jurors.

When the jury box and alternate juror seats are filled, the real qualifying process begins, the process called *voir dire*. These are two French verbs, "to see" and "to tell," which when loosely translated means "to understand and tell the truth."

This is a questioning process in which the judge asks each prospective juror a series of questions, depending on the nature of the case, to determine whether the person can be fair and unbiased in considering the evidence and can abide by the judge's instructions on how to assess the evidence and the law in reaching a verdict. The two opposing attorneys may either submit questions for the judge to ask or might be able to ask some questions directly of the prospective jurors, depending on the court and the policy of the judge.

CHALLENGING THE PROSPECTIVE JUROR

When the *voir dire* is over, each attorney in turn may **challenge** and excuse any of the potential jurors in two ways, similar to how they can challenge a judge. Each attorney may challenge and have the judge excuse any number of prospective jurors **for cause**. That is, any number can be challenged for demonstrating that they cannot be fair and unbiased and cannot accept the adversary system of justice, with its attending protections against the accused, especially the defendant's right to remain silent. However, the attorney will have to convince the judge that his or her reasons for claiming bias, and so on, are sound. In addition, each attorney may exercise a limited number of **peremptory challenges**, challenges without giving a reason. When a juror is challenged and excused, a new prospective juror is randomly chosen and *voir dired*.

The defense attorney may also challenge the entire jury and claim that the entire venire list has a bias against the defendant, usually because of pretrial publicity. In this case, the defense would make a motion for a **change of venue**. The judge is well aware of the delicate balance between freedom of the press and a fair trial for the accused. The judge cannot control the press because the First Amendment gives the press the right to investigate and publish the news freely. However, the judge may control the information available to the press by issuing what is called a **gag order**, limiting the release of information by all the parties that have a legal role in the case (*Rideau v. Louisiana*, 1963, *Estes v.Texas*, 1965; *Sheppard v. Maxwell*, 1966). Attorneys frequently rely on hunches, experience, and old wives' tales about what makes a good jury in deciding who to challenge. In some cases, an attorney will hire a jury watcher or jury consultant to assist in assessing the types of responses that jurors make during the *voir dire*. In the past, this left a great deal to chance and to gut feelings. Today, a more sophisticated method is available.

The traditional method of selecting jurors is giving way to science. What is termed **scientific jury selection** is the use of some type of social science research method(s) to assess the attitudes of persons within the venire list or within the community at large. Such methods include field interviews and/or questionnaires within the population at large, random surveys, or questionnaires given to a large portion of people from the venire list who are summoned as potential jurors. The method got its start in the mid-1970s in a small county in North Carolina.

On January 15, 1974, a 20-year-old black woman, Joan Little, and her younger brother were arrested for stealing $850 from two mobile homes and were booked into the Beaufort County Jail in North Carolina. Both were charged with burglary. The brother worked out a plea bargain and was granted probation. She demanded a jury trial, was convicted, and was sentenced to prison for seven to 10 years. She appealed and had to remain in jail pending her appeal. On her eighty-first night in jail, a 62-year-old white night jailer entered her cell; she stabbed him 11 times with an ice pick, took his jail keys, and escaped. She turned herself in to the state police about a week later and was returned to Beaufort County to face trial on a charge of first-degree murder (Robin, 1987, p. 285).

The prosecutor claimed that she had the ice pick hidden in her cell and lured the jailer in on a pretext, then killed him. She claimed that he entered her cell, threatening her with the ice pick (which had come from the jail kitchen), and demanded sexual favors. She acted as though she was giving in, then at the right moment, in his heat of passion, the jailer dropped the ice pick. She picked it up and stabbed him in self-defense. (Robin, 1987, p. 285).

The Joan Little case was an early *cause célebre* in the woman's rights movement, and sympathetic persons from around the nation responded with both moral and financial support. In fact, this writer can recall having students at California State University, San José, who collected and contributed to the Joan Little Defense Fund. These funds probably went to the Southern Poverty Law Center, the organization that helped fund her eight-member defense team, the social science experts, and field interviewers. They raised substantial funds and hired several social science researchers from local universities and 70 interviewers to conduct public opinion surveys among the Beaufort County residents. The survey results showed that most people had heard of the case because of extensive pretrial publicity and that they had already made up their minds. The survey also showed a strong racial bias against blacks in the community (Robin, 1987, p. 285). Armed with this information, the defense requested and was granted a change of venue to Wake County. There, the team of social science researchers conducted another survey to assess the community attitudes and to attempt to develop a profile of a favorable juror. They hired 20 interviewers, who interviewed 954 potential jurors, collecting demographic information on them and asking questions to learn of their attitudes and activities.

These surveys did not show the racial bias that had existed in Beaufort County, so the venue was acceptable. However, their questions did reveal characteristics of favorable jurors for the defense and favorable jurors for the prosecution. Therefore, during the *voir dire*, which was conducted primarily by the attorneys, the defense team asked questions similar to those asked in the survey. When the responses matched those of a favorable juror, they did not use a challenge, but if the responses were unfavorable, they would exercise one of their peremptory challenges. Eventually, the jury was acceptable to both parties, and the trial continued.

Joan Little was found not guilty of any crime because the jury was not convinced by the circumstantial evidence that she was guilty beyond a reasonable doubt. Her defense team credited the scientific survey and jury selection process for the verdict. The cost of her defense was approximately $325,000 (Robin, 1987, p. 286).

From that humble but expensive beginning, the use of **jury questionnaires** has grown until today, it is the common method in serious cases in which a large jury pool is needed to be certain that a fair and unbiased jury is selected. Instead of using private funds or allowing one side to have the advantage of the information gathered, a standard questionnaire is administered at county expense, completed by all those summoned in a case, and both sides share in the results. However, each side can still use the information as a basis for further questioning in the *voir dire* process.

A recent example of this is the O. J. Simpson case in Los Angeles, in which the jury questionnaire had 94 pages of questions and required about four hours to complete. Similar examples can be found in courts throughout the country. The uses of these questionnaires are still the same: to eliminate obviously biased or unqualified persons, to move for a change of venue if it is appropriate, and to attempt to select the most favorable jurors, and challenge the unfavorable ones, by asking questions from the information given in the answers.

COURT TRIALS

The Sixth Amendment guarantees an accused person the right to a jury trial. However, there are times when it is in the best interests of the defendant not to have a jury trial but to have the trial by a judge sitting alone. This is called a **court trial**; the terms *judge* and *court* are used interchangeably within this context. In situations where the accused faces heinous charges that might stir the emotions of people on a jury, or where they might find the defendant, or his or her appearance, offensive, the jury might find it difficult to render a fair verdict. Theoretically, a judge can rise above the emotions of a case and rule on the factual evidence and the law.

The defendant may waive his or her right to a jury (*Patton v. United States*, 1930), and proceed with a court trial, if the prosecutor agrees to the waiver.

Ironically, the U.S. Supreme Court has ruled that although the Constitution guarantees the accused the right to a trial by jury, it does not give him or her the right not to have a jury. Consequently, the district attorney (DA) must concur with the defendant's waiver (*Singer v. United States*, 1965), and the waiver must be made personally by the defendant in open court.

In a northern California case, a defendant appeared in superior court for arraignment on information charging two counts of second-degree (vehicular) homicide. The attorney waived his client's right to a jury, with the client standing alongside him, and requested a court trial. The attorney affirmed this request at a later hearing, with the defendant again standing beside him. However, the defendant did not say a word in court, and the judge did not ask him if he personally agreed to the waiver. The defendant was convicted and sentenced to prison for two terms of 15 years to life. Approximately five years later, on appeal, the state supreme court reversed the conviction because the waiver was not personally made in court by the defendant (*People v. Ernst*, 1994). The California Constitution expressly states that "a jury may be waived in a criminal cause by the consent of both parties expressed in open court by the defendant and the defendant's counsel" (Cal. Const., art. I, §16). Eventually, he was recharged, but a plea bargain was arranged where the defendant pled guilty in exchange for a suspended sentence and four years of probation.

LET THE TRIAL BEGIN

It is not uncommon to have all the parties assembled and ready for trial only to have the attorneys agree to a last-minute plea bargain. The jurors are stunned, but they are thanked for their time and willingness to serve. If the trial does take place, it is the responsibility of the judge to control and orchestrate the events to ensure a fair trial, to rule on the admissibility of evidence or on the questioning practices of the attorneys, and to serve as arbitrator in disputes between the attorneys.

The prosecutor has the responsibility to prove the state's case beyond a reasonable doubt. It is the responsibility of the defense to challenge the presentation by the DA on his or her case every time there are questions of fairness or the rights of the client.

THE ATTACHMENT OF JEOPARDY

In a court trial, jeopardy attaches when the first witness is sworn in and seated. In a jury trial, jeopardy attaches when the jury is sworn and seated. The phrase **jeopardy attaches** means that the defendant has been placed in a position of jeopardy at that moment, and the trial must continue to a conclusion. From that moment on, the defendant cannot be retried if the conclusion is a not guilty verdict. However, if proceedings are stopped at any time before jeopardy attaches to the defendant, proceedings against the accused usually may be resumed or renewed by a new complaint.

If the trial is stopped at the end because of what is termed a **hung jury**, a jury that cannot decide on a verdict, it is not considered to be a conclusion of the trial. A trial concludes only when there is a verdict. Consequently, the DA may refile the charges, and the judge may start the trial over again with a new jury and not place the defendant in double jeopardy, as defined under the Fifth Amendment. Legally, it is single jeopardy over again.

THE CASE-IN-CHIEF

The prosecutor begins the presentation of the trial because it is the state that charged the defendant, and it is the responsibility of the DA to prove that charge without the help of the defendant. If the DA fails to prove the state's side of the case, the matter may be dismissed without the defense ever having to present their side. The entire case presented by the prosecutor, including all the witnesses and other evidence, is called the **case-in-chief**.

A trial is similar to a college term paper. It is composed of three parts: the introduction, body, and conclusion. A term paper without a good introduction becomes a maze of meandering verbiage. Thus a good introduction sets the jury's focus and thinking as to what will be shown in the body of the trial. The prosecutor begins his or her introduction, called an **opening statement**, or opening remarks, to the jury. This outlines the state's case and tells the jury what the DA thinks the evidence will show and how he or she intends to show it. The defense attorney may follow with his or her own opening statement, or he or she may wait until the DA has finished with the state's case.

The prosecutor attempts to prove the truth of the charges by the presentation of three types of evidence: physical, confessional, and testimonial.

PHYSICAL EVIDENCE

Physical evidence is evidence that is physical in nature, such as solids or liquids, and includes bodies, blood, semen, bullets, empty shell casings, fingerprints, hair, writings, documents and records, photographs, and other tangible items, such as weapons or stolen property. Some of these are known as **fruits of a crime**, such as the stolen property. Others are called the **instrument of a crime**, the item used to force open a door or window, or the weapon used in an assault or homicide.

Another category of evidence is called **transferred evidence**. This includes any physical item left at the scene by the suspect, such as hair, blood, or semen, or any items removed from the scene, such as stolen property, particles of material from a rug, or blood from the victim.

The careful collection, analysis, and preservation of any physical evidence is crucial in obtaining a conviction. Care must be taken not to break the **chain of evidence**, which means to break the continuity of its possession so as to cast doubt that the evidence in court, before the jury, is the same evidence taken at the scene or from the suspect, and that it has not been tainted in any way. This also includes the care that must be given in lab analysis and the testimony used about it.

The DA usually will introduce the physical evidence into trial by the person who first obtained it, followed by the one who controlled it pending trial, and ending with the one who performed any analysis or testing of it, in order to maintain the integrity of the evidence presented.

The prosecution would be barred from admitting any physical evidence that had been seized illegally, obtained in violation of the exclusionary rule and the Fourth Amendment, discussed at length in Chapter 2.

CONFESSIONAL EVIDENCE

Confessional evidence comprises confessions or incriminating statements made by the defendant to peace officers during their investigation. Obviously, the exclusionary rule is an overlay used by the court in determining the legality of confessions or admissions by the defendant. If statements were made while the defendant was in custody, the defendant must have been *Mirandized* (Chapter 4) before questioning.

If a confession is used as evidence when it should have been suppressed, it does not necessarily mean that the conviction is not valid or that the conviction will be reversed. On any appeal, it will be up to the appellate court to determine whether the defendant would have been convicted anyway, regardless of the admissibility of the confession (*Arizona v. Fulminante*, 1991). If the appellate court is convinced that the defendant would have been convicted anyway, use of the illegally obtained confession is called a harmless error, and the conviction need not be reversed.

TESTIMONIAL EVIDENCE

Testimonial evidence refers to the testimony given in court by witnesses. The term witnesses does not mean just those who witnessed the crime, as there are two types of witnesses: expert witnesses and lay witnesses.

An **expert witness** is a person who has special understanding or knowledge about a particular subject and/or aspect of the crime because of special training or education in that subject. This includes such people as physicians, DNA experts, crime lab analysts, accident reconstruction specialists, and fingerprint and other forensic experts. These persons may offer opinions and conclusions based on the facts of the evidence, and their opinions are considered to be evidence. However, the jury is advised that they are the ones who determine how much weight to give the opinions of any expert.

The judge will determine if the witness is to be considered an expert. One consideration will be whether the witness has ever testified as an expert in any other court. In addition, the opposing attorney may *voir dire* the witness, that is, question the person as to his or her expertise by asking about the person's education and/or training; or the opposing attorney may stipulate (agree) that the witness is an expert.

A **lay witness** is a person who might have some knowledge about the events of the crime but has no special training or education in any aspect about which he or she will testify. Most witnesses are lay witnesses, including a majority of the police officers involved in the case. These witnesses may testify about what they have personal knowledge of by virtue of the five senses: what they heard, saw, tasted, touched, or smelled. They cannot offer opinions that would be beyond the common knowledge of a layperson.

Direct and Indirect Evidence

Evidence of any type may be placed into one of two additional categories: direct and indirect evidence. **Direct evidence** is evidence that proves a specific fact directly. **Indirect evidence** does not stand on its own as a relevant fact or truth. It requires the jury to make the connection between sets of facts, or to logically infer that something probably is true. For example, if a man testifies that he saw the defendant coming out of his neighbor's house at 8:00 P.M. of the evening that the house was burglarized, it is direct evidence. It stands alone as a fact and puts the defendant directly at the scene of a burglary, leaving the house at a specific time. However, when the fingerprint expert testifies that the prints he found on the outside rear door handle and on a glass in the kitchen sink match those of the defendant, it is indirect evidence in that the jury must infer or conclude that the defendant's prints must have been left at the scene that same evening, during the burglary.

Indirect evidence is also called **circumstantial evidence** because whether it is relevant to consider as evidence depends on the total circumstances in which it is included and considered. It requires the jury to infer the connection between it and some more tangible direct evidence.

Scientific Evidence

Science and technology have advanced at a rapid pace during this century, particularly during the past 25 years. Today, physical evidence can be collected and tested by methods that would have been impossible only a few years ago. The newest scientific method for testing evidence, and the one about which there is still argument, concerns the reliability of DNA testing. The analysis of a person's DNA can either place him or her at a crime scene or prove conclusively that he or she was not the offender by a method that only the analysts seem to understand. Just how accurate it is and how much weight to give the results as evidence in a criminal matter is still arguable in some quarters. The traditional standard for determining the reliability of any scientific method, known as the *Frye test* or **Kelly–Frye test** (*People v. Kelly*, 1976), was described initially almost 75 years ago, in the decision *Frye v. United States*, (1923). The court stated:

> Just when a scientific principle or discovery crosses the line between the experimental and demonstrable stages is difficult to define. Somewhere in this twilight zone the evidential force of the principle must be recognized, and while courts will go a long way in admitting expert testimony deduced

from a well-recognized scientific principle or discovery, the thing from which the deduction is made must be sufficiently established to have gained general acceptance in the particular field in which it belongs.

The use of fingerprint analysis met that test many years ago. The use of a lie detector test has not, and probably never will, because it is the polygraph operator who interprets the results. The use of DNA print testing, although still questioned by some, apparently has crossed "...the line between the experimental and demonstrable stages..." and is fairly well accepted in most states.

HYPNOTICALLY ENHANCED MEMORY AS EVIDENCE

The reliability of **hypnotically enhanced memory** is another area where even the "experts" disagree. The issue seems to center around whether testimony given after hypnosis is really enhanced memory or memory created by the hypnotist or by the subject to please the hypnotist. Some state courts have ruled that induced memory might be tainted; therefore, it is not reliable because the truth of it cannot be validated. If the defendant wants to testify at trial, and has had his or her memory enhanced through hypnosis, he or she must be allowed to testify. Otherwise, it would deny him or her the right to testify on his or her own behalf (*Rock v. Arkansas*, 1987). Enhanced memories can be very useful in situations where a witness saw a license plate or a person, but just cannot recall. The vision is still there and can be recalled by hypnosis.

VIEWING THE CRIME SCENE

The members of the jury are instructed by the judge not to visit or view the crime scene on their own. In fact, they are not to receive any evidence on their own outside the courtroom, unless the judge directs them. If the judge thinks that the jury needs to view the actual crime scene in order to better understand the testimony of witnesses, the judge will arrange for all the jurors to view it together in the presence of the two attorneys, the defendant and the judge.

DIRECT AND CROSS EXAMINATION

When used in this context, the word *examination* means questioning of a witness in court by an attorney. **Direct examination** is the questioning of a witness by the attorney who called the witness to help prove his or her side of the case. For example, when the prosecutor is attempting to prove the guilt of the defendant, he or she will call and question by direct examination such witnesses as the arresting police officer, the victim, and any eyewitnesses to the crime. When the opposing attorney questions the witnesses, it is called **cross-examination**. Therefore, when the defense attorney questions the victim or the police officer who arrested his or her client, in order to show that his or her client is not guilty, it is cross-examination.

After one attorney completes his or her cross-examination of a witness, the other attorney may re-question his or her own witness. This is called **redirect**. Following that, the other attorney may requestion the witness by **recross**, and so it can go until the witness's testimony has been exhausted.

During direct examination, an attorney may not ask what are called **leading questions**, questions in which the desired answer is stated or implied. It is assumed that this witness is friendly to the attorney and will cooperate because he or she was called to testify by that attorney. If that witness becomes uncooperative in answering the attorney's questions, the attorney may ask the judge to declare the person to be a **hostile witness**. Then the attorney may ask leading questions because that may be the only way to get that witness to testify. In addition, attorneys may ask leading questions during their cross-examinations.

Before any witness is allowed to take the stand, he or she will be sworn in as a witness. A witness may **swear** an **oath** before God that he or she will tell the truth, or if a witness prefers not to include God in the process, he or she may simply **affirm** that the testimony will be the truth. Some courts have even allowed witnesses to make up their own affirmations.

Witnesses are directed to come to court to testify by the use of a legal document that commands their appearance called a **subpoena**. Failure to respond to a subpoena is contempt of court. When an attorney wants to have the court command a witness to bring certain documents with him or her to court, the attorney has the court issue a *subpoena duces tecum*, meaning, "bring the documents."

OBJECTIONS TO THE QUESTION

During the questioning of a witness by one attorney, the opposing attorney might challenge the admissibility of a particular question of the witness or the answer by the witness. The attorney does this by filing an **objection** with the court: "I object to that question, your Honor."

The basis for making an objection might be that the question calls for a conclusion or opinion from a lay witness, is a leading question, has been ruled as inadmissible, or would call for hearsay information. Hearsay information is what a witness might have learned from another source but does not know it firsthand. There are a few exceptions to this hearsay rule, such as a dying declaration by one person to another, certain business records, or a spontaneous statement made by the victim or some witness.

Each attorney might argue his or her positions on whether to allow the question or to admit the answer. Finally, the judge will rule on the objection. If the judge says "**I sustain the objection**," it means that he or she agrees with the attorney who made the objection and the question may not be asked or answered. If it already had been answered, the judge will order that the answer be stricken from the record and will tell the jury to disregard it. Of course the jury cannot disregard it because they heard it. However, they may not refer to it or use it in their deliberation over the guilt of the defendant. If the judge does not agree with the attorney who made the objection, and will allow the question and answer, the judge says "**I overrule the objection**."

PRIVILEGED COMMUNICATION

Not all testimony can be admitted at trial. Some people are protected by law against having to testify, even though they might know what happened. For example, the defendant is protected against having to testify by the Fifth Amendment to the Constitution. If the state accuses a person of a crime, the state must prove it without that person's help.

There are others who know the defendant and might have communicated with the defendant about the crime, but they do not have to testify because of what is termed **privileged communication**, a vestige from common law. They have a privileged relationship with the defendant and may not reveal anything they know about the matter. These privileged communication relationships include those between husband and wife, attorney and client, doctor and patient, therapist and patient, clergy and penitent, sexual assault victim and counselor, and domestic violence victim and counselor.

CONDUCT OF THE JURY

As stated above, the jury may not receive any evidence or information outside the courtroom. For example, a petite female of 98 pounds was on trial for killing her husband by shooting him with his Ruger .44 caliber magnum revolver, a large gun. The defense claimed that she did not have the strength to pull the trigger alone, and that her husband was pulling the trigger during a struggle in which she was trying to defend herself, and the gun went off. The jury was deadlocked in its deliberation, with some of them believing the defense's theory. However, one of the jurors, also a small and lightweight female, dry-fired her husband's Ruger .44 caliber revolver and told the other jurors how easy it was. The verdict was a quick *guilty*, until the defense learned about her telling the jurors of her experience. The error was grounds for a new trial. In addition, the jury must be attentive during the trial, must not hear or read about the case, and must not discuss the case among themselves or with anyone else during the trial, and must not form any opinions as to the defendant's guilt until the jury begins its deliberation.

In some instances, a judge will sequester a jury, either during the entire trial or just during the jury's deliberation. To **sequester a jury** means to isolate them from outside influences, such as requiring them to return to a hotel room at the end of each day.

THE PROSECUTION RESTS

The *prosecution rests* when all the evidence has been presented and the state's case is over. At this point the jury has heard only one side of the matter, the prosecution's case-in-chief. Also, by this time, the defense has determined what would be the best defense strategy to counter what the prosecutor's evidence has shown.

DEFENSE STRATEGIES

The basic role of the defense attorney is to defend the rights of the accused. It is not to defend what the client is alleged to have done. This is done by challenging the prosecution at every turn, and to force him or her to present enough legal evidence to prove the client guilty beyond a reasonable doubt. Once the prosecution has rested and this part of the defense's challenge is over, the attorney will counter the state's case by presenting some form of defense. There are three general **defense strategies** categories discussed below, with several specific defenses under each category. However, before the defense attorney needs to present an active defense, it may make a motion to the court to dismiss the case, as follows.

MOTION FOR A DIRECT VERDICT

The defense might believe that the evidence presented was not sufficient to prove his or her client guilty, or he or she might just want to test what the judge's thinking is about the sufficiency of the evidence. The defense may make a **motion for a direct verdict** or direct verdict of acquittal, as it is also known, a motion for a judgment of acquittal by the judge. Before making such a motion, the attorney will either ask that the jury be excused or will indicate to the judge what the motion will be; then the judge will excuse the jury.

The defense does not want the jury to hear what will occur during this process. In making this motion, the defense attorney is claiming that the prosecution did not present enough evidence to prove his or her client guilty legally—that the state did not make its case. Therefore, there is nothing to defend. The judge can respond with one of three rulings:

1. The judge may grant the motion, thus finding the defendant *not guilty* and dismissing the case. Obviously, this means that the judge agrees that the state did not prove its case.

2. The judge may reduce the crime to a lesser but included crime. This means that the state did not prove all the elements of the crime charged, but did prove the elements of the lesser crime.

3. The judge may deny the motion and order the trial to continue. In doing this, the judge is in effect saying that the state did prove its case and that the defense attorney should prepare a defense. Obviously, the defense would not want the jury to know if this is the judge's thinking.

NOT GUILTY BY THE EVIDENCE

The strategy of claiming not guilty by the evidence might be used by the defense when the state's case is based primarily on circumstantial evidence; there is no direct evidence or eye witnesses to prove the matter conclusively or to connect the defendant with the crime. The defense might attempt to cast doubt on the state's argument and create another reasonable explanation for what occurred, through the presentation of his or her own witnesses, or through the cross examination of the state's witnesses. This could include the specific arguments that the victim consented, the defendant was framed, there was a mistake in the identification of the suspect, the defendant did not have guilty knowledge of a crime (e.g., had no way of knowing that he or she was committing a crime at the time), or the defendant is of such good character that he or she could not possibly have done it.

GUILTY, BUT TO A LESSER CHARGE

A claim of guilty, but to a lesser charge, is a strategy that the defense might use when the direct evidence is strong, and there is no doubt that a crime occurred and the defendant committed it.

However, "what did he or she really do?" The person did the act, but what he or she did does not fit the degree of the crime charged. It fits some lesser crime. As an example, a defendant charged with first degree murder might admit the killing, but try to prove that it was in the heat of passion and lacked the specific intent of first degree. If the defense is successful, it might substantially reduce the penalty the defendant will receive. Maybe that is the best that the defense can hope for.

Not Guilty Because of Legal Justification

In the two defense strategies discussed above, the defense often can succeed just by weakening the argument of the prosecution. However, under the third category, the defense must offer what is termed an affirmative defense; it must actually present a real defense. This would be a situation in which the prosecution's evidence proved beyond the doubt of anyone that an act occurred and the defendant did it. However, the defense will attempt to prove that the defendant had a legal right to do what he or she did. This would include self-defense, insanity, accident or misfortune, entrapment, the defendant acting under a threat or duress, the defendant being unconscious of the act (through intoxication or a drug overdose induced by someone else), so as to not understand his or her own actions, or that he or she had a legal duty, privilege, or immunity. For example, a police officer or state correctional officer facing a homicide charge could argue that he or she had a legal right to shoot a person, or in the case of carrying a concealed weapon, a person could argue that they had a permit, or even had a fear of immediate harm, or other legal excuse.

It is beyond the scope of this book to discuss the juvenile justice system in any detail. Nevertheless, one aspect of it should be noted here. In theory, juveniles do not commit crimes; they commit delinquent acts. However, most state laws now allow the juvenile court to find that certain minors (ages vary with the states) can be tried as adults. The court will conduct what is called a *fitness hearing* and will consider the evidence presented as to the fitness of the minor to remain within the jurisdiction of the juvenile court. If the minor is found unfit, he or she will be bound over to adult court for trial just like any other adult. In any juvenile case in which the minor is under the age of legal adulthood, the minor will remain within the juvenile court's jurisdiction regardless of what type of offense he or she committed. In these cases, however, the defense might be that the minor did not have the capacity to appreciate the nature and consequences of his or her act. The burden of proof is on the state to prove by clear and convincing evidence that the minor did have this capacity (*In re Manuel L.*, 1993). In whatever defense the attorney uses, the process of presenting the witnesses and other evidence will be the same as it was during the case-in-chief.

TESTIMONY BY THE DEFENDANT

One of the most important decisions that the defense attorney must make is whether to put the defendant on the witness stand to testify in his or her own behalf. The defendant does not have to testify, and the prosecution is prohibited from making any comment to the jury if the defendant does not take the stand (*Griffin v. California*, 1965). If the defense plans to put the defendant on the stand, the attorney must consider how the defendant's testimony will affect the jury. The defendant also will be available for cross-examination by the prosecutor, which will really test the facts given by the defendant. Also, if the defendant made any incriminating statements to police during their investigation that were ruled inadmissible because they were obtained in violation of *Miranda*, they may be used to **impeach** the defendant's story if what he or she says on the stand is different than what he or she told the police (*Harris v. New York*, 1971; *People v. May*, 1988).

REBUTTAL

Once the defense has presented its side of the case and has rested, the prosecution may have another turn to convince the jury of its argument. The DA may present witnesses to **rebut** (counter) the version of the truth created by the defense. These witnesses may be cross-examined by the defense as well. Following that, the defense also may present rebuttal witnesses, which in turn may be cross-examined by the prosecution. Finally, when all the witnesses have been exhausted, literally, the trial is over.

CLOSING ARGUMENTS

Closing arguments are similar to the summary and conclusion of a term paper. It is the opportunity for each attorney to address the jury and to summarize what the evidence has shown. Each will stress the strong points of their case and draw attention to the weakness of their opponent's case. The prosecutor must be careful not to make what is termed a **prejudicial error** by stating something inadmissible that might prejudice the jury against the defendant.

For example, the prosecutor cannot mention the defendant's prior record, refer to him or her in repugnant terms, or say that he or she has personal knowledge of the defendant's guilt. If the prosecutor makes a prejudicial error and the defendant is found guilty, the defense has grounds for an appeal. On the other hand, if the defendant is found not guilty, nothing said by the defense attorney is appealable. Consequently, the defense has far greater latitude in wording his or her summary of what occurred.

INSTRUCTIONS TO THE JURY

The judge must explain to the jury what its responsibilities are. This includes giving them an explanation of the laws in the case, the elements of each possible crime that might be considered (the *corpus delicti*), and any other instructions requested by the attorneys. Specifically, the judge must **instruct the jury on the laws** that apply in any situation related to the defense theory offered during the trial. When there have been expert witnesses, the judge might clarify for the jury that just because someone is called an expert, it does not mean that what that person says is true. The jury must decide how much weight to give to the testimony by any expert. In addition, the judge must instruct them which side has the burden of proof and on what is meant by the phrase *beyond a reasonable doubt*.

The legal language of what constitutes reasonable doubt might not be clear to a layperson. Consequently, the judge should describe it in lay terms for jurors because it does little to explain the concept. The clarity of the instructions of the judge is crucial to the jury's proper interpretation of the laws and the evidence. Improper or incomplete instructions could be the basis of a later appeal after conviction.

JURY DELIBERATION

In the discussion on jury selection, it was noted that several alternate jurors were selected in addition to the regular panel, in case a regular juror becomes ill or is disqualified from the jury for some reason. Now, at this point in the proceedings where the jury sits alone in that closed room to **deliberate** on a verdict, the alternates cannot participate. Only the seated panel members deliberate. They must deliberate until they reach a verdict or until they are sure that they cannot reach a verdict.

The jurors first select a foreperson by an election process. Then it is the responsibility of the jurors to review and weigh the evidence objectively, decide on the credibility of any testimonial evidence, and judge the facts within the limits of the law as explained to them by the judge.

There will be two possible results from the jury's deliberation. If a jury finds that it cannot reach a verdict because the jurors disagree on what the verdict should be, they will inform the judge. The judge probably will explain to the jury that they are a panel of reasonable people and that there is no reason to believe that any other chosen panel could make any better judgments. He or she will encourage the jury to continue its deliberation. If the jury absolutely cannot decide on a verdict, the judge will declare a hung jury, dismiss the jurors, and allow the DA to decide on whether to prosecute the case again with a new jury.

If the jury has reached a **verdict**, the judge is informed, and all the participants gather in the courtroom. When everyone is there and the judge is seated, the jury is brought into the room by the bailiff. The judge asks if the jury has reached a verdict, and the foreperson says "yes." Then the judge instructs the foreperson to hand the signed verdict to the bailiff, who hands it to the clerk, who hands it to the judge, who either reads it or hands it back to the clerk to read. In many courts, the judge asks the defendant to rise and face the jury while the judge reads the verdict.

Once the verdict is read, the jurors think that their services are over. They deliberated in secret, and let someone else tell the defendant what the verdict was. Now they are ready to go home. However, in many cases the attorneys have one more procedure for them to complete.

POLLING THE JURY

Each attorney may **poll the jury**. This is a process in which an attorney faces each individual juror and asks the juror how he or she voted. The jurors must respond. The defense attorney is looking for some hesitation, some expression of doubt from a juror, something to indicate that the deliberation was not done legally or that duress was used to force a change of vote by some juror. Then the attorney will pursue that line of questioning.

If the attorney is able to find some irregularity in the deliberation, or it is disclosed that the jury received information or evidence outside the courtroom, it might be grounds for a motion for a new trial.

If some irregularity is discovered during the trial, before the verdict is in, it would have been grounds for what is called a **mistrial**.

The prosecution probably will poll the jury in the case of a hung jury. The DA will want to know what the actual vote was in order to determine whether it is worth trying the case again. If a verdict is 11 to 1 for conviction, it might indicate that some holdout hung the jury. In that case, the DA probably would recharge the defendant. However, if the verdict is 8 to 4 for acquittal, the DA knows that either the evidence was weak or that his or her presentation was not adequate.

After the jury is polled and both attorneys are satisfied that the jury's services are no longer needed, the judge will dismiss the jury, commending them on how well they fulfilled their civic responsibility. In a guilty verdict case, the defense might follow the jurors out of the courtroom, hoping to speak with one or more of them, again seeking to find some irregularity in the deliberation process.

UNANIMOUS VERSUS NONUNANIMOUS VERDICTS

Many people think that a **unanimous verdict** is always required in a criminal trial. It is required by the law in some states, but it is not required under any constitutional guidelines. In fact, the U.S. Supreme Court ruled in two cases (*Johnson v. Louisiana*, 1972, and *Apadoca v. Oregon*, 1972) that a unanimous verdict is not required to ensure a fair trial for the accused. A verdict may be delivered by a three-fourths majority. However, in a follow-up case (*Burch v. Louisiana*, 1979), the Supreme Court did rule that a unanimous verdict is required in non-petty cases with a jury composed of only six persons. Nonpetty cases are those in which the possible penalty is longer than six months' incarceration.

The use of a **nonunanimous verdict** is still controversial because its use can discount the opinions of some jurors, and it also means that there is doubt in the minds of some jurors. Several states, including Louisiana and Oregon, used nonunanimous verdicts before 1972, and others have adopted them since that date. Its use has shortened deliberations and resulted in an increased conviction rate. It has also saved counties money in jury and trial expenses. In addition, one could argue that since we live in a democracy where majority rules in the political arena, why not apply this to the legal arena? As an example of majority rule, the Supreme Court justices decided the Johnson case by a vote of 5 to 4. It would have been ironic if they had ruled to require a unanimous verdict by the same vote.

ANOTHER MOTION FOR A DIRECT VERDICT

After the verdict is in, and if the verdict is guilty, the defense may make another motion for a **direct verdict**. As before, the defense is claiming that the state did not prove its case. In addition, the defense is claiming that the jury made an error of law in reaching its verdict. The judge, being the expert on how the law should be applied in the case, may make the same three rulings as were cited above in the section "Motion for a Direct Verdict." The defense might make this motion just for the record, realizing full well that the trial judge will deny his or her motion. In this case, the defense is thinking ahead toward an appeal, and the federal appellate courts will not hear a case on the issue of the sufficiency of the evidence to prove guilt unless the defense has made this motion during trial.

SUMMARY

This chapter began by quoting the Sixth Amendment to the Constitution, which contains most of the rights a person has when accused of and tried for a crime. Within this context, we presented the trial procedures, beginning with a definition of a speedy and public trial and the state's burden of proof in a criminal case, then compared the relative advantages of a court trial and a jury trial. Next, we discussed the process of selecting jurors, by both the traditional method and a scientific selection process. It also examined the issues surrounding the use of less than 12 on a jury, then later the use of nonunanimous verdicts, both of which are controversial and both of which lead to an increase in conviction rates.

The entire trial process was detailed step by step, from the point when jeopardy attaches, through the presentation of a case by the prosecution and defense, and concluding with the verdict. This included the types of evidence presented and the strategies used by the defense in countering the prosecution's case-in-chief.

The verdict in a criminal case is either guilty or not guilty. No one is ever found innocent, because that means that they did not commit the crime. The jury has no way to determine that. The term *not guilty* means that the state did not prove that the person did it, a far cry from actual innocence. If the person is found not guilty, the matter is dismissed and everyone goes home. If the verdict is guilty, the case is set for the next stage in the proceedings, sentencing. That is the subject of the next chapter.

KEY TERMS AND CONCEPTS

Affirmation
Assistance of counsel
Case-in-chief
Chain of evidence
Challenges
Change of venue
Circumstantial evidence
Closing argument
Conduct of a jury
Confessional evidence
Court trial
Cross examination
Defense strategies
Deliberation
Direct evidence
Direct examination
Direct verdict
Expert witness
Fruits of a crime
Gag order
Hostile witness
Hung jury
Hypnotically enhanced memory
Indigent
Indirect evidence
Instructions to a jury
Instrument of a crime
Jeopardy
Jury of one's peers
Jury selection
Jury size
Kelly–Frye test
Lay witness

Leading questions
Miranda impeachment
Mistrial
Nonunanimous verdict
Oath
Objection
Opening statements
Peremptory challenge
Physical evidence
Polling the jury
Prejudicial error
Privileged communication
Public trial
Rebuttal
Recross examination
Redirect examination
Scientific evidence
Scientific jury selection
Scottsboro Boys
Sequester a jury
Sixth Amendment
Speedy trial
Subpoena
Subpoena decus tecum
Summons
Testimonial evidence
Transferred evidence
Unanimous verdict
Venire list
Verdict
Viewing the crime scene
Voir dire

REFERENCES

HOLTEN, N. GARY, and LAWSON L. LAMAR. *The Criminal Courts: Structures, Personnel, and Processes.* New York: McGraw-Hill, 1991.

LEWIS, ANTHONY. *Gideon's Trumpet.* New York: Random House, 1964.

ROBIN, GERALD D. *Introduction to the Criminal Justice System*, 3rd ed. New York: Harper & Row, 1987.

RUBIN, H. TED. *The Courts: Fulcrum of the Justice System, 2nd ed.* New York: Random House, 1984.

SCHEB, JOHN M., and JOHN M. SCHEB II. *Criminal Law and Procedures*, 2nd ed. St. Paul, MN: West Publishing, 1994.

ZALMAN, MARVIN, and LARRY SIEGEL. *Key Cases and Comments on Criminal Procedures.* St. Paul, MN: West Publishing, 1994.

CASES

Apadoca v. Oregon, 406 U.S. 404 (1972)

Argersinger v. Hamlin, 407 U.S. 25 (1972)

Arizona v. Fulminante, 499 U.S. 279 (1991)

Ballew v. Georgia, 435 U.S. 223 (1978)

Betts v. Brady, 316 U.S. 445 (1942)

Burch v. Louisiana, 441 U.S. 130 (1979)

Duncan v. Louisiana, 391 U.S. 145 (1968)

Estes v. Texas, 381 U.S. 532 (1965)

Frye v. United States, 293 F. 1013 (D.C. Cir. 1923).

Gannett v. DePasquale, 443 U.S. 368 (1979)

Gideon v. Wainwright, 372 U.S. 335 (1963)

Griffin v. California, 380 U.S. 609 (1965)

Harris v. New York, 401 U.S. 222 (1971)

In re Manuel L., 11 Cal. 4th 529 (1993)

Johnson v. Louisiana, 406 U.S. 356 (1972)

Patton v. United States, 281 U.S. 276 (1930)

People v. Ernst, 8 Cal. 4th 441 (1994)

People v. Kelly, 17 Cal.3d 24 (1976)

People v. May, 44 Cal.3d 309 (1988)

Powell v. Alabama, 287 U.S. 45 (1932)

Richmond Newspapers v. Virginia, 448 U. S. 555 (1980)

Rideau v. Louisiana, 373 U. S. 723 (1963)

Rock v. Arkansas, 483 U.S. 44 (1987)

Sheppard v. Maxwell, 384 U. S. 333 (1966)

*Singer v. U. S. *, 380 U.S. 24 (1965)

Williams v. Florida, 399 U.S. 78 (1970)

SENTENCING PROCEDURES AND ALTERNATIVES

This chapter deals exclusively with sentencing and the alternative procedures, including the types of sentencing laws, sentencing options in both misdemeanor and felony cases, and the primary alternative to sentencing, probation. The roles of probation in the sentencing process, as well as in the procedural aspects of supervision, revocation, and honorable termination are detailed, as are the legal aspects of probation that effect police procedures. A brief summary of federal sentencing procedures is included as well.

Sentencing is one of the most important functions of the justice system because it affects not only the punishment for the offender, but the feelings of the victim and the safety of the community. There are three basic types of felony sentencing laws: mandatory, indeterminate, and determinate. Each is often related to a particular goal that the legislature had in mind when it enacted a particular type of sentencing law. Sentencing in misdemeanor cases usually is limited to a fine and/or jail sentence. It might also include some sort of community service work.

THE GOALS OF SENTENCING

The **goals of sentencing** include the following:

Incapacitation. This means to neutralize the defendant's capacity to commit further crimes, by imposing strict custody requirements, and has the public safety as its primary concern.

Retribution. This is similar to revenge, or the belief of an *eye for an eye.* The offender is made to pay harshly for the crime committed, and the victim often feels better, thinking that justice has been done.

Deterrence. This means to stop criminal behavior. This is further divided into **general deterrence**, which is the deterrent effect the punishment of an offender has on the general public at large, and **specific deterrence**, which is the deterrent effect that the punishment has on the specific defendant who is punished.

Rehabilitation. This means to effect a change in a person's attitude and/or conduct so that he or she changes from criminal to noncriminal behavior in a lasting way.

Vindication. This means to make the law right, or to uphold or support the value of the law broken, by giving a sanction to one who violates the law.

Punishment. This is a *just desserts* approach that seeks to punish each offender fairly and equally for the crime committed. Punishment usually is equated with years of prison time. It does not take into account any consequences that might result from the punishment time given.

TYPES OF SENTENCING LAWS

THE MANDATORY SENTENCE LAW

A **mandatory sentencing law** is a law enacted by a state legislature or Congress in which specific sentences are mandated for certain crimes, and no judge has any discretion. Or it could be a situation in which the legislature designates mandatory prison sentences for certain types of crimes and prohibits the judge from granting probation as an alternative.

THE INDETERMINATE SENTENCE LAW

Various states have enacted an **indeterminate sentence law** (ISL), which initiates **parole**, as an extension of the offender's sentence into the community, after serving some portion of it in prison. Both parole and the ISL were products of the reform model that entered U.S. corrections in 1870, when it was first established by Zubalon Brockway, Warden at New York's Elmira Reformatory. This is not to say that parole originated in America. It had been in use in Australia, England, Ireland, and France long before it came to this country. Historically, parole has always been associated with some type of ISL, and the goal of both were rehabilitation.

An ISL is a sentencing law in which the legislature sets a minimum and a maximum for the offender to serve, and a parole board conducts an annual review of the inmate's progress toward rehabilitation to determine when the optimum time is for his or her release. For example, a sentence might be from five years to life or one to 10 years. Somewhere within those limits, the offender knew that he or she could get parole when he or she was rehabilitated. If an offender was kept too long, he or she might become bitter and angry. If released too soon, he or she might not yet be rehabilitated.

Use of this law created a great deal of **disparity** (wide differences in the time that people served for the same crime) and did not prove effective in the rehabilitative process. Approximately 70 percent of those released returned to crime within a two-year period. **Recidivism** is the return to crime by a person released from prison, and the person who fails and returns to prison is a **recidivist**.

During the 1970s, there were many individuals and groups criticizing the ISL and attempting to enact a replacement law. They represented a wide spectrum of interests: conservative lawmakers, law-and-order lobbyists, and members of humanist organizations, such as the American Friends Society (Quakers), all calling for abolition of the ISL. The conservatives wanted longer prison terms and the Quakers wanted fair and equal punishment. By the mid-1970s, their influence combined with the strong punitive feelings within state governments and an increasingly punitive public to abolish the ISL and enact its replacement, the determinate sentencing law. Maine was the first state to act, followed by California and a majority of other states. Maine also abolished parole, but no other state did. However, the ISL is still used in the states of Alabama, Alaska, Connecticut, Georgia, Missouri, Nevada, Massachusetts, Ohio, Oklahoma, South Carolina, South Dakota, and Vermont.

THE DETERMINATE SENTENCE LAW

The two primary goals of a **determinate sentence law** (DSL) are a punishment for each crime in proportion to its seriousness, and the elimination of disparity in sentencing. Such laws were enacted because the legislatures and the governors had given up on the ideal of rehabilitation. They concluded that the only thing one can accomplish for certain is to take away some years from a person's life. That we can do well.

A DSL applies to felony sentencing and equates punishment with time: time out of a person's life, without regard for the results of what occurs to the person during that time. However, 98 percent of all those sent to prison return some day to the community, and the public would be safer if they came back better instead of worse.

The laws vary to some extent between the states, but basically, the legislatures have provided three specific times that a convicted felon may serve and the sentencing judge chooses the most appropriate time, after conducting a hearing and considering all the relevant factors. The middle time (or term) is called the **presumptive term** because it is presumed that the judge will impose the middle term if everything else is equal. The upper time is called the **aggravated term** because the judge may impose it if there are factors about the crime or the role of the defendant that make it aggravated. The lower time is called the **mitigated term** because the judge may impose it if there are factors about the crime or role of the criminal that make it less serious than the average.

It would be interesting for the reader to refer to the penal codes within his or her own state to compare what any given felony sentence is today with what it was 20 years ago. Needless to say, the prison times have changed dramatically, especially the maximum number of years—they have increased in most states. In addition, under a DSL, parole eligibility is no longer connected to the sentence. Now all one needs to do is to serve the time, and release is automatic and cannot be denied, regardless of attitude or intentions. In addition, there are work-time laws that allows an inmate to earn up to one day off his or her sentence for each day worked, and everyone is given the opportunity to work. Participation in educational or vocational programs usually is equated with working for purposes of earning half-time off a sentence.

THE SENTENCING PROCESS

After a felony conviction, either by verdict or plea, the matter is set for sentencing at a later date, often four to six weeks from the date of the verdict. During the time between the verdict and sentencing, the case is referred by the court to the probation department for an investigation and report as to the proper sentence. Often this is termed a **presentence investigation** (PSI) or a **report of the probation officer** (RPO).

THE PRESENTENCE REPORT

The probation officer, and his or her deputies, serve as both the investigative and enforcement arms of the court. When a felon has been referred for the sentencing investigation, the case is assigned to one of the deputy probation officers who works in the investigation unit. This assignment usually is given to the deputy who has investigated the fewest cases so far during the month. This keeps the workload even.

The probation officer will conduct a thorough investigation into the nature of the crime, the role of the defendant and codefendants, if any, and the social and personal life of the defendant. Any and all the significant information collected by the probation officer is summarized in a **presentence report**. The report contains the details about the offense, the defendant's statement as to his or her role in it and motives for it, a **victim impact statement**, an assessment of the prior record, if any, and the potential of the defendant to reform.

This is one of the most important documents filed with the court. Since the judge knows nothing about those 90 percent (plus) of the cases that are convicted by plea bargain, he or she must rely on the RPO to provide all the relevant information upon which to base a sentence. The information also will be used later, either in developing a plan for probation supervision or for prison classification. It will be considered later in determining parole conditions, and perhaps much later in preparing any subsequent presentence reports if the defendant reoffends. In many states the law requires a RPO in felony cases, and makes it discretionary in misdemeanor cases. However, most probation departments are too busy and overworked with felony matters to have the time to deal with misdemeanor investigations.

The probation officer evaluates the case to determine if the defendant is eligible for probation and, if so, whether he or she will make a good candidate for probation. If so, and if the probation officer recommends probation, he or she will include a list of the terms and conditions that he or she thinks should be made a part of the probation order. If the defendant is not eligible for or deserving of probation, the probation officer will recommend whatever sentence is legally required and/or appropriate in the case.

The probation officer might also include in the RPO an assessment of the defendant's ability to repay any of the cost of any appointed counsel services, any restitution to the victim or the state's restitution fund, and/or in some states, a victim penalty assessment fund. The probation officer also must advise the victim of the hearing date, and usually the victim will be allowed to address the court personally as to the impact the crime had on him or her, or the victim's family.

THE SENTENCING HEARING

The presentence report is filed with the court, and the judge must sign it stating that he or she has read and considered the report. Copies are also given to the prosecution and the defense so that they can prepare any arguments about sentencing at the **sentencing hearing**. At the hearing, either side may present additional evidence that they want the judge to consider, and they may argue for or against the recommendation of the probation officer. They may also put the probation officer on the stand and question him or her about the information contained in the report.

Following the arguments or comments on the RPO, the judge will pronounce the sentence. Or, if he or she does not want to sentence the defendant, or if he or she does not want the defendant to serve a sentence that has been given, the judge may instead grant probation. The details of probation as the alternative to sentencing are presented in a subsequent section of the chapter.

SENTENCING OPTIONS

The law is very clear about what sentences crimes may receive. Misdemeanors are punishable by a jail term of up to one year (or in some cases, up to six months), or by fine, or by both jail and fine. Felonies are punishable by one of the prison times provided by the law. Often, felonies can be punishable by a term in county jail, which makes the crime a misdemeanor.

If a judge desires more information about a felon than that provided in the RPO, he or she may suspend criminal proceedings and refer the defendant to the state's department of corrections for a diagnostic study. Similar referrals may be made to youth facilities for juveniles. The report from either facility will provide a diagnostic evaluation of the defendant and a recommendation about the appropriate sentence.

THE GRANT OF PROBATION

Probation is not a sentence. No one is ever sentenced to probation. It is an alternative to, in lieu of, and instead of, a sentence. Loosely translated from the Latin, *probation* means "I prove." It is used as an opportunity for the defendant to prove himself or herself worthy to remain in the community and not have to be sentenced or to serve a sentence. Probation may be defined as *the suspension of the imposition or execution of a sentence and the order of conditional and revocable release in the community under the supervision of a probation officer.*

The legal definition means that, one way or another, there is a "suspension of...a sentence...." The words *imposition* and *execution*, as they are used here, require further explanation. *To impose a sentence* means to give one. Therefore, to suspend the imposition means that no sentence is given, pending successful completion of probation. If all goes well during the period of probation, it will terminate without the person ever being sentenced. If all does not go well, and the defendant's probation is revoked, the judge will choose what the sentence is to be.

To execute means to carry out. Therefore, when a judge wants to give a sentence but not have it carried out, pending successful completion of probation, he or she imposes a sentence but suspends the execution of it. If all goes well, the defendant will never have to serve the sentence imposed. However, if probation is revoked, the judge will order that the sentence previously given be carried out. The defendant knows the entire time that he or she is on probation how much time he or she must serve if probation is revoked.

Two other words in the definition given above need an explanation: *conditional* and *revocable*. The word **conditional** means that the judge will grant probation but conditions will be attached. If the defendant breaks one of the conditions, the judge can find that the defendant is in violation of probation and may revoke probation. If the defendant does not like the conditions required by the judge, the defendant may refuse probation, leaving the judge no alternative but to sentence the person. Consequently, when a defendant accepts probation, he or she freely and voluntarily agrees to abide by the conditions imposed and not to object when the probation officer enforces them (*People v. Bravo*, 1987).

The meaning of the word **revocable** is self-evident. It means that if probation is revoked, it is taken away and a sentence will follow.

TERMS OF PROBATION

Misdemeanor probation may be granted for a term usually up to three years. If a condition is imposed, a defendant must be reasonably able to complete that condition during that period, or it is unfair and illegal to impose it. Probation in a felony case may be granted for terms of varying lengths, depending on the state and the type of crime. Usually, however, felony probation is granted for terms of three to five years. That is a long time for a person to abide by the conditions imposed, and it is sufficient time for a person to prove himself or herself worthy to remain in the community. The majority of convicted felons are granted probation.

TYPES OF PROBATION

The definition of probation given above refers to supervision by a probation officer. This is known as **formal probation** because the person is formally supervised by an officer of the court (the enforcement arm of the court) in those states that operate probation at the county level, or is supervised by a state agent in those states that operate probation at the state level. In either case, the probation officer wears two hats. He or she is responsible to supervise and help the defendant while enforcing all the judge's orders.

In granting probation, the judge may order what is called **straight probation**, which is probation straight out of the courtroom and into the community, or **shock probation**, which is probation with some time in jail as a condition of probation. In felony cases, this time may be up to one year, and it still is not considered a sentence. Frequently, the jail time ordered is 30, 60, or 90 days. It is done either to shock the defendant out of a criminal lifestyle or to add a little punishment to the probation.

In reporting these cases, the media often confuses the issue by reporting them inaccurately. In the press it usually will say, "John Doe was sentenced to 90 days in jail, followed by three years on probation." Of course, that is not what happened. Actually, the judge suspended the sentence and granted probation for a term of three years, subject to the condition that the defendant serve 90 days of jail time. If John Doe's probation is later revoked, he will be given whatever the sentence is for his crime. He will, however, be given credit for the 90 days served, as he would for any days served after the initial arrest.

Not all probationers are supervised, particularly those granted misdemeanor probation. Unsupervised probation is called **court probation**, because he or she is on probation directly to the court. A **conditional sentence** is another phrase meaning court probation.

WHO RECEIVES PROBATION

It is a common misconception that once a person is convicted of a felony, he or she automatically goes to prison. According to the Bureau of Justice statistics in 1996, there were about 3.2 million individuals on probation in 1996; 55 percent of all adult probationers had been convicted of felonies, 26 percent of misdemeanor, and 17 percent of felony or misdemeanor DUIs. Women accounted for 21 percent. About 65 percent were white, 35 percent black, and 15 percent were Hispanic.

Generally speaking, the southern states made more use of probation as an alternative to sentencing, with Texas leading the way. California was second. There are 2000 probation agencies in the nation, and probation is sometimes operated at the individual county level and sometimes at the state level, depending on the state in question.

CONDITIONS OF PROBATION

The conditions ordered with any grant of probation are of two types: standard and special. **Standard conditions** are the requirements that every probationer must follow, such as reporting to the probation officer, obeying all laws, avoiding evil associates, and advising the probation officer of any change in address or employment. **Special conditions** are the requirements uniquely chosen for a particular defendant or class of defendants.

These conditions must be constitutional, reasonably related to the crime or criminality of the defendant, and must be possible to complete within the term of probation. For example, a bad-check writer might be ordered not to possess any checks except payroll checks on which he or she is named as payee. A credit card offender might be ordered not to possess any credit cards or open any time payment accounts. A drug offender undoubtedly will be ordered to submit to random chemical testing for the continued use of drugs. Both adult and juvenile probationers associated with gang offenses will be prohibited from possessing gang paraphernalia or associating with known gang members.

Special conditions that are frequently ordered include community service work, psychiatric treatment, electronic monitoring with or without house arrest (confinement), and restitution. Many conditions are required, depending on the nature of the case.

PROBATION SEARCHES

The most controversial special condition is one that allows the probation officer to **search** the probationer and his or her possessions. States vary in the authority given probation officers to search and they vary also in the grounds needed by the officer to initiate a search. The procedural guidance has come from the legislatures and/or the state appellate courts rather than from the U.S. Supreme Court. In California, for example, where probation is conducted at the county level, the probationer is ordered to *submit his or her person, automobile, or place of residence to search by any peace officer at any time of the day or night without a warrant*. This is termed a **three-way search clause**.

Not all states go this far in allowing probation officers to search their clients. In Wisconsin, for example, where probation comes under the authority of the State Department of Health and Social Services, a probation officer may search a probationer's home as long as the officer has approval from his or her supervisor and has *reasonable grounds* to believe that contraband exists. Wisconsin law also makes a probation violation for refusing to submit to the search of one's home.

This *reasonable grounds* standard satisfied the thinking of the U.S. Supreme Court in one of the few such search cases taken before it. In 1983, a probationer named Griffin was on probation in Wisconsin for resisting arrest, disorderly conduct, and obstructing an officer. One day while Griffin was on probation, Michael Lew, the supervisor of Griffin's probation officer, received information from a detective on the Beloit Police Department that there were or might be guns in Griffin's apartment. Unable to secure the assistance of Griffin's own probation officer, Lew, accompanied by another probation officer and three plainclothes policemen, went to the apartment. When Griffin answered the door, Lew told him who they were and informed him that they were going to search his home. During the subsequent search they found a handgun.

Griffin was charged with possession of a firearm by a convicted felon, a felony in Wisconsin. He moved to suppress the evidence seized during the search. The trial court denied the motion, concluding that no warrant was necessary and that the search was reasonable. A jury convicted Griffin of the firearms violation, and he was sentenced to two years' imprisonment. The conviction was affirmed by the Wisconsin Court of Appeals.

On further appeal, the Wisconsin Supreme Court also affirmed. It found denial of the suppression motion proper because probation diminishes a probationer's reasonable expectation of privacy, so that a probation officer may, consistent with the Fourth Amendment, search a probationer's home without a warrant, and with only *reasonable grounds*, not probable cause, to believe that contraband is present. It held that the reasonable grounds standard of Wisconsin's search regulation satisfied this reasonable grounds standard of the federal Constitution, and that the detective's tip established reasonable grounds within the meaning of the regulation since it came from someone who had no reason to supply inaccurate information, specifically identified Griffin, and suggested a need to verify Griffin's compliance with state law.

On further appeal, the U.S. Supreme Court agreed and concluded that this warrantless search did not violate the Fourth Amendment. In his opinion, (*Griffin v. Wisconsin*, 1987) Justice J. Scalia stated:

> To reach that result, however, we find it unnecessary to embrace a new principle of law, as the Wisconsin court evidently did, that any search of a probationer's home by a probation officer satisfies the Fourth Amendment as long as the information possessed by the officer satisfies a federal *"reasonable grounds"* standard. As his sentence for the commission of a crime, Griffin was committed to the legal custody of the Wisconsin State Department of Health and Social Services (the agency under which probation is operated), and thereby made subject to that Department's rules and regulations. The search of Griffin's home satisfied the demands of the Fourth Amendment because it was carried out pursuant to a regulation that itself satisfies the Fourth Amendment's reasonableness requirement under well-established principles.

> In searching a probationer's house, the probation officer may search the rooms under the control of the probationer, such as the bedroom, and any common areas shared with others in the house, such as the kitchen and living room. If the probation officer is at the residence to make a search, giving him or her a legal right to be there, any evidence or contraband of other people, in plain view, may be seized. The same requirement applies to juvenile probationers, whether the parents like it or not.

POLICE SEARCHES OF PROBATIONERS

Using the *Griffin* case cited above as the standard, one would conclude that any probation search must be based on *reasonable grounds*, which is the same standard as *reasonable suspicion* discussed in Chapter 3. However, that case did not set national precedent, and states must then rely on their own procedures.

The wording used in probation search clauses in California includes "any peace officer." Consequently, if a police officer on patrol stops a person and detains him or her for any lawful purpose, runs a record check and it comes back showing that the person is on probation with a three-way search clause, the officer may conduct the search, without having any reason, as long as it is for *some legitimate law enforcement purpose* (a broadly worded caution).

As another example, probationers in Arizona are required to submit to search of their person or possessions by a probation officer if the officer has reasonable suspicion of a violation. Police officers may not stop and search a probationer, although probation officers often have a police officer accompany them on house searches because police officers are better trained in enforcement and restraint techniques that might be necessary to complete the search.

One note of caution needs to be included. Any search, whether by a police or probation officer, may not exceed the **scope of the search** clause. If the search order limits the search to a search for stolen property, for example, officers may not search for drugs, or if it is limited to searching the person, they may not search the car or residence. Therefore, it is always better to know of the probation status and of the wording used in the search clause before effecting any search. If the suspect is on federal probation, police officers probably will not be able to search him or her at all because the scope of the search clause is usually limited to "...search by any federal probation officer...."

MODIFICATION OF PROBATION ORDERS

The conditions of probation are the orders of the court, and as stated above, it is the responsibility of the probation officer to enforce those orders. However, any of the conditions may be modified or deleted, and others may be added at any time during the period of probation. If the **modification** favors the probationer by removing some restraints, it can be done easily and often without a formal hearing.

Examples of this would include deleting a curfew order or an order for drug testing, vacating a fine or restitution order, or changing the time given in shock probation from 90 days to time served. The probation officer will merely submit a brief report to the court explaining the change wanted, with a copy of the new order for the judge to sign. The appearance of the probationer might be a mere formality. However, if the modification will impose more restraint on the probationer, a formal hearing will be required. A copy of the report recommending these changes will be sent to the defense attorney of record.

VIOLATIONS OF PROBATION

A probationer may be found in **violation of probation** for two reasons. If he or she violates one of the conditions of probation but is not arrested for a new crime, it is called a **technical violation**. As an example, if the probationer is on probation for drug use, and a drug test comes back from the lab showing the use of a drug or narcotic, the probation officer may discuss it with him or her and reinforce what the judge said about not using drugs, or he or she may arrest the probationer for violating that condition against using drugs and return the probationer to court. If the probationer is arrested and charged with a new crime, it is called a **formal violation**.

In either type of violation matter, the probation officer will decide whether he or she thinks that probation should be modified, to add restraints, such as 30 days in jail to dry out, or to revoke probation and have the probationer sentenced. The judge will usually agree with the recommendation. A violation is a very formal proceeding. It actually requires a two-stage hearing process: an initial probable cause hearing followed by a revocation hearing, with most of the due process afforded in the original proceedings, short of a jury trial (*Gagnon v. Scarpelli,* 1973). In an earlier decision, the Supreme Court granted probationers the right to be represented by an attorney in a probation violation hearing where the judge might revoke probation and impose or execute a sentence (*Mempa v. Rhay*, 1967). That right was made retroactive in another case the following year (*McConnell v. Rhay*, 1968).

RECORD EXPUNGMENT

In any case where the probationer has completed the period of probation and fulfilled all the conditions, or has been discharged from probation prior to its full completion, many states provide for a process known as **expungement**, the reversal of the conviction. He or she is allowed to withdraw his or her plea of guilty or no contest entered at the time of conviction and to enter a new plea of not guilty. The judge will then dismiss the original complaint, information, or indictment, and the probationer no longer has a criminal conviction.

The probationer has proven himself or herself worthy not only to remain in the community, but to have his or her criminal record reversed. Any rights lost because of the conviction are restored. Except, that he or she is told that he or she still must reveal the facts of the conviction when applying for any public office or with any public agency.

There was a time when a person could have his or her record expunged and become a peace officer. However, most states have modified their laws to prohibit a felon from possessing a firearm, regardless of any expungement. A federal law has had the same effect within all the states. Also, most state laws require sex offenders to continue to register as a sex offender even after receiving an expungement. Consequently, once an offender is required to register as a sex offender the requirement lasts for a lifetime, unless a full pardon is granted, which does not happen often. This registration requirement alone will limit the type of employment available to former sex offenders. New federal law prohibits anyone from possessing a firearm who has been convicted of domestic battery. This law is beginning to have sweeping implications for those currently employed in law enforcement or corrections.

FEDERAL SENTENCING PROCEDURES

THE FEDERAL SENTENCING COMMISSION

Until about 10 years ago, the federal version of the penal code, Title 18 of the *United States Code*, provided the maximum prison time a felon could serve, but the sentencing judges had the discretion to choose the actual time up to that limit. Disparity was a serious problem. A simple drug possession offender might be granted probation from a federal judge in San Francisco, whereas the sentence for a similar offense in a Texas district might be 10 years in a penitentiary. Finally, after decades of research and debate about this disparity, Congress established the U.S. Sentencing Commission as a part of the Comprehensive Crime Control Act of 1984.

The commission is an independent agency in the judicial branch of the federal government. Its purpose was to create sentencing policies and practices and uniform detailed **sentencing guidelines** for all the federal courts. These guidelines became effective on November 1, 1987, as a part of the **Sentencing Reform Act**. Almost immediately this act was appealed by federal defendants across the country. In fact, the judges of the federal district court in

San Francisco declared the act unconstitutional, citing the separation of powers doctrine, because of the way Congress had constituted the membership of the commission. The judges did not want to follow the mandatory guidelines and give up their cherished discretion. However, on January 18, 1989, the U.S. Supreme Court upheld the constitutionality of the act and the commission, making the sentencing guidelines binding on all federal courts.

FEDERAL SENTENCING GUIDELINES

The complete guidelines take up a large volume in book form, and determining a sentence in an involved case can be very complex. Hopefully, the following explanation can be understood without providing any complex examples. The guidelines consider the offender's **instant offense** (crime of conviction) and the nature of the criminal conduct by assigning a base-level number to each crime that serves as a starting point. This base level can be increased or decreased depending on the particular circumstances of the case. Factors that can modify it are called *specific offense characteristics* (a.k.a. *harms*), which are prescribed in the guidelines. The base level has a range from 1 (least serious) to 43 (most serious) that forms one axis (list down the side of a page). A second axis is laid out across the top of the page in six categories to reflect the offender's prior record. In the box at the point where these two axis intersect is the prison time range from which the judge must choose to impose. The sentencing judge has a narrow window to exercise some discretion within that range.

RESULTS OF THE GUIDELINES

The use of these guidelines has accomplished one of the commission's primary goals by reducing disparity in the time people serve for the same crime. However, it has also resulted in very long and harsh sentences for most crimes. For example, consider the sentence for the least serious crime of transporting drugs for a defendant with no prior record. Prior to the guidelines, the defendant could receive probation. Now the offense carries a minimum of 10 years in prison. Consequently, the federal prison population has nearly tripled since the guidelines were implemented. By the end of 1997, the Bureau of Prisons housed 101,845 inmates in its 92 facilities nationwide. Over 70 percent of these were serving five years or longer, and over 40 percent were serving over 10 years.

Prison inmates can earn up to 53 days off their sentence a year, which means that they will serve most of their sentence time. The federal government abolished parole shortly after the guidelines were initiated because it did not think it was necessary. Federal officials soon learned, however, that it was a mistake to abolish parole, so they replaced it with a procedure called *supervised release* (which is parole). The use of the guidelines, with their many mandatory prison sentences, has also reduced the use of federal probation.

SUMMARY

In this chapter we presented many of the post-conviction procedures associated with sentencing and the primary alternative to sentencing, probation. We began with a list of the possible goals of sentencing, followed by the types of sentencing laws used over the years to achieve one or more of those goals.

Sentencing options in both misdemeanor and felony cases were summarized. Probation, as the primary alternative to sentencing, was presented in some detail, including the roles of a probation officer in the sentencing process, as well as in the procedural aspects of supervision, revocation, and honorable termination and expungement. Also included was an examination of the legal aspects and requirements in some states of probation searches by probation officers and by police officers.

KEY TERMS AND CONCEPTS

Aggravated term	Punishment
Conditions of probation	Recidivism
Determinate sentence law	Recidivist
Deterrence	Rehabilitation
Expungement	Retribution
General deterrence	Revocation of probation
Goals of sentencing	Sentencing guidelines
Incapacitation	Sentencing hearing
Indeterminate sentence law	Sentencing options
Mandatory sentence law	Sentencing Reform Act
Mitigated term	Shock probation
Modification of probation	Specific deterrence
Police search of parolees	Straight probation
Police search of probationers	Terms of probation
Presentence investigation	U.S. Sentencing Commission
Presentence report	Victim impact statement
Presumptive term	Vindication
Probation	Violation of probation

REFERENCES

COHEN, NEIL P., and JAMES J. GOBERT. *The Law of Probation and Parole*. New York: McGraw-Hill, 1983.

SCHEB, JOHN M. and JOHN M. SCHEB II. *Criminal Law and Procedures*, 2nd ed. St. Paul, MN: West Publishing, 1994.

CASES

Gagnon v. Scarpelli, 411 U.S. 778 (1973)

Griffin v. Wisconsin, 483 U.S. 868 (1987)

McConnell v. Rhay, 393 U.S. 2 (1968)

Mempa v. Rhay, 389 U.S. 128 (1967)

People v. Bravo, 43 Cal.3d 600 (1987

9

POSTSENTENCING PROCEDURES

In this chapter we describe a variety of procedures that occur after the formal sentencing of a defendant has been completed. In misdemeanor cases, this includes county parole and, later, reversing the conviction. In felony cases, it includes the role of the parole board in granting parole and/or setting its conditions, or revoking parole. In this portion of the chapter we also explain the legal conditions and requirements by which a peace officer may stop, detain, and search a parolee. It also presents the procedures for the honorable termination of parole and an application for pardon.

This is followed by a historical overview of the death penalty, along with a short review of selected appellate cases that have affected death penalty procedures.

The law gives the executive branch of government, the governor or president, the discretion to affect criminal procedures through the exercise of four acts of clemency (leniency): a pardon, reprieve, commutation, and amnesty. These discretionary acts are described, along with the regular appellate process, and four writs. The chapter concludes with a description of the procedure of indemnification, paying back a person who has been wrongly convicted and imprisoned.

Sentencing Review

MISDEMEANOR CASES

The procedures described in this section refer only to those cases in which a misdemeanant is sentenced and not granted probation or given a conditional sentence, such as court probation. Those matters were described in Chapter 8. In the grand scheme of things, this does not amount to many people. Of all the persons convicted of crimes, only about 5 percent are misdemeanants sentenced to jail. And of that small amount, about 10 percent are wobblers, sentenced to jail after receiving felony convictions, automatically changing their crimes to misdemeanors.

When a person is sentenced to jail, the term will be up to one year. In some cases the person might be serving multiple-year sentences, with an order to serve them consecutively, which means that he or she could remain in jail for one year on each sentence. However, when a person is sentenced to jail, in most states he or she is eligible for release on county parole after serving some portion of the sentence, usually half. The county parole board or commission is usually composed of representatives from county justice agencies, such as the sheriff and probation officers, a deputy district attorney, and sometimes a local defense attorney.

County parole commissions or boards meet from time to time during the month to consider applications for parole. They operate as independent bodies, with the authority to grant or deny parole. **County parole** is defined as the *conditional and revocable release from county jail of a sentenced misdemeanant into the community under the supervision of an agent of the county parole commission.* As such, the conditions are similar to those imposed on probationers. Standard conditions for the parolee might include not leaving the county, obeying all laws, seeking employment, and keeping the parole commission informed of his or her residence. Special conditions might be added, similar to probation cases, such as drug testing and a three-way search clause.

County parole supervision often is provided by a public officer who works with limited peace officer powers under the direction of the county parole commission. Usually, this is a deputy probation officer designated as the county parole agent, who supervises the parole caseload instead of, or in addition to, a probation caseload. Any violation of the parole conditions may result in the parolee being returned to jail to complete the remaining portion of his or her jail sentence.

FELONY CASES

In the discussion of felony sentencing in Chapter 8, the elimination of disparity was one of the goals of sentencing under the Determinate Sentencing Law. Disparity means the wide and discriminatory terms that people serve for the same crime. Under the old ISL, inmates often were kept in suspense for years, not knowing when they would be paroled or what they had to do to win parole. Parole was granted at the discretion of one or two parole board members who heard the case. In many cases, parole came at the whim of a board member. This practice was eliminated under the DSL, because discretion as to the length of a sentence is limited, and the sentencing judge must state on the record the factors considered in choosing the time given.

Regardless of this caution, the legislatures in many states have provided additional checks on sentencing so as to further minimize disparity. First, the sentencing judge often retains jurisdiction for a short period of time. This allows him or her time to reflect on and reconsider the sentence chosen, and the opportunity to recall the person to court for resentencing as long as the new sentence is no greater than the original one.

THE BOARDS OF PAROLE

The second check on the existence of disparity in sentencing often is given to the **parole board**, hereinafter called the board, although the specific names given to these agencies among the states do vary. One of their responsibilities often is to review each prison sentence given within the first year of the sentence to determine the existence of any unreasonable differences in time that people receive for similar crimes from courts around the state. One way to assess this is to be certain that each judge follows the rules provided by the state's court administrative body as to how sentences are to be determined and what factors are to be considered in mitigation and aggravation. In some states, the board has the authority to return the inmate to the court for resentencing. Any new sentence may not be longer than the original one.

State parole boards are composed of persons usually appointed by the governor, with the advice and consent of the senate. Their terms are staggered so that they do not all coincide with any one governor's term. Some states have separate boards for men and women, and separate ones for juveniles.

Membership on the board is the result of a political appointment, not necessarily professional qualifications. Consequently, the membership often reflects the political philosophies of the governors who appointed them. In addition to reviewing the sentences of inmates, parole boards have several other significant responsibilities. For one, they consider applications for parole from any inmate sentenced under the ISL in those states that use that type of sentencing law. It sets the conditions of parole for all parolees upon release.

Another responsibility of the board usually is to hear all allegations of parole violations and to decide on whether to revoke parole. The board must also conduct annual reviews as to the degree of adjustment in the community of each parolee and will terminate parole if the adjustment has been satisfactory. The board also reviews each case in which the person was given life without the possibility of parole, for a possible recommendation to the governor to change the sentence, allowing for parole. When a person has been discharged from parole and is crime free for several years, the person may apply to the governor for a pardon. All such applications are reviewed by the board, with a recommendation to the governor about granting the application.

PAROLE PROCEDURES

Parole is defined as the conditional and revocable release of a prison inmate into the community after serving some portion of a sentence, under the supervision of a parole agent. The parole agent is an agent of the executive branch of state government, as opposed to a probation officer, who might be under the judicial branch of government in those states that operate probation at the individual county level. He or she has peace officer powers that are limited to his or her occupational needs and conditions. Anyone sentenced to prison with a maximum term of life often will be on parole, if parole is granted, for the remainder of his or her life. The length of regular parole runs from one to five years, depending on the state and the parolee's adjustment within the community.

As stated above in the discussion of the DSL, parole is automatic in many states. It cannot be denied by any authority. However, an inmate sentenced to any life term, such as 25 years to life or 15 years to life, is sentenced under the ISL and might be considered for parole after serving two-thirds of the minimum term. The grant of parole under the ISL is known as **discretionary release**, because it is at the discretion of the board.

The parole of all other inmates sentenced under the DSL is called **mandatory release**, because their parole is mandatory. The board cannot deny parole, and the inmate cannot refuse parole. The board can only set the conditions that the parolee must follow. This can pose a risk to the community if a violent inmate is paroled and has not changed his or her behavior.

A classic example of this situation is the Singleton case, making the news all the way from California to Florida in 1998. In 1978, a 15-year-California old girl accepted a ride in a van from a 50-year-old man named Larry Singleton. He drove her to an isolated place, raped her, hacked off her forearms with an ax, and left her laying beside the road to bleed to death. Fortunately, she lived. He was caught and convicted of mayhem, for which he received the relatively short determinate sentence of seven years instead of a life sentence that he could have received under the ISL. He was paroled early, in fact, because of good time/work time credits. However, state parole authorities had to hide him and move him from town to town because of the public outrage over his parole. The public did not understand that under the DSL the law required his parole. He was discharged from parole two or three years later and moved to Florida. On February 20, 1998, he was convicted of murdering a woman in Tampa, Florida, who had taken a ride in his van. The jury voted 10 to 2 on February 25 to recommend the death penalty (only a majority vote is required in Florida in death penalty phases of a trial). Singleton was sentenced to death on March 30. Incidentally, Singleton's 15-year-old California victim, now a 35-year-old mother of two who is doing well with prosthetic forearms, went to Florida to give dramatic testimony to the jury during the penalty phase of the trial.

When a person is released from prison on parole, the board will set the **parole conditions**, which are similar to those granted a probationer: standard and special conditions. Standard conditions usually include reporting to the parole agent within 72 hours of release, not leaving the state or parole district without permission, and not possessing any weapons. Special conditions might include drug testing, mandatory mental health treatment, a three-way search clause, mandatory attendance at Alcoholics Anonymous or Narcotics Anonymous meetings, electronic monitoring, or registering as a sex offender, as required under the state's registration statute.

SEXUALLY VIOLENT PREDATOR LAWS

On July 29, 1994, a 7-year-old New Jersey girl named Megan was kidnapped and killed by a paroled sex offender named Jesse

Timmendquas, who had moved into her neighborhood. Soon after, the New Jersey legislature enacted a law that requires all convicted sex offenders to **register** with the law enforcement agency having jurisdiction in the area where they live. After registration, the danger potential, the risk posed by the offender, is rated. If the risk is moderate, the police are required to notify the local schools, daycare facilities and youth organizations of the offender's identity. If the risk is high, police may publicly post the identity of the offender and may even make door-to-door identifications in the offender's neighborhood. This New Jersey law is now known as **Megan's Law**. Now, all states, and the federal government, have some form of Megan's Law, designed to protect the public from sexual predators.

After the passage of Megan's Law, officials in many states began questioning why their sentencing laws allowed the parole of these offenders in the first place. They thought that if an offender posed a risk of reoffending against another child, he or she should not be released. Consequently, many states enacted sexual predator laws which allow state officials to detain sex offenders in locked hospital facilities after the completion of their determinate sentence. A jury trial and a burden of proof beyond a reasonable doubt is required to certify a person as a **sexually violent predator** and to be so confined. However, almost immediately, defense attorneys and civil rights attorneys contested these laws, claiming that they punished the offender twice for the same offense, constituting double jeopardy. Attorneys also claimed that the new laws could not be applied to offenders whose original offense was committed prior to the enactment of the law.

In a test case in 1996, the state of California filed petitions against a sex offender named Rasmuson and 14 others convicted of sexual assault, whose prior acts were committed before the enactment of this law. They appealed, claiming that the law could not be applied to them retroactively, that it could not use offenses committed before the "predatory" (SVP) law was enacted. The trial court agreed, because the *ex post facto* law does prohibit the imposition of punishment on crimes committed before the new predatory law was enacted. However, the 2nd DCA reversed and upheld the application of the SVP law because the law was enacted under a civil code, and that predatory proceedings are civil and not subject to the *ex post facto* clause (*Garcetti v. Superior Court*, 1997).

In a recent Kansas case, the Kansas court held that a similar practice was unfair and unconstitutional. That case went before the U.S. Supreme Court (*Kansas v. Hendricks*) during the 1997 session. By a vote of 5 to 4 on June 24, 1997, the Court upheld the Kansas law, ruling that extended confinement was a civil commitment for treatment, not a criminal punishment. Justice Clarence Thomas wrote the opinion for the conservative majority, stating that "even though they may be confined against their will [in mental hospitals], they are not being punished."

In Arizona, the Department of Corrections has referred the cases of 19 sex offender prison inmates to local prosecutors for civil commitment proceedings. On March 16, 1998, attorneys for nine of the inmates appealed to the Arizona Supreme Court for relief, claiming that the state's sexual predator law that allows a civil commitment after completion of a criminal sentence is unconstitutional because it constitutes double jeopardy. The court agreed to hear arguments in the cases, after which it declined to accept jurisdictione nine cases. However, with the Kansas case as precedent, there does not appear to be grounds to argue.

POLICE SEARCHES OF PAROLEES

Interesting legal issues surround the **three-way search** condition for parolees. One issue centers on requiring the parolee to waive his or her Fourth Amendment protection against unreasonable search and seizure when he or she cannot refuse parole. Also at issue is whether the standard of **reasonable suspicion** of a parole violation is required before an officer may search a parolee. States differ in their procedures. In 1986 in California, the state supreme court held:

The conditional nature of a parolee's freedom may result in some diminution of his reasonable expectation of privacy and thus may render some intrusion by parole officers "reasonable" even when the information relied on by the parole officer does not reach the traditional level of "probable cause." However, the search must be related to the proper purpose of parole supervision and *requires a standard of "reasonable suspicion" of criminal activity.* (*People v. Burgener*, 1986)

A majority of states have agreed with the view of parole in this context. This distinguished a probation search from a parole search as to the cause required by police. Parole searches had to meet the standard of *reasonable suspicion* of criminal activity. States such as Colorado, Massachusetts, Michigan, Montana, Nevada, South Dakota, Utah, and Wisconsin have either administrative directives or state court decisions that require a similar standard. However, California enacted a law effective on January 2, 1998, that requires a prison inmate who is granted parole to sign parole orders that allows for the search of his or her person, place of residence, or automobile without any cause or suspicion.

Pennsylvania already had a similar parole law, requiring an

inmate to sign parole orders accepting a search clause that does not require reasonable suspicion (or any suspicion, for that matter) by a peace officer before that officer may conduct a search. In 1997 a prison inmate named Scott came up for parole but objected to signing his parole orders allowing the three-way search. However, if he refused to sign, he would have had to serve 10 more years of his sentence. He signed the orders and was granted parole. He also agreed to a parole condition that prohibited him from possessing any weapons.

In a subsequent search of Scott's home, police and parole officers found firearms and a bow and arrows. He was arrested on a parole violation. At his parole revocation hearing, he objected to the admission of the evidence based on grounds that the search violated his Fourth Amendment rights. The parole board rejected his challenge, revoked his parole, and recommitted him to prison. He appealed to the Commonwealth Court of Pennsylvania, which agreed that his rights had been violated and reversed the parole board's decision. The state appealed to the Pennsylvania Supreme Court, but it agreed with the lower court, so the state appealed Scott's case to the U.S. Supreme Court.

The U.S. Supreme Court had already ruled that the Fourth Amendment does not allow the search of a probationer's home without reasonable suspicion (*Griffin v. Wisconsin*, 1987). It was hoped that the *Scott* case would provide a federal precedent for states to follow in parole searches. The case was argued in March 1998 and decided in June 1998. The U.S. Supreme Court held that the exclusionary rule does not apply to parole searches (*Pennsylvania Board of Probation and Parole v. Scott*, 1998), and it reversed the Pennsylvania Supreme Court's decision which had overturned Scott's parole revocation. Not only did this case fail to set a national standard, it threw open the door for states to allow parole searches without cause.

Almost immediately, the California Supreme Court decided a case (*People v. Reyes*, 1998) that had been on hold, so to speak, pending the *Scott* decision. A California prison inmate named Rudolfo Reyes was released on parole after signing his parole orders, which included a three-way search clause as a condition. In a subsequent search of a shed on his property, Woodlake police officers found a small amount of methamphetamine. He was charged with a new crime of possession, and the evidence obtained by police was admitted at his trial over his objections, and he was convicted. The court of appeals reversed his conviction because the state's *Burgener* decision, cited above, required reasonable suspicion of criminal activity before police could search. The state supreme court, however, reversed the lower appeals court and its own precedent, and upheld Reyes' conviction. In a 4 to 3 decision the court majority dismissed its own argument in *Burgenger* and referred to a juvenile probation search case (*In re Tyrell*, 1994) as precedent and stated that

> [t]the search here appears to be for a proper purpose and we hold that in the absence of particularized suspicion (reasonable suspicion), the search did not intrude on any expectation of privacy "society is prepared to recognize as legitimate."

Consequently, in California and Pennsylvania, at least, parolees do not have any Fourth Amendment protection and may be searched by any peace officer without cause. Other states might follow this lead, tipping the scales (the social contract) in favor of social protection rather than individual liberty.

PAROLE REVOCATION PROCEDURES

A parolee may violate his or her parole by either committing a new offense or by breaking one of the conditions of parole, a technical violation. There was a time when parole was considered to be a mere extension of an inmate's cell out into the community rather than a release from confinement. As such, one did not get back any freedoms, and any **revocation of parole** simply moved the person's cell back behind the prison walls. All this was done without due process.

In 1972, however, a paroled robber named Morrissey had his parole revoked and was returned to prison to serve the remaining portion of his sentence. He claimed that he had been deprived of his freedom without due process, using the Fourteenth Amendment as the basis of his appeal. The U.S. Supreme Court agreed (*Morrissey v. Brewer*, 1972) and established a two-stage hearing process as a requirement in all parole revocation cases.

The first stage, called a ***Morrissey hearing***, is a probable cause hearing before a representative of the parole board, in which the parole agent must establish probable cause to believe that a violation occurred. The second stage is similar to a trial, only without a jury and before a parole board member or panel of three members. The parolee has the right to discovery, to cross-examine witnesses against him or her, and to present witnesses on his or her own behalf. The board must state its reason for revoking parole, with its decision based on a preponderance of the evidence. It was these same procedures that the Supreme Court extended to probation revocation hearings in its *Gagnon* decision in 1973.

SEX OFFENDER REGISTRATION

Anyone convicted of the commission or attempt to commit certain sex offenses listed in the penal codes of various states is required to register with the local law enforcement agency having jurisdiction where the offender lives. These registration laws are designed to control all convicted sex offenders, whether the victim is an adult or a child. Most states' laws require that the offender register if convicted and released into the community on probation, released from jail, prison, a youth facility, or a mental hospital.

Each convicted offender is informed of this requirement before release and must sign a form acknowledging that he or she understands the law. The form contains the offender's intended address upon release and is sent to the state's department of justice (DOJ) for the purpose of tracking the offenders. The appropriate law enforcement agency is notified of the offender's pending release and address.

If a sex offender relocates, he or she must not only register with the law enforcement agency in the new jurisdiction, but must notify the present agency of the move and new address. DOJ is also notified of each new registered address. In many states, anyone convicted of failing to register is guilty of a felony, punishable by a prison term. However, if they have two prior violent felonies that count as strikes, this might count as the third strike in those three-strike states. Also, any person on probation or parole who fails to register will have his or her probation or parole revoked. Anyone required to register will, at the time of release into the community, be required to provide two samples of blood and a saliva sample for DNA analysis by DOJ.

These sex offender registration laws are designed to keep the identity and presence of sex offenders visible within the law enforcement community. In states with a *Megan's Law*, local law enforcement agencies have a list of sex offenders registered within their jurisdiction on file on a computer disk. The list is divided into three categories: serious risks, average risks, and others. Officials may circulate or cause to be published the names and pictures of those in the serious risk category. Any person from the public may go to a law enforcement facility and use the disk on a computer to scan the average risk category to determine if anyone lives within their area or within the area where they work, or where their children attend school. It is a criminal offense, however, for anyone to take any action against the person or property of a sex offender based on the information learned from such a public inquiry.

Apparently, most offenders do register when first required, but for many reasons, do not reregister upon relocation. This makes tracking and/or locating sex offenders within a community very difficult. It is particularly difficult in large urban areas with a large transient population. However, some states have formed sexual predator apprehension teams to assist local law enforcement in locating unregistered offenders and arresting them individually, or in sweeps within a jurisdiction. Some jurisdictions now report that unregistered sex offenders who have heard about the sweeps are voluntarily reregistering to avoid a third-strike arrest.

THE DEATH PENALTY

Use of the **death penalty** is one of the most controversial issues in the field of criminal justice. Feelings about it run high, and it is seldom that one person can convince another to change his or her views through argument. The reasons for and against it have remained the same for many years and are detailed in much of the literature on the death penalty as an issue (Katsh, 1994). The scope of this book is not issue oriented, and there is no intention here to argue the merits of the death penalty.

BRIEF HISTORY OF THE DEATH PENALTY

Executions have been carried out by a number of gruesome methods throughout history. In early America, the methods included hanging, burning, stoning, and the swallowing of pins. As society allegedly became more sensitive about how it carried out its executions, hanging became the predominate method, although the firing squad remained in common use in Utah. Hangings used to be a public display, and the last public hanging was carried out in Owensboro, Kentucky in 1939. Uses of the electric chair, firing squad, and gas chamber replaced hanging, and now lethal injection is replacing those other methods in many states. Since 1608, when execution records first became available (Schmalleger, p. 305), approximately 19,000 people have been executed. The controversy over its use has been argued at length in recent years (Katsh, 1994).

During the past 26 years, the U.S. Supreme Court has decided a number of death penalty cases that created significant precedent.

The case that led the way is *Furman v. Georgia* (1972). Georgia's death penalty law gave the jury complete discretion as to whether to impose death or life in prison. Furman, a 26-year-old black man, killed a homeowner during the commission of an attempted burglary and was sentenced to death. His attorney appealed on the grounds that the penalty constituted *cruel and unusual punishment*, in violation of the Eighth Amendment.

Four Supreme Court justices believed that Georgia's law was legal. Justices Thurgood Marshall and William J. Brennen, Jr., thought that the death penalty in any form was cruel and unusual, and three remaining justices believed that the death penalty per se was legal but that the procedure used in Georgia, giving full discretion to the jury, was unlawful. Consequently, by a vote of 5 to 4, Furman's sentence was disallowed and Georgia's death penalty law was declared unconstitutional. The death penalty laws in most other states were similar to Georgia's and were also found to be unconstitutional.

The *Furman* decision meant that the death penalty of all inmates who had been sentenced using these unconstitutional procedures had his or her sentence reduced to life. They were removed from death rows and placed in the prison systems' regular populations. The decision also created a moratorium on imposing the death penalty until the states enacted new laws that met the constitutional test. The new laws had to provide for the presentation to a jury of both mitigating and aggravating factors, and the sentences had to receive mandatory appellate review.

By 1976, many states had enacted new and lawful death penalty statutes in cases of homicide with special circumstances. In 1976, the U.S. Supreme Court approved of a death penalty law that provided a two-stage hearing process: the trial and a sentencing hearing in which evidence could be provided as to the appropriate sentence in a case (*Gregg v. Georgia*). In 1977, the Supreme Court ruled that the death penalty could not be imposed on persons convicted of rape (*Coker v. Georgia*). The case also implied that the death penalty could only be used in homicide cases.

By 1988, the 37 states that had reinstated the death penalty had condemned 2124 persons to death, and had actually executed 100. By the end of 1998, over 500 had been executed. The popular mood today seems to favor the death penalty, and most politicians would not risk their careers by opposing it. Also, there are efforts at both the federal and state levels to expedite the appellate process so as to avoid the long delays, often between nine and 14 years, from sentencing and execution.

Writs and the Appellate Process

A convicted person may **appeal** his or her conviction based on a denial of procedural rights guaranteed in the state or federal constitutions or on the question of the legality of the law itself. An appeal usually questions some procedural aspect of the arrest, trial, or sentencing, and rarel, questions the legality of the substantive law that the person was convicted of violating.

An appeal that questions the law itself is made on the basis of one of three claims: that the wording of the law is too vague for an ordinary person to understand what behavior is prohibited and is declared to be **void for vagueness** (*Maillard v. Gonzales*, 1974; *Kolendar v. Lawson*, 1983), that the law is unconstitutional in that it prohibits a right or freedom otherwise guaranteed, or that the law criminalizes behavior that was either not a crime or not a separate crime but a part of another crime.

The first two situations in which the law would be questioned need no explanation. The latter situation requires clarification. As an example, the mere act of forcibly moving a person from room to room in order to complete a robbery used to be sufficient to meet a legal definition of kidnapping. In one case, a man attempted a robbery of a local hofbrau, during which he forced the cook, a waiter, and the manager to move from room to room to open the safe and collect all the available cash. He was charged with attempted robbery and kidnap. The kidnap portion of the charge was reversed because it was not a separate crime but was a necessary part of the crime of robbery.

A conviction in municipal court, or other lower court, may be appealed to superior court, then to the courts of appeal, then to the state supreme court if the appeal involves a state constitutional question. A felony conviction in superior court may be appealed in the same manner. If either appeal is based on an issue that arises out of the U.S. Constitution, it may be appealed up the federal appellate ladder, from the district court, to the federal courts of appeal, and finally, the U.S. Supreme Court.

Very few cases reach the top level. The Supreme Court has discretion in accepting cases on appeal and only select those that have a significant constitutional question. Over 5000 cases are appealed to the Supreme Court in a year, and it agrees to hear fewer than 200. Nevertheless, it maintains a full schedule and will hear those cases that undoubtedly will establish procedural precedents that all the states must follow.

WRIT OF CERTIORARI

A **writ of certiorari** is the basic document used to appeal a conviction. A writ is a legal request, when filed. It is a legal order when granted, permitting review by the higher court of the decision of the lower court. The purpose of appealing any conviction is to have it overturned, regardless of whether the case will be retried. At the U.S. Supreme Court level, it takes a vote of four to *grant cert*—to agree to hear the case.

WRIT OF HABEAS CORPUS

A **writ of habeas corpus** is a writ filed by a person who claims to be held in custody without due process or by the denial of a constitutional right. If a person wants to appeal his or conviction and is already in custody because of it, he or she will file both a writ of certiorari and a writ of habeas corpus. In the latter writ the person filing the writ is named first and the person who has custody of him or her is named second. For example, in the *Gideon* case described in Chapter 7, Gideon was in custody in a prison in Florida and wanted to have his conviction reviewed because of his claim that he should have been appointed an attorney. The writ cited when discussing his case is the writ of habeas corpus, naming Wainwright as the second party because he was the director of the Florida Department of Corrections.

WRIT OF MANDAMUS

A **writ of mandamus** is a request made to compel a lower court to perform an action or duty. It might be used when a person requests a lower court to do something, and it refuses. The matter is appealed to a higher court on the hope that the higher court will order the lower court to comply with the request. For example, it might be used to mandate the return of evidence that is no longer relevant, that an agency otherwise will not return.

WRIT OF PROHIBITION

A **writ of prohibition** is a writ, or request, that is the opposite of a writ of mandamus. It is a request to prohibit a lower court or justice agency from taking an action or performing a duty. For example, it might be used to ask a higher court to prohibit a lower court from admitting certain evidence at trial.

EXECUTIVE CLEMENCY

The executive of a state is the governor, and of the United States it is the President. Each has the authority to exercise **executive clemency**, or leniency, in only one of four ways: pardon, reprieve, commutation, and amnesty, as described below. Their authority in these areas is without question or accountability.

PARDON

A pardon is an act of forgiveness in which the offense is erased as if it never happened. To qualify, a person must have been crime-free for an extended period of time, depending on their offense and the state. Most states provide that an application for a pardon will be filed with and reviewed by a board, often the parole board or board of prison terms. If the pardon is granted by the executive, most of the civil rights lost as a result of the conviction are restored. The right to possess or carry a firearm is excluded from this restoration in many states.

REPRIEVE

A reprieve is a temporary delay or postponement in carrying out a sentence, pending a final decision. For example, the governor might grant a reprieve to a person who has been given an execution date and faces immediate execution. However, the person also has an appeal pending before a court that could affect his death sentence.

COMMUTATION

A commutation is a lessening or shortening of a sentence. The usual grants of commutation are to **time served**, or from life without parole to life with parole. As mentioned above under the discussion of the board of prison terms, one of their responsibilities is to review all sentences of life without the possibility of parole and to recommend to the governor the desirability of commuting it to life with the possibility of parole. The governor may also commute any death sentence to life. This is one reason that political opponents in a governor's race for election question each other as to their stand on the death penalty.

AMNESTY

Amnesty is an executive act of freeing a person, often a group of people, from prosecution. People might be pending trial or prosecution and for political or other reasons, the governor or President thinks that they deserve not to be prosecuted. This writer equates it with the childhood game of hide-and-seek and use of the phrase (phonetically) *olly-olly-oxen-free*. The executive is calling the game over, either to forgive the players or because he cannot find them. All the players are safe from capture and can return home to start a new game. An example is the act of President Carter granting amnesty to all those who did not register for the draft, and instead, fled the country. It was as if he stood at the border of Canada and yelled "olly-olly-oxen free," and they all came home.

INDEMNIFICATION

Indemnification is money paid as compensation to a person who was convicted of a felony and imprisoned, then later pardoned by the governor, either because no crime was ever committed, or if it was, the convicted person did not commit it. If a person thinks that he or she qualifies, he or she can file a claim with the state board designated to hear such matters, with evidence presented by the claimant, and by the attorney general if the claim is disputed. If the board finds in favor of the claimant, it will award compensation. The amount varies among the states.

SUMMARY

In this chapter we described many of the procedures that occur after formal sentencing of a defendant. In misdemeanor cases, this included county parole and reversing the conviction. In felony cases it included the role of the parole board in granting parole to ISL inmates and setting the conditions of parole for both ISL and DSL inmates, along with hearing all parole violation matters and revoking parole.

We also explained the legal conditions by which a peace officer may stop, detain, and search a parolee. The chapter included a summary of the death penalty and a discussion of the procedures by which a governor or President may exercise four acts of clemency (leniency). The meaning of these acts was described, as were the writs used in the appellate process. The chapter concluded with a review of the act of indemnification, compensation to a person who has been wrongly convicted and imprisoned, then pardoned, for a felony that either never occurred or, if it did, was committed by another person.

KEY TERMS AND CONCEPTS

Amnesty
Board of parole
Commutation
County parole
County parole commission
Death penalty
Death penalty appeals
Discretionary release
Executive clemency
Indemnification
Mandatory release
Morrissey hearing
Pardon

Parole
Parole conditions
Police searches of parolees
Reasonable suspicion
Reprieve
Revocation of parole
Sex offender registration
Sexually violent predator law
Void-for vagueness doctrine
Writ of certiorari
Writ of habeas corpus
Writ of mandamus
Writ of prohibition

REFERENCES

Cohen, Neil P., and James J. Gobert. *The Law of Probation and Parole*. New York: McGraw-Hill, 1983.

Katsh, M. Ethan (ed.) *Taking Sides: Clashing Views on Controversial Legal Issues*, 4th ed. Guilford, CT: Dushkin Publishing, 1994.

Scheb, John M. and John M. Scheb II. *Criminal Law and Procedures*, 2nd ed. MN: West Publishing, 1994.

Stuckey, Gilbert B. *Procedures in the Justice System*, 3rd ed. Columbus, OH: Charles E. Merrill, 1986.

Tewksbury, Richard A. *Introduction to Corrections*, 3rd ed. New York: McGraw-Hill, 1997.

CASES

Coker v. Georgia, 433 U.S. 584 (1977)

Furman v. Georgia, 408 U.S. 238 (1972)

Garcetti v. Superior Court, 49 Cal. 4th 1533 (1997)

Gregg v. Georgia, 428 U.S. 153 (1976)

Griffin v. Wisconsin, 483 U.S. 868 (1987)

In re Tyrell 8 Cal. 4th 68 (1994)

Kansas v. Hendricks, 521 U.S. 346 (1997)

Kolendar v. Lawson, 461 U.S. 352 (1983)

Mailliard v. Gonzales, 416 U.S. 918 (1974)

Morrissey v. Brewer, 408 U.S. 471 (1972)

Pennsylvania Board of Probation and Parole v. Scott, No. 97-581 (1998)

People v. Burgener, 41 Cal. 3d 505 (1986)

People v. Reyes, 19 Cal. 4th 299 (1998)

REFERENCES

ARTICLES

CAVIN, JEFFERY D. "Waiver of a Juvenile's Fifth and Sixth Amendment Rights," *Journal of Juvenile Law*, Vol. 13, 1992.

KAMISAR, YALE. "The Exclusionary Rule in Historical Perspective: The Struggle to Make the Fourth Amendment More Than an Empty Blessing," *Judicature*, November 1978.

MOORE, DELANCEY H. "The Complexity of Jail Classification of Gang Members," *American Jails*, March/April 1997, pp. 81–84.

ROWAN, JOSEPH R. "Corrections in the 21st Century," *American Jails*, March/April 1997, pp. 32–34.

WILKEY, MALCOLM RICHARD. "The Exclusionary Rule: Why Suppress Valid Evidence?" *Judicature*, February 1979.

REFERENCE WORKS

COHEN, NEIL P., and JAMES J. GOBERT. *The Law of Probation and Parole.* New York: McGraw-Hill, 1983.

DEL CARMEN, ROLANDO V. *Criminal Procedures: Law and Practice,* 3rd ed. Belmont, CA: Wadsworth, 1995.

HOLTEN, N. GARY, and LAWSON L. LAMAR. *The Criminal Courts: Structures, Personnel, and Processes*. New York: McGraw-Hill, 1991.

ISRAEL, JEROLD H., YALE KAMISAR, and WAYNE R. LaFAVE. *Criminal Procedures and the Constitution: Leading Supreme Court Cases and Introductory Text*. St. Paul; MN: West Publishing, 1991.

KATSH, M. ETHAN (ed.). *Taking Sides: Clashing Views on Controversial Legal Issues*, 4th ed. Guilford, CT: Dushkin Publishing, 1994.

PEOPLES, EDWARD E. *Criminal Procedures in California*. Forestville, CA: Meadow Crest Publishing, 1997

PEOPLES, EDWARD E. *Juvenile Procedures in California*. Forestville, CA: Meadow Crest Publishing, 1995

ROBIN, GERALD D. *Introduction to the Criminal Justice System*, 3rd ed. New York: Harper & Row, 1987.

RUBIN, H. TED. *The Courts: Fulcrum of the Justice System*, 2nd ed. New York: Random House, 1984.

SCHEB, JOHN M. and JOHN M. SCHEB II. *Criminal Law and Procedures*, 2nd ed. St. Paul, MN: West Publishing, 1994.

STUCKEY, GILBERT B. *Procedures in the Justice System*, 3rd ed. Columbus, OH: Charles E. Merrill, 1986.

TEWKSBURY, RICHARD A. *Introduction to Corrections*, 3rd ed. New York: McGraw-Hill, 1997.

ZALMAN, MARVIN and LARRY SIEGEL. *Key Cases and Comments on Criminal Procedures*, 1994 ed. St. Paul, MN: West Publishing, 1994.

PUBLISHED ACCOUNTS

FRIENDLY, FRED W., and MARTHA J. H. ELLIOTT. *The Constitution: That Delicate Balance*. New York: Random House, 1984.

LEWIS, ANTHONY. *Gideon's Trumpet*. New York: Random House, 1964.

ROTHWAX, HAROLD J. *Guilty: The Collapse of Criminal Justice*. New York: Random House, 1996.

SIMON, JAMES F. *The Center Holds: The Poser Struggle inside the Rehnquist Court*. New York: Simon & Schuster, 1995.

WOODWARD, BOB, and SCOTT ARMSTRONG. *The Brethren: Inside the Supreme Court*. New York: Simon & Schuster, 1979.

CASE INDEX

I

Illinois v. Krull, 1987, 45
In re Alonzo C., 1978, 59
In re Gault, 1967, 87
In re Manuel L., 1993, 151
In re Tyrell, 1994, 183

J

Johnson v. Louisiana, 1972, 154

K

Kansas v. Hendricks, 1997, 180
Knowles v. Iowa, 1998, 57
Kolandar v. Lawson, 1983, 187

M

Mailliard v. Gonzales, 1974, 187
Mallory v. United States, 1957, 75
Mapp v. Ohio, 1961, 30
Maryland v. Wilson, 1997, 57
Massiah v. United States, 1964, 81
McConnell v. Rhay, 1983, 170
McKaskle v. Wiggins, 1984, 114
McNabb v. United States, 1943, 75
Mempa v. Rhea, 1967, 170
Michigan v. Tucker, 1974, 80
Miranda v. Arizona, 1966, 74–87
Moran v. Burbine, 1986, 81
Morrissey v. Brewer, 1972, 183

N

New York v. Quarles, 1984, 40, 81
Nix v. Williams, 1984, 39
North Carolina v. Butler, 1979, 85

O

Ohio v. Robinette, 1996, 55
Oregon v. Elsted, 1985, 82
Oregon v. Mathiason, 1977, 84
Ornelas v. United States, 1996, 61

P

Patton v. United States, 1930, 135, 140
Payton v. New York, 1980, 67

Pennsylvania Board of Probation and Parole v. Scott, 1998, 182
People v. Bravo, 1987, 164
People v. Burgener, 1986, 181
People v. Ernst, 1994, 140
People v. Kelly, 1976, 144
People v. May, 1988, 151
People v. Ramey, 1976, 67
People v. Reyes, 1998, 182
People v. Torres, 1989, 82
Peterson v. Robinson, 1954, 64
Powell v. Alabama, 1932, 131

R

Richmond Newspapers v. Virginia, 1980, 130
Richards v. Wisconsin, 1997, 69
Rideau v. Louisiana, 1963, 137
Rock v. Arkansas, 1987, 145

S

Sheppard v. Maxwell, 1966137
Silverthorne Lumber Co. v. United States, 1920, 39
Singer v. United States, 1965, 140
State v. Lindusay, 1930, **NEED PAGE**
State v. Smith, 1956, 70
State v. Williams, 1970, 37
Steagald v. United States, 1981, 67

T

Terry v. Ohio, 1968, 50
Thompson v. Keohane, 1995, 82–84

U

Unites States v. Brady, 1987, 42
Unites States v. DeSantis, 1989, 42
Unites States v. Carillo, 1994, 42
Unites States v. Gonzalez, 1990, 82
Unites States v. Leon, 1984, 42
Unites States v. Ramey, 1976, 67
Unites States v. Robinson, 1973, 53
United States v. Verdugo-Urquidez, 1990, 82

W

Weeks v. United States, 1914, 27
Welsh v. Wisconson, 1984, 68
Whren v. United States, 1966, 57

Williams v. Florida, 1970, 135
Wilson v. Arkansas, 1995, 67
Wolf v. Colorado, 1949, 29
Wong Sun v. United States, 1963, 39

SUBJECT INDEX